Privacy, Surveillance and Public Trust

Privacy, Surveillance and Public Trust

Daniel Neyland

Senior Research Fellow, Said Business School
University of Oxford, UK

First published in 2006 by
PALGRAVE MACMILLAN
Houndmills, Basingstoke, Hampshire RG21 6XS and
175 Fifth Avenue, New York, N.Y. 10010
Companies and representatives throughout the world.

PALGRAVE MACMILLAN is the global academic imprint of the Palgrave
Macmillan division of St. Martin's Press, LLC and of Palgrave Macmillan Ltd.
Macmillan® is a registered trademark in the United States, United Kingdom
and other countries. Palgrave is a registered trademark in the European
Union and other countries.

ISBN-13: 978–1–4039–4670–6 hardback
ISBN-10: 1–4039–4670–1 hardback

This book is printed on paper suitable for recycling and made from fully
managed and sustained forest sources.

A catalogue record for this book is available from the British Library.

Library of Congress Cataloging-in-Publication Data

Neyland, Daniel, 1973–
        Privacy, surveillance, and public trust / Daniel Neyland.
            p. cm.
        Includes bibliographical references and index.
        ISBN 1–4039–4670–1 (cloth)
            1. Electronic surveillance – Case studies. 2. Closed-circuit
        television – Case studies. 3. Electronic surveillance – Moral and ethical
        aspects – Case studies. 4. Privacy, Right of – Case studies. 5. Trust. I. Title.

TK7882.E2N487 2006
323.44′8—dc22   2005056599

10   9   8   7   6   5   4   3   2   1
15   14   13   12   11   10   09   08   07   06

Printed and bound in Great Britain by
Antony Rowe Ltd, Chippenham and Eastbourne

Contents

Acknowledgements   vi

1   Introduction   1

2   Who are These Kids and Why are They Standing
    Still? Questions on the Telling of CCTV Stories   19

3   CCTV Modes of Action: Accountability,
    Surveillance and Privacy   46

4   Trust and Informational Mobility: CCTV, Local
    Retailers and Local Residents   75

5   'We Sold Pictures of a Man Cutting His Hands
    Off For Entertainment Purposes': The Story of
    Mr. B and CCTV   96

6   Constituting the Town Centre: Space, Trust
    and Accountability   116

7   Conclusion   151

Appendix   175

Notes   176

References   180

Index   190

Acknowledgements

I would like to thank the following for their contribution to this book: the ESRC, Kevin Hetherington, Christine Hine, Ian Hutchby, Mike Lynch, Lucy Suchman, Andrea Whittle and Steve Woolgar.

1
Introduction

Privacy, surveillance and trust form a burgeoning presence within debates surrounding technological developments, particularly in the current war on terror environment. Recent years have seen a huge growth in demands for: certainty in the verification of identity; accountability in individual and organisational activity; and mechanisms designed to accumulate knowledge of what individuals and groups will do next. Across Europe and the United States, these demands have been implicated in, amongst other things, increasing numbers of security cameras (Norris and Armstrong, 1999), a proliferation of forms of biometric identifiers (Adey, 2004), enhanced border crossing security (Collier, Lakoff and Rabinow, 2004), more frequent and detailed use of a variety of profiling and categorising techniques (Lomell, 2004) and a growth in automated scanning systems (Heath and Luff, 1999). These technological developments do not stand alone, but form the focus for a rapidly expanding legislative environment, the production of new and amended forms of expertise and the swift generation of means of assessment (to cover everything from the legality of a system (Taylor, 2002) to its value for money (Neyland and Woolgar, 2002)), alongside an expansion of the industry of protest and movements to enhance civil liberties.

These developments signal ever increasing state and organisational attempts to capture, store and categorise information about everyday activities. Travel, shopping, work and leisure activities are all implicated, on occasions, in this growth of socio-techno-legal systems. However, what is it that we know about the everyday activities that go into the establishment and maintenance of these systems? In what ways are our daily activities subtly (and not so subtly) re-oriented in relation to the development of these systems?

1

These questions are undoubtedly complex, particularly with regard to the number of different technological developments, legislative environments, forms of accountability and everyday activities that are implicated in the systems outlined previously. However, this complex mass of activity will form the backdrop in this book for a close and detailed interrogation of one technological system: Closed-Circuit Television cameras (CCTV) in the United Kingdom. A detailed analysis of CCTV will provide the means to engage with this complex mass of issues.

The United Kingdom leads the world in deploying CCTV systems with four million cameras[1] in operation 24 hours a day, 365 days a year. However, it is too simplistic to assume that either the cameras provide a solution for social problems or act as a harbinger of a future Orwellian dystopia. Instead, this book actively engages in an assessment of the ways in which CCTV has been established, maintained and questioned, through a detailed ethnographic study of surveillance in practice. It suggests that Closed Circuit Television systems involve the complex plaiting of social and technical entities which together form a closed-circuit of interaction. Opening up these closed-circuits for sociological analysis offers an opportunity to develop a sophisticated empirical interrogation of the legislative and policy environments of CCTV and day to day surveillance activities that take place both inside and outside the system (see later for more on why CCTV was selected as a focus; for studies which engage in less detail but on a broader scale with a range of surveillance technologies see for example Gandy, 1993; Lyon, 1994; Poster, 1990). This chapter will, first, suggest that an interrogation of CCTV can be organised around three principle issues: privacy, surveillance and trust. Second, the methodological practicalities involved in studying privacy, surveillance and trust will be considered. Third, the structure of this book will be presented.

Privacy

What is the analytical utility of focusing on issues of privacy, surveillance and trust? Privacy is perhaps the most frequently referenced issue with regard to the practices of those involved in technological systems implicated in the regulation, accounting and categorising of the population. Questions are asked of the possibility of maintaining privacy and CCTV (see Soetnan, Lomell and Wiecek, 2004 for a discussion) and suggestions are made regarding policy and legislation in order to protect privacy (Stalder, 2002; Taylor, 2002). As an issue, privacy forms a concept around which multiple concerns are organised. Talk of privacy and

CCTV involves talk of integrity, reliability, civil liberties and legality. Privacy thus offers a means to organise engagement with the mass of socio-techno-legal issues involved in systems developed for accumulating and analysing forms of information on the population. However, what is privacy? How could it be adequately legislated for in relation to CCTV? Is it something to be owned, can it be held or given up in return for some other good?

Privacy and public

On occasions talk of privacy involves the constitution of a binary opposition between 'the private' and 'the public' (e.g. Benn and Gauss, 1983; Fahey, 1995; see McCulloch, 1997 for a response). Within this opposition, what is present under one category acts as evidence of what will form an absence under the other category (for an interesting example, see Fraser, 1994; and for a discussion, see Sheller and Urry, 2003). The following quote from Higgs, talking of privacy in the wake of the September 11th attacks on the United States, sets out many constituents of arguments relating 'the private' and 'the public':

> The government has declared war on 'terrorism', but because terrorists assume many guises and operate in many places, the only way to ensure that no terrorist escapes notice is to watch everyone, everywhere. Lacking the patience and the wit to focus its surveillance on only the most likely suspects, the government will regard all of us as potential terrorists or as their potential providers, unwitting perhaps, of aid and comfort. Our communications by ordinary mail, telephone, fax, and e-mail will be scrutinized or at constant risk of scrutiny; our homes and places of business will be searched or at constant risk of search; our personal contacts, financial affairs, and travel by airliner, train, and ship will be closely monitored and restricted. (Higgs, 2001)

In this quote from a civil liberties advocate certain activities (such as 'communications') and certain spaces (such as 'the home') are presented as indicative of areas which should be free from forms of external data collection, storage or calculation (at least if consent has not been granted for this collection). In this sense the home, for example, is private in terms of the presence of boundaries, control over potential incursions through those boundaries (whether physical or informational) and the possibility of self-regulation of the activities that take place within those boundaries. In the work of McCulloch (1997) and Fraser

(1994), these presences can be noted as unlike their opposite, 'the public', where a notable absence of boundaries highlights the greater likelihood of incursion, information collection and categorisation and delegated forms of regulation. This representation of private and public as co-constituted opposites can also be noted in relation to forms of information, such as medical records (Privacy Rights, 2004); an individual's genetic make-up (American Civil Liberties Union, 2005); and shopping habits collected through loyalty cards (BBC, 2004). It is frequently claimed such information is personal and so should not flow beyond the confines of a strictly bounded set of legitimated viewers/users. The private/public co-constitution also forms the basis for debates such as: should employers have access to employees' activities (Zuboff, 1988; and for a discussion of privacy in the workplace see Mason, Button, Lankshear and Coates, 2002); which activities airport security staff utilise in order to render certain passengers in need of closer inspection; which activity CCTV staff focus their cameras on (see Chapter 3). Thus the representation of private/public can relate to space (e.g. the claimed privacy of the home), information (e.g. the claimed privacy of medical records) and action (e.g. the claimed right to walk through a town centre, see Chapter 5).

Privacy and legislation

However, this by no means exhausts notions of privacy. While privacy is frequently constituted in opposition to ideas of 'the public', it can also be construed in terms of rights and legislation (for a discussion see Bennett and Grant, 1999). Taylor (2002) offers a useful summary of the variety of forms of privacy legislation that relate to CCTV in the United Kingdom, which legislation has precedence and the questions such legislation poses for CCTV. Stalder (2002), however, suggests that forms of privacy legislation are 'not the antidote to surveillance' (2002: 120). He suggests that in place of a focus on individual acts of privacy transgression, we have to start considering such acts as 'part of a new landscape of social power' (2002: 123). Stalder suggests that in place of conventional legislative approaches to privacy, we need to consider broader forms of accountability mechanisms that might limit the extent of the power of those handling personal information. Raab and Bennett (1998) conversely suggest that, as yet, we know little in detail about risks posed to privacy, about the social distributions of such risks and who is in greatest need of legislative privacy protection. Bennett and Raab (2003) advocate the adoption of Fair Information Principles (FIPs) by states and organisations involved in the collection and analysis of information about people. FIPs are designed to cover the extent of information an organisation would hold, the reliability and integrity of information storage, the use to which information would be put and agreements on transparency and accountability of information practices. However, Bennett and Raab (2003) argue that even in cases where organisations are willing to adopt FIPs, further research is required on the adequacy of mechanisms for assessing the extent to which organisations comply with the principles adopted.

Privacy as a contingent accomplishment

While these forms of legislation are discussed further in Chapters 5 and 7, it is worth noting the diversity of forms of action and possible remedy that are articulated under the rubric of privacy. Activities related to privacy range from corporate accumulation of data (see Milberg, Smith and Burke, 2000; Garfinkel, 2000) through to state regulation of activities (see Agre, 1997; Braithwaite, 2000; Rose, 2000). As Viseu, Clement and Aspinall (2004) argue privacy is 'a loose concept encompassing a variety of meanings' (2003: 2). Possible remedies to threats of privacy range from encouraging organisations to adopt Fair Information Principles (Bennett and Raab, 2003) through to declarations of the impossibility of maintaining privacy in the face of technological developments (Sykes, 1999). This diversity suggests that privacy could be considered as a contingent accomplishment (see Hine and Eve, 1998). In line with such a claim, Sheller and Urry (2003) suggest there are multiple 'privates' and 'publics' leading to the 'complex and fluid hybridizing of public-and-private life' (2003: 108). Reflecting this multiplicity, Gallagher (2004) discusses privacy and personal rights held in relation to particular spaces, held by particular groups or weighed up in cost-benefit assessments. Given the number of variants on what privacy might be, when privacy could or should be considered and what should be the outcome of particular claims for privacy, it is difficult to find certainty in talk of privacy. Relating the sense of a particular setting or sequence of action as private might be contingent upon the interactivity of that setting and action. That is, clarity on what privacy is, and who has a right to make a claim to privacy and what the outcome of a claim should be, may not retain stability across activities or find resolution in universally agreed upon and accepted rights to privacy. Privacy may remain uncertain until decided by a forum, such as the legal system, deemed appropriate by the various protagonists involved in a dispute (although even then disputes can remain, see Chapter 5). In this sense, privacy might be radically situated (Hine and Eve, 1998) and only available as a post-hoc rationale for understanding any particular setting and sequence of action as pertaining to notions of privacy, as legitimating a particular claim to privacy and hence initiating a series of subsequent privacy-considered actions. Such an approach to privacy raises a series of questions for the appropriateness of CCTV activity, regulation and policy (see Chapter 3 for more on these questions and the issue of privacy).

The three broad areas of privacy presented in this chapter – as a co-constitution with notions of 'the public', as a focus for legislation and rights, and as radically situated and contingent – suggest both the conceptual importance (privacy is discussed to such an extent) and difficulty of utilising privacy as an organising principle for interrogating CCTV (privacy is discussed in so many different forms). In researching CCTV and in asking questions of the ways in which recent technological developments collect, store and categorise information on the population, what we need to know are details of sites of interaction where questions of privacy are asked, where formulations of possible threats to privacy are made, maintained and challenged. Such an analysis of interaction, focusing on the ways in which privacy is produced and reproduced on a day to day basis, can be organised around the concept of surveillance.

Surveillance

The term surveillance is used in relation to a variety of contexts, by a range of social science research and is oriented towards diverse claims regarding the actions of particular technologies, places and people. While privacy can act as a useful organising principle in analysing claims regarding who should *have* what (in terms of rights, protections and remedies) and how these claims might be decided, surveillance can act as a useful organising principle for analysing claims about who *does* what (in terms of day to day activities inside and outside technologies involved in collection, storage and categorisation of information on the population).

It is not the case however, that there is agreement on which activities should form the focus for analysing surveillance. Rule (1973) considers surveillance as an embedded aspect of relations between the state and the population. 'Surveillance entails a means of knowing when rules are being obeyed, when they are broken, and most importantly, who is responsible for which' (1973: 22). While Rule focuses on social order and possible punishment, McCahill (2002) focuses on the ambivalence of surveillance technologies. He argues that 'The introduction of new surveillance technologies always has a social impact, and this impact can be both positive and negative' (2002: xi). However Lyon (2001) shifts debate towards the practices of information collection and analysis involved in surveillance, suggesting a definition of surveillance as: 'any collection and processing of personal data, whether identifiable or not, for the purposes of influencing or managing those whose data have been garnered' (2001: 2). This view is contrasted by Bennett (2005) who suggests that Lyon draws his definitions too broadly and that greater attention needs to be paid to the details of exactly who has their personal data scrutinised, and to what effect.[2] For Bennett most data collected is entirely routine and free from further scrutiny, both for the collectors and subjects of collection. Bennett suggests, however, that this is a highly selective, contingent process and forms the point at which questions should be asked of whose information is selected for greater scrutiny, why and for what end. This selectivity involves issues of identity (who someone is) and claims about likely future action (what threat they might pose).

These are not the only views on surveillance. Poster (1990) draws on the work of Foucault (1977) in considering the panopticon and what Poster terms the 'super-panopticon'. This idea is drawn on subsequently by Norris and Armstrong (1999) in their analysis of the United Kingdom as a surveillance society. Norris and Armstrong (1999) suggest that developments in CCTV form examples of state-driven, mass categorisation and information management mechanisms which act on the actions of the population. Marx (2002) adopts a similarly broad approach to surveillance. He argues attention should be paid to the 'places, spaces, networks and categories' of surveillance, beyond any focus on the individual (2002: 9). Marx links this shift in research attention to a shift in developments of the technologies and techniques of surveillance (these issues will be discussed further in Chapter 2).

What these approaches suggest is a variety of approaches to surveillance. It can be broadly construed to incorporate information collection and processing. Alternatively, surveillance can be utilised to consider the problematic aspects of more specific and narrowly drawn activities of selective attention and threat assessment, within broader practices of information collection. Or surveillance can be considered as a highly politicised act, closely integrated into the management of the population. This range of approaches to surveillance and the breadth of surveillance considerations will be of utility to this book. From the variety of approaches presented, we can see recurring questions of identity, assessments of 'what is going on', and suggestions regarding the importance of deciding what might happen next. The focus of subsequent chapters will be on the actions of surveillance, through which these commonly recurring themes can be witnessed. Surveillance will be treated as an empirical matter, with talk of surveillance – documents about surveillance and actions considered by participants in relation to surveillance – analysed in terms of what they reveal about the day to day actions of surveillance. The variety of approaches to surveillance and commonly recurring themes in surveillance work will then be utilised in relation to this empirical data in order to interrogate which approach might shed most light on the activities to hand. This pragmatic and practical approach to surveillance frees the research from the necessity of a priori definitions of what surveillance is, how it is accomplished and with what outcomes. In place of a singular definition of surveillance, it will be treated as a field of action with a variety of possible claims, counter claims and views as to what is going on in any particular setting or sequence of action. Rather than leave surveillance as an entirely open concept however, the regularly recurring themes of information collection, storage, analysis and prediction will be used to organise the on-going discussion of surveillance. The subsequent chapters will use empirical data and the variety of current views on surveillance from social science research to get to grips with surveillance in action.

Thus privacy will be utilised in order to interrogate claims regarding what people do and do not have (and possibly should have), in relation to further claims about the integrity and justifiability of boundaries surrounding forms of activity. Surveillance will be utilised in order to interrogate a field of action involving the constitution of identities for individuals and groups, establishing 'what is going on' in any particular setting and launching claims about what might happen next. This suggests that privacy and surveillance are not easily separable, but neither is one reducible to the other. While this does not establish clear definitions for what precisely constitutes privacy and surveillance, subsequent chapters will be used to assess existing social science conceptualisations of privacy and surveillance (as briefly outlined) in addressing the empirical data (see Methodology section for more on empirical data). This focus on privacy and surveillance is marked by notable absence concerning both the work done by those in what might be termed a surveillance system such as CCTV to promote an identity for the system and work done by individuals and local populations not part of the system to produce an identity for CCTV. This identity work can be analysed through a consideration of trust.

Trust

Social scientists often consider trust in relation to expectations regarded as constitutive of the social order (see for example, Garfinkel, 1963;

Barber, 1983; Shapin, 1994; Misztal, 1996; Luhman, 2000).[3] In analysing the relations between a CCTV system and local populations, what expectations might there be and how might these be constitutive of social order? How would individuals and populations render these expectations relevant to constituting identities for CCTV and how might CCTV systems attempt to promote particular identities?

Garfinkel (1963) suggests that social order involves a multitude of trust expectations and accountability relations which characterise mundane day to day interactions. For example, in a conversation the first speaker will hold to account the second speaker's response, assessing the extent to which the second speaker has demonstrably understood the first speaker, displayed this understanding in their response and thus accomplished the expectations of the first speaker. Such mundane expectations are forms of trust and such forms of trust hold the social order together. Garfinkel (1963) argues that at moments where expectations breakdown, further assessments of trust are initiated and repair sequences are entered into in order to get the interaction back on track. To explore these arguments, Garfinkel (1963; 1967) designed a series of breach experiments where expectations would be undermined in order to highlight the ways in which 'trust is a condition for "grasping" the events of daily life' (1963: 190; for more on Garfinkel, see Chapter 2).

The work of Garfinkel has been utilised in a variety of ways. Using Garfinkel's work, Shapin (1994) suggests that 'To accept the relation of another ... is to give that other the right to furnish our minds' (1994: 38). In this sense, to trust CCTV would be to constitute expectations of CCTV in line with what a CCTV system claims to be doing. Identity work for the CCTV system, then, would involve work to promote 'what goes on' in the CCTV system and work to repair any breaches to expectations established between the system and local populations. Barber (1983) utilises the work of Garfinkel to consider alternative modes of trust looking at, first, a person's expectations regarding others' technical competence and, second, expectations that contractual obligations would result in an organisation placing the person's interest ahead of the organisation. Here identity work would not just involve relations between a CCTV system and individuals, but would involve assessments of CCTV's competence (can the system do what it claims and, for example, reduce crime?) and the legislative environment of CCTV (including considerations of what the legislation covers and whether or not it would place an individual's interest ahead of the CCTV system).

These forms of socio-technical assessment suggest recent social science research on trust and risk (see for example, Beck, 1992; Giddens, 1990) might have some utility for considering relations drawn between CCTV systems and individuals or local populations. In such studies, notions of trust have been tied into considerations of scientific or informational uncertainty (Frewer, Howard, Hedderley and Shepherd, 1996), calls have been made for policy developments to enhance trust (Jasanoff, 1990) and it has been linked to brand loyalty (Chaudhuri and Holbrook, 2001), particular forms of communication (Rowe, Marsh, and Frewer, 2004) and regulation (Shapiro, 1987; Boyd, 2002; Gambetta, 2000). Although this literature is diverse, many of these areas of trust overlap and there are common threads that can be drawn out. The emphasis in these approaches is placed upon decisions as to what to trust in the face of increasing risk, uncertainty, rapid changes and multiple sources of expertise. However, Hilgartner (1990) warns against buying into a deficit model, where various groups and individuals are assumed by institutions to have inadequate understanding of risk or inadequate knowledge to judge whether or not to place trust in an organisation, event or source of information. Frewer (2004) suggests that the deficit model assumes there is a stable and available, possibly scientific, 'truth' in the hands of institutions of which most people are not aware or are poorly informed. In line with the claim (see for example, Latour and Woolgar, 1979 and also see Chapter 2 for a discussion) that 'science' is not involved in the production of neutral facts, but is rather a messy and contingent social activity, the idea of a neutral and available truth in the hands of organisations may be somewhat misleading. Furthermore, it is suggested by Wynne (1996) and Frewer (2004), amongst others, that the constitution of trust is not characterised by a deficit of information but rather by the drawing together of multiple sources of information in complex decision-making (and perhaps the social science emphasis should be placed on the making). Thus trust in CCTV may involve the drawing together of multiple claims, based on multiple forms of information, forming on-going assessments and decisions regarding what CCTV is doing, what it could do and whether or not it works.

An emphasis on complex decision-making in relation to trust appears to fit with the work of Barber (1983) and to suggestions that a variety of considerations might be entered into in constituting an identity for an organisation such as a CCTV system. To return to Garfinkel's (1963) work it will be important to consider the ways in which such forms of trust are dependent on assessments and expectations through which CCTV might enter into routine and mundane, day to day activities or constitute breaches in those routines. On occasions of breach in the social routine, it would then be important to consider what repair mechanisms a CCTV system could enter into to shift back into a position of trust.

Using these ideas, trust will be treated as a central consideration in a variety of different forms of identity work that goes on in and through CCTV. It will be argued that publicity activities engaged in by CCTV managers involve the constitution of audiences (such as local residents, retailers, shoppers) and attempts to communicate trust relations with those audiences. However, these 'audiences' prove to be complex and diverse collectives, active in producing responses to these attempts to constitute trust (see Chapters 3 and 4 for more detail). In this sense, trust will be considered as 'performative' (Szerszynski, 1999: 244) and 'an active political accomplishment' (Misztal, 1996: 7).

In sum, this chapter suggests that a variety of questions can be engaged through the concepts of privacy, surveillance and trust. From the preceding discussion, we can see that privacy, surveillance and trust need not be tightly defined at the outset of research, but can be utilised as organising principles for grouping, analysing and asking questions. Privacy can be articulated in terms of boundaries, rights and legislation, particularly focusing on claims regarding what people should *have*. Surveillance can be interrogated as a field of action, particularly focusing on what individuals and the CCTV system *does*. Trust can form the basis for analysing identity work in and around CCTV, particularly on the *relations* drawn between people and the CCTV system. Such analytical activity will form the site in subsequent chapters for drawing together the variety of social science approaches introduced previously in order to consider their relevance and value. Although such an approach offers three organising principles for considering the day to day activities in and around CCTV through which information on the population might be collected, stored, categorised and analysed, we still need to know why CCTV is a compelling example to analyse, how such an analysis should be completed and what issues this might introduce.

Methodology

Why study CCTV?

CCTV forms the focus for analysis in this book as it represents an example of the growing number of technological developments oriented towards the collection, production, storage, categorisation and analysis of information on the population. As such it is implicated in a range of developing social (such as new forms of employment, questions of interaction and engagement, means of protest), technical (such as biometrics, technologies of identification, predictive modelling) and legislative (such as changes in law, policy and formations of regulation) arrangements. What we currently lack is a detailed understanding of how these arrangements are made and maintained on a day to day basis. It would prove impossible within the confines of a single book to interrogate these activities in detail across a broad range of technological forms. Selecting CCTV as a focus offers an opportunity to engage with the ways in which such an analysis can be achieved in relation to one technology, the theoretical forms of engagement this can produce and the policy outcomes such research can initiate.

How to analyse CCTV

While forming a suitable focus for a dynamic range of analytical activity, questions could be asked of the possibility of studying CCTV in detail. It is claimed there are over four million CCTV cameras in operation in the United Kingdom and there is little agreement over the boundaries of what counts as CCTV (city centre systems, shop security, residential camera networks, or all of these). Furthermore, CCTV systems do not just involve a range of cameras linked in a network, but incorporate CCTV operatives, police officers, documents and so on. CCTV systems also engage with a variety of target audiences whether they are drivers (such as the London traffic camera network), residents (such as camera systems in housing estates, see McGrail, 2002), retailers or residents (see Chapter 4). Given this interactive mass and ever growing number of CCTV cameras and systems, it might seem difficult to consider such a diversity of day to day activity.

It is possible to narrow this focus. Amongst the four million CCTV cameras, CCTV systems, people and documents associated with CCTV, the main focus for social, technological and legislative developments have been public area CCTV systems. These provide a compelling means to engage with day to day activity which can be understood in relation to privacy, surveillance and trust. Thus this book takes as its focus a town just east of London with a population of around 65,000 residents, a town centre with shops and leisure facilities and a local authority run CCTV system. The town of Burbville (named for the purposes of anonymity in this research) will form the representative focus for getting to grips with the ways in which recent developments in social, technical and legislative arrangements are constituted through day to day activity.

Burbville CCTV system is funded by the local authority. It incorporates 32 cameras on a fibre optic network linked to a control room. In the control room there are 16 small split-screen monitors and two large monitors (one to increase the size of smaller images and one that is mirrored in the local police station). Staff work in teams of two on 8-hour shifts, 24 hours a day and talk to local shops and police officers on a radio system. The system constantly runs time-lapse recorders, which compress an image from each camera, every few seconds, onto a single tape. The staff can also switch on a real-time recorder if they perceive an event is happening or is likely to happen. They are also expected to keep a log of incidents to report to their managers. There are two CCTV managers involved in the day to day operation of the system, gaining publicity for the system and dealing with enquiries. The CCTV managers view their role as operating in between a variety of systemic documents (including CCTV guidelines produced in association with the local police, finance guidelines produced in line with UK national government initiatives and local documents produced in meetings between the managers and local councillors) and the CCTV staff.

This brief introduction to Burbville CCTV suggests a study of privacy, surveillance and trust focused on day to day CCTV activities would need to engage with a range of social and technical entities. CCTV mangers and staff, local police officers, members of the local political authority, alongside a variety of documents, need to be drawn into the analysis. Beyond the confines of CCTV, in Burbville there are residents who live in the town centre, retailers who work in the town centre and shoppers who visit the town centre who could also be said to engage in the day to day activities of CCTV. How can such a diverse array of people, practices and technical entities be accommodated into this research?

There are many statistical accounts of CCTV such as the Home Office pamphlet, 'Understanding Car Park Crime and CCTV' (Home Office, 1993), which suggests that 'CCTV does not create a physical barrier directly stopping car-crime' (1993: 2) and needs arrest results to maintain its 'credibility' (1993: 24). The statistics in this pamphlet provide neat factual totems to support these conclusions, but only go a small way towards explaining the detail of the situations; the 'why', 'how' and 'for what reason' of any CCTV action. Another Home Office pamphlet, 'Closed Circuit Television In Public Places' (Home Office, 1992), suggests 36 per cent of people asked felt the cameras were an invasion of privacy, 54 per cent were against government installed systems and so on. It is not clear from such statistical analyses how respondents formed their views of CCTV. Are these issues those which respondents have previously considered or might they be responding to the categories offered to them by the survey? It is also unclear whether respondents' views of

CCTV differ by time, location or recent experience. Similar questions could be asked of statistical research that looks at the internal activity of CCTV systems, where the researchers' own categories appear to play an important role in the constitution of research outcomes (see Norris and Armstrong, 1999 and Chapter 2).

In place of such a statistical focus, this research utilised ethnography as a means to capture and analyse a variety of forms of interactivity focused around the technological system of CCTV. Ethnography has frequently been used to interrogate such socio-technical interaction. For example, Suchman's (1987) study of the use of photocopiers, Woolgar's (1991) study of configured computer users and Hirsch's (1992) study of familial use of technology each utilise an ethnographic approach. These studies engage with in-depth details of how technologies are understood by participants to the research and attempt to re-present the basis for interaction between people, technology and documentary sources.

Ethnography is based on 'description from the natives' point of view, rather than imposing one's own framework upon the situation' (Woolgar, 1988: 84). Ethnography requires the researcher to enter the field of research for a prolonged period, engaging with relevant data and becoming an integral part of the field setting. It also requires work to translate field notes, observations and documentary analysis into a representation of the setting. In studying the CCTV system this involved gaining access to the system, engaging with members of the system (CCTV staff, CCTV managers, police officers) and collecting and analysing documents produced within the system. However, this was not straightforward. The CCTV managers and CCTV staff occupied different offices within the local council building, and police officers spent their time in the police station (a separate building) or out on the town centre beat. Such a picture also draws a limited boundary around CCTV. Beyond the CCTV managers, staff and police, local retailers had their security staff connected to the CCTV system by radio and formed a group asked to help finance the system by the CCTV managers. Local residents and shoppers in the town centre also regularly featured on CCTV monitors and did a great deal of work in producing identities for CCTV.

How could this variety of settings, people and documents be incorporated into the study? Hirsch (1992) recommends a form of multi-site ethnography in his study of families' use, consumption and negotiation of technologies in the home. Hirsch identifies himself as the link between the families of his research, and as the link between the various sites in which the families negotiate understanding of technology. In multi-site ethnography links are drawn between a variety of settings, and multiple forms of data collection and analysis are utilised to shed light on the focus of study. Multi-site ethnography is discussed further by Hine (2000). For Hine's study of internet sites, she uses the term 'mobile rather than multi-sited' ethnography (Hine, 2000: 64). The mobile ethnography consists of following connections, linking up groups and crossing conventional boundaries. This has the advantage of treating ethnography as an 'experiential and engaged exploration of connectivity' (Hine, 2000: 61), in which the connections and boundaries are up for analysis, not just the content or actions that occur within those boundaries.

Multi-site and mobile ethnography were used in the study of CCTV to draw together multiple settings and forms of engagement. The CCTV managers and Burbville police officers were drawn into the research through extended, semi-structured interviews in their places of work, in return for which they were offered a report on the outcomes of the research. These interviews were repeated at early, mid and later stages of the fieldwork (for more on this see Chapter 3). The CCTV staff were observed for a prolonged period in the CCTV control room. This enabled an analysis of their day to day activities of identity production and interaction with local police officers and their own managers (for more detail, see Chapters 3 and 5 particularly). A variety of system documents, from operational guidelines to minutes of local council meetings, was collected and analysed (these feature in subsequent chapters). Local retailers (see Chapter 4) and residents (see Chapters 3, 4 and 6) were also interviewed using extended semi-structured interviews. In order to foster interaction and discussion between residents, a video was also made of Burbville and shown to residents in discussion groups (see Chapter 6).

This approach, drawing together multiple settings and forms of analysis, provided dynamic data for engaging with the day to day activities of privacy, surveillance and trust. However, the approach also raised several methodological issues.

Methodological issues

First, it might be asked how representative is one town of CCTV activity more broadly? Undoubtedly, as with any social science research, questions can legitimately be asked about representative adequacy. A survey which covered every CCTV system in the United Kingdom could still be interrogated in relation to whether or not the researchers' questions, time of year when the research was carried out or means of engagement, amongst many other things, influenced the adequacy of material collected. In this research the focus has been on producing an adequate representation of Burbville (see second point). An alternative reorientation for these questions of representation is: how useful is this study for shedding light on the subject matter to hand? The utility of selecting and analysing Burbville lies in the opportunities presented to produce a highly detailed engagement with the developing social, technical and legislative arrangements involved in day to day activities of privacy, surveillance and trust. The following chapters stand as demonstrations of this utility.

Second, consideration needs to be given to the choices of what was included and not included in this book, when analysis was initiated and drawn to a close, and what constituted an adequate re-presentation of Burbville. The research took place over several years (see for example Chapter 5), covering important legislative changes regarding CCTV (such as the 1998 European Human Rights Act, for more on this see Chapters 5 and 7) and significant changes in attitude toward the purposes, legitimate targets and practices of surveillance (particularly in relation to the post-September 11th period, see Chapter 7). The time-frame for this research, 1997–2005, was an integral feature of constituting the relevance of the research. Decisions over what to collect were informed by Hammersley and Atkinson's assertion of ethnographic flexibility, 'collecting whatever data are available to throw light on the issues that are the focus of the research' (1995: 1). Decisions on what to include and what not to include were taken in line with Atkinson's (1990 and 1992) suggestions on textual representation and Hine's (2000) approach to ethnography as 'experiential and engaged exploration' (Hine, 2000: 61). This resulted in as much of the original data as possible being incorporated in the text to enable readers the chance to engage with the data and engage with assessments of the data's utility.

Third, given the mass and variety of data collected, how could this be organised into a coherent and detailed study of the day to day activities of CCTV? Briefly stated, privacy, surveillance and trust were utilised as three organising principles for categorising the data into themes and interrogating the data (this is dealt with in more detail in Chapter 3). An outline of the structure of the book can prove useful in considering how these themes and organising principles provide coherence for the textual representation of the research.

The structure of the book

Chapter 2 picks up on the organising principles outlined in this chapter and initiates a detailed analysis of the theoretical frameworks which can

be brought to bear on privacy, surveillance and trust. Rather than instigate a straightforward run-through of current literature, this chapter
draws on an exemplar from the ethnographic study of CCTV in order to
dynamically engage with the literature. This exemplar (of kids standing
still) is used to evaluate three different ways of analysing the 'same'
CCTV story using currently available theoretical approaches (a critical
surveillance approach, an ethnomethodological approach and a Science
and Technology Studies (STS) approach).

Chapter 3 focuses on the internal interactivity of CCTV and how that
interactivity operates through modes of accountability to produce particular representations of CCTV, public and private. Entangled in this
representational identity work are on-going concerns for the CCTV
managers of privacy and trust. Rather than analysing a single notion of
public and private, this chapter suggests a means of coping with multiple
modes of accountability involved in the production of forms of public
and private. Producing a representation of *members of* public *in* public
spaces and producing a representation of CCTV *for* public audiences are
important and very different concepts in CCTV interaction. This interactivity forms the focal point for elaborating notions of privacy (who
should have what, when, providing boundaries for what kind of
action?) and trust (how can the CCTV managers foster a sense of trustworthiness of CCTV?).

Chapter 4 moves from the internal operations of CCTV to an analysis
of external relations between the CCTV system and local retailers.
This change in focus is used to consider the extent of informational
mobilisation around Burbville and the extent to which CCTV manages
to accomplish the kind of automated functioning of power some
surveillance analysts focus on (this idea builds on Chapter 2). The suggestion is made that the absence of such automated functioning raises
questions for retailers and residents about how to understand trust in
relation to CCTV. The views of residents and retailers are used to underscore the argument that trust and surveillance are not fixed and neither
are they stable concepts that can simply be applied to interactions
between, for example, bank managers and CCTV managers. Rather trust
and surveillance are the product of on-going negotiation.

In order to highlight the connectivity of the CCTV system and the
town to wider circuits of the criminal justice system and the media,
Chapter 5 looks at the story of Mr. B. He was filmed attempting to commit suicide in Burbville and was then shown without his consent on
national television. The CCTV managers hoped to use these images to
promote the caring aspects of the system, that it can save lives as well as
reduce crime. Simultaneously civil liberties groups hoped to promote

the privacy invading aspects of CCTV, that lives can be ruined through lack of regulation. The chapter follows the Mr. B story from its local setting, through local and national media, to the High Court and eventually the European Court of Human Rights. Issues of privacy, surveillance and trust, and who gets to decide what an image represents are analysed. This analysis draws on the conflicting viewpoints of CCTV managers and staff, local police, local residents, High Court judges, a civil liberties group and the media.

Chapter 6 focuses on interactivity between local residents and the CCTV system. It argues that an important feature of the complex interplay of CCTV, local residents, retailers and police is focused on the space in which the CCTV system operates. An attempt was made by the author to produce a video of this space to show to local residents in focus groups. The difficulties posed by making the video (including resistance by the local authority who run the CCTV system) and responses to the film (including claims that it misrepresented the town) form the basis for the development of a spatial component to the analysis building through the book. It further enhances the notion that who gets to speak for images and attempts to decide their content is highly contentious. The chapter concludes by suggesting that local residents understand privacy and trust in relation to how they construct detailed elaborations of the spaces of Burbville.

Chapter 7 is divided into three sections. The privacy, surveillance and trust sections pull together the insights developed in preceding chapters into a coherent, incisive and robust means of interrogating the principle issues of this book. The CCTV legislation section of the chapter then uses this analysis to highlight the policy implications of this research. Considerations of the ways in which privacy might be regarded, surveillance engaged and trust fostered are offered in relation to the insights offered by the preceding chapters (particularly Chapters 5 and 6). The Futures of privacy, surveillance and trust section of Chapter 7 finishes the book by outlining a possible future research agenda, taking up many of the ideas presented. This final section suggests that the rapidly expanding privacy, surveillance and trust environment requires an array of research projects, policy engagements and theoretical developments.

2

Who are These Kids and Why are They Standing Still? Questions on the Telling of CCTV Stories

Introduction

CCTV systems form one example of the recent and rapid expansion of technological systems involved in the collection, storage, categorisation and analysis of information on the population. These technological developments (which also include, for example, biometric technologies, organisational accountability mechanisms, border crossing systems, traffic control and automated scanning systems, amongst other things) form the focus for a range of new and developing technical, social and legislative arrangements. Chapter 1 suggested we have little idea of how these arrangements are made and maintained on a day to day basis. The argument was made that an ethnographic approach to CCTV can reveal much about its day to day activity and that privacy, surveillance and trust can form organising principles for analysis. However, while CCTV cameras are an increasingly prevalent feature of Britain's town centres (it is claimed there are four million cameras in operation in Britain), closer inspection of these cameras suggests there are a variety of on-going ambiguities and uncertainties surrounding CCTV images, what they represent and how they are utilised. Alongside the growing presence of cameras, there is an increasing sociological literature on CCTV.

This literature, however, unveils a multitude of ways in which CCTV stories can be told. There is, then, ambiguity and uncertainty both in the operation of CCTV and in what might form the most effective means of analysing CCTV.

In order to address these ambiguities and uncertainties, this chapter asks what four approaches to telling CCTV stories can achieve. The chapter will do this by initially offering an ethnographic rendition of a CCTV story produced from the field notes of a study of Burbville CCTV system (see Chapter 1 for more on methodology). The chapter will then look at three further ways this story can be told utilising what can broadly be termed a critical approach, an ethnomethodological approach and a Science and Technology Studies (STS) approach. The Chapter will conclude with suggestions on addressing the ambiguity of CCTV images, activities and theoretical approaches. These suggestions will form the basis for initiating a theoretical means for engaging with CCTV through notions of privacy, surveillance and trust.

The story

Burbville CCTV system incorporates 32 cameras in a fibre-optic network connected to a control room operated by teams of two staff, working in 8-hour shifts, 24 hours a day, 365 days a year. The staff sit behind a desk which features 16 small split screen monitors (showing activity from each of the cameras) and two large monitors (one for close-ups of town centre activity and one mirrored in the local police station). The CCTV staff also have a PC for logging notes on events and pens and paper for making notes prior to PC entries. The system constantly runs time-lapse recorders, which compress an image from each camera, every few seconds, onto a single tape. The staff can also switch on a real-time recorder if they perceive an event is happening or is likely to happen. The staff are connected to local shops and police on the beat by a radio system. The staff are also frequently visited by the CCTV managers who take an interest in 'what is going on'. There are two CCTV managers who are involved in the day to day operation of the system, gaining publicity for the system and dealing with enquiries. The following story is the product of field notes taken from a study of the CCTV control room.

Friday evening and kids standing still[1]

On a Friday night shift (10 p.m. to 6 a.m.), all cameras were focussed on pubs, the one nightclub in the town and the town's eateries. On Friday night McDonald's was a popular place for kids to go. It was also a popular time for young men and women to go to pubs, clubs (etc.). Between about 9 p.m. (when a previous team were finishing their shift) when most people who were coming into town had arrived and around 11 p.m. when the pubs closed, there was a hiatus in activity. The pubs were fairly full, but we could not see in; the one nightclub in town hadn't really got going yet, people hadn't drunk enough to require a kebab and the taxi rank was full of cars waiting for business which hadn't arrived yet.

A sequence which filled this lull was the identification of several kids as 'suspicious'. Although they did not look significantly different to the few other groups of people walking the streets, they appeared to have made the mistake of standing still. Standing still was a worrying activity for the CCTV staff. Outside take-away food places and pubs it was not something the CCTV staff could do very much about, but in the middle of the High Street, for 'no good reason' it had to be closely observed. I estimated the four kids to be about 13, but the CCTV staff guessed at 14. They were swiftly approached by a police car and its two officers who happened to be passing and could respond to the CCTV staff's radioed message of 'kids standing still'. There was no commentary on this 'event' in the control room from the police in the High Street,[2] but it seemed that the police were asking many questions and the kids were vehemently shaking their heads. This appeared to annoy the police, and the CCTV staff switched on the real-time recorder; a few tuts and exhalations were heard in the control room. The impression seemed to be that these kids must be doing something.

A second police car arrived, which seemed a little excessive as the kids were quite small and didn't appear to be going anywhere, but this was very much a personal opinion, not widely shared in the control room. The police officers stepped out of the second car and one promptly fell over the curb. The kids found this very amusing. The kids had to empty all their pockets and were talked to for another ten minutes or so. The policeman who fell over asked most questions. Eventually the kids were told to go on their way and there was some disappointment in the control room. The kids were followed down the street by the cameras and when one pulled something out of his pocket, camera 17 zoomed in from 200 feet and in full fibre-optic, digitally enhanced close-up, highlighted the sweet he was about to unwrap.

A critical story

There are a range of sociological studies of CCTV which take what could be termed a critical approach (Norris and Armstrong, 1999; Norris, Moran and Armstrong, 1998; Crang, 1996; Davies, 1996; Goombridge and Murji, 1994). The term 'critical' here is intended to convey the sense that these researchers do not restrict their analyses to questions of 'what is going on', but use such studies to form a critical viewpoint of CCTV, legislation, number of cameras (etc.). Such studies engage with CCTV in a variety of ways, including studying CCTV in European cities (Lomell, 2004), in train stations (Muller and Boos, 2004), during street protests (Coleman, 2004), in relation to the media (Goombridge, 2002) and in combination with identity tracking technology (Cameron, 2004).

These works frequently refer to and centre their analyses on terms such as surveillance and privacy. As noted in Chapter 1, however, these terms can be used in a variety of ways. Privacy can be utilised to talk of the relation between notions of 'public' and 'private' (Fraser, 1994), forms of legislation (Taylor, 2002) and can be approached as a contingent accomplishment (Hine and Eve, 1998). Surveillance can be considered in relation to, amongst other things, a broadly conceived field of information collection (Lyon, 2001), a narrowly conceived approach to information selection and threat assessment (Bennett, 2005) or in terms of mechanisms for managing populations (Poster, 1990). For the purposes of this study of privacy, surveillance and trust in action, a tight definition of these terms will be resisted prior to engaging in more detail with empirical data (see subsequent analysis and Chapter 3). However, for this chapter the approach taken by critical analysts to CCTV can be useful for further considering current social science approaches to privacy and surveillance. The work of Norris and Armstrong will be considered in detail here as broadly representative of this critical approach to CCTV. Certainly their work is the most widely developed with two books concentrating solely on CCTV (Norris and Armstrong, 1999; Norris, Moran and Armstrong, 1998) and can form the basis for initiating a discussion of the critical approach to CCTV, privacy and surveillance.

Norris and Armstrong are critical 'of a tendency towards technological determinism: an unquestioning belief in the power of technology' (1999: 9). They suggest that 'there is a common assumption: CCTV actually produces the effects claimed for it' (1999: 9). In order to avoid simply accepting claims made about CCTV, they embark on a rigorous empirical investigation of the practices of CCTV staff. The upshot of these investigations is the identification of a set of rules which drive CCTV staff activity in the operation of equipment. These rules are developed through ideas drawn from the work of Sacks (1972, see also 'An ethnomethodological story' section given later). As Norris and Armstrong state: 'Drawing on the work of Harvey Sacks ... we present and document a set of seven working rules which inform operators' choices as to whom ... should be subjected to extended targeting and surveillance' (1999: 11). It is 'an occupational necessity that [CCTV operatives] develop a set of working rules and procedures which seek to maximise their chances of selecting those most likely to be involved' in any incident (1999: 117).

The CCTV staff have to make predictions, according to Norris and Armstrong, about who is likely to be involved in a future event, who is most likely to require close observation, in order to make multiple, rapid judgements. In this view, the CCTV staff are presented with so many images of so many people, selections must be made and those selections must adhere to regularly repeated criteria. The criteria allow for the mass of images to be reduced to a manageable workload which will subsequently allow for the CCTV staff to operate effectively in between their own managers and the police. In this sense the mass of images is managed by appearances, which are categorised by simplifying criteria of 'certain appearances are likely to lead to certain activities'.

What are the results of such subjection to targeting, surveillance and categorisation? 'The human targeting conducted by CCTV operatives is … inherently discretionary and the result is discriminatory target selection based on crude indices of race, age, gender and appearance' (Norris and Armstrong 1999: 225). The mass of images the CCTV staff are presented with are categorised by a variety of criteria requiring a variety of response or non-response according to regularly repeated predictions, or rules, of the likely future activity of certain age, racial or gender based groupings.

Norris and Armstrong (1999) utilise an interpretation of Foucault's (1977) work on the panopticon and Poster's notion of the 'super-panopticon', in producing this analysis of CCTV activity. Foucault (1977) used the example of Bentham's prison designs in considering the ways in which populations are actively involved in forms of self management, paying attention to their own activity and how it might be assessed. In Bentham's designs prison cells surround a central watchtower from where a guard can see into every cell. Foucault suggests that because prisoners can only see the tower (not the inside of the tower), they do not have any basis for judging whether or not they are being watched at any time. Foucault suggests this encourages prisoners to consider the possibility that they are permanently potentially under scrutiny and should adjust their activities accordingly. Foucault suggested the panopticon involved three elements: first, making disciplinary connections to specific bodies; second, producing more and more data of particular areas; and, third, convincing people to pay attention to, or internalise, their own visibility and how they might be assessed. Norris and Armstrong's (1999) interpretation of the panopticon is restricted to the ways in which CCTV is implicated in gathering data (the second area of Foucault's approach; for a broader consideration of such governance issues, see Governance and governmentality section).

Norris and Armstrong use this focus on data collection to argue that increasingly important power relations are 'based on the collection of vast amounts of information on individuals and populations which is then used to manage the activities of the state' (1999: 223). This focus on information collection leads Norris and Armstrong to ask: does the increase in use of CCTV signal moves towards what Poster (1990) has called the 'super-panopticon'? Poster's version of the panopticon (the 'super-panopticon') is also intentionally restricted to the production of mass data. Poster suggests computers, for example, enable more data to be tabulated and thus increase surveillance capacity, leading towards a super-panopticon in which we will all be traceable. Norris and Armstrong (1999) suggest CCTV is a similar accounting, mass accumulating device. However, Norris (2003) suggests that the use of panoptic metaphors requires broader study. He suggests that, currently, CCTV has not achieved panoptic status, but suggests new technological developments signal moves in that direction.

Thus Norris and Armstrong (1999) focus on the potential for CCTV to become a panopticon, at least in relation to the mass accumulation of data. Their version of CCTV does not focus on people being encouraged to pay attention to their own activities (although see Fyfe and Bannister (1996) for an account of this), but instead considers in detail the ways in which particular areas are being made increasingly surveyable. They then tie this surveying into political issues (suggesting for example that CCTV can have racial implications). Norris and Armstrong suggest this activity fits within 'a type of government power, which has become increasingly important during the twentieth century, [and] is based on the collection of vast amounts of information on individuals and populations which is then used to manage the activities of the state' (1999: 223). This governmental focus is taken up by McCahill (2002) who suggests CCTV is involved in shifting responsibility and power from national government to multiple, regional, locales.

In sum, for the critical approach CCTV is a system implicated within a range of governance practices that seek to collect and categorise information for the activities of the state. The CCTV staff are at the centre of a mass of images which require simplification into broad categorisations based on criteria of age, race, gender (etc.) which can be used to predict future actions and decide upon suitable responses. Suitable responses often involve the passing of these predictive categorisations onto further areas of state activity such as the police. The categorisation of images by CCTV staff is a local manifestation of a broader goal of the state to collect and manage information on the population.

What does this imply for the story of kids standing still? Using Norris and Armstrong's (1999) work, it is possible to retell the story as a critical tale of categorisation.

Friday night and the categorisation of ill-disciplined youth

The CCTV staff scanned the monitors of Burbville town centre, surveying the mass of images the monitors' offered. This surveying activity was not neutral or apolitical. It was carried out via the regularly repeated rules for categorising images that the CCTV staff developed in several years of operating the CCTV equipment. They were looking for certain age, race and gender groupings.

The CCTV staff began surveying a group of young males. Drawing upon their regularly repeated rules for categorisation, the staff noted that these were young males, out at night, loitering not by McDonalds or a pub, but in the middle of the High Street. In terms of likely future behaviour, the CCTV staff were certain that something would occur here. Young males were frequently picked out for observation by CCTV staff as the staff tried to maximise their chances of selecting those most likely to be involved in a future incident. Using the radio and large monitor which connected the staff to the police, images of the kids were mobilised to the police with the message that they were likely to be the cause of some unspecified future unrest. This mobilisation of images called for a further mobilisation of police officers in response.

The CCTV staff were presented with such a range of images from the town centre that, inevitably, they had to make selections about which images to look at for a prolonged time and which to mobilise for a response. The categorisation of these kids as problematic was made according to their age (teenagers), gender (male) and position in the High Street (in the middle). While there were a range of other people in the High Street, these people were standing outside McDonalds or outside pubs and so were (according to the CCTV staff) less likely to be the future cause of an incident.

Eventually after a significant and prolonged targeted surveillance and police response, the kids were told to go on their way. This highlighted the pervasiveness of state requirements for gathering and processing information. The uncertainty presented by kids standing still in an unusual position required a response which categorised behaviour according to CCTV's rules of engagement with the town centre (based on age, gender, geographical location and likely future action). In this way the state managed the activities of the populace by constantly providing categories into which the population were entered.

An ethnomethodological story

While the critical approach is useful in initiating discussion of the basis of discrimination, categorisation and identification in CCTV, this approach is not without criticism. In particular, Lyon (1993) asks questions of Poster's (1990) approach to the super-panopticon. Lyon asks what form of social power is implicated within this theoretical model, how broadly influential is the super-panopticon across social relations and on what grounds might it be resisted? For the purposes of developing an approach to privacy and surveillance in action we also need to ask: how, in detail, do CCTV staff build and (importantly) maintain any forms of categorical suspicion and how are these made evident in day to day CCTV activity? These questions can be addressed by turning to an ethnomethodological approach to CCTV.

Ethnomethodology began with Garfinkel's (1967) work on courtroom activity. He drew on the work of Parsons on the reproduction of stable social orders and encounters (see Coulon, 1995, for a discussion) and the work of Alfred Schutz (see Sudnow, 1972, for a discussion). Ethnomethodology is focused on practical accomplishment and 'permanent tinkering' in social life (Coulon, 1995: 17). Concepts of reflexivity, accountability and indexicality are utilised in considering the ways in which members of a social group or exchange can be seen or heard to be producing representations of, and in, that event. As Strum and Latour suggest (1999), within Garfinkel's ethnomethodology there is no society or social relations until they are performed and recognised as such. Being a member of society is itself an on-going accomplishment with people managing their own 'observability' (Rogers, 1983: 81). Thus ethnomethodology is concerned with the ways in which social interaction is made and maintained through on-going and everyday accountability relations made available in forms of interactivity. As Heritage suggests, Garfinkel's concern was 'directed at examining how various types of social activity are brought to adequate description and thus rendered "account-able" ' (Heritage, 1984: 136). However Garfinkel was clear that in producing an account of, in this case, a conversation, 'Many of its expressions are such that their sense cannot be decided by an auditor unless he knows or assumes something about the biography and the purposes of the speaker, the circumstances of the utterance, the previous course of conversation, or the particular relationship of actual or potential interaction that exists between user and auditor. The expressions do not have a sense that remains identical through the changing occasions of their use' (in Sudnow, 1972: 5). This contingent accomplishment of accountable interaction will form the basis for outlining an alternative to the critical approach to CCTV. The 'Ethnomethodology and CCTV' section will begin with an introduction to ethnomethodological engagement with CCTV and then consider the ways in which this work fits into broader ethnomethodological concerns of, first, visual representation and, second, the accomplishment of walking.

Ethnomethodology and CCTV

Heath and Luff (1999) produce an analysis of CCTV from an ethnomethodological remit. Their concern lies in how CCTV is used as a tool in the London Underground by station operatives to assess how platform conditions can be rendered controllable. Heath and Luff suggest that station supervisors in the Underground often have to deal with quick glances at scenes displayed on monitors and less than complete information. They subsequently need to make guesses about what might be happening just beyond a camera's viewpoint. Heath and Luff argue that 'video technologies used in concert with other devices, like radio, form a critical resource for collaborating with colleagues and developing a coordinated response to an emerging incident' (1999: 3). Such social and technical coordination can help to produce a relatively coherent and seemingly complete response to an incident.

The station supervisors put together a range of claims in these responses. Claims are made about 'unusual passenger behaviour' (1999: 3) including passengers standing still or dawdling, carrying large packages, being over or under dressed for the time of year, wavering close to the platform edge and so on. 'Control room staff practically discriminate apparently routine behaviour for organisational purposes' (1999: 3). This appears very similar to the work of Norris and Armstrong (1999). However, the emphasis here is a little different. Although both draw on Sacks, the work of Heath and Luff, unlike Norris and Armstrong, emphasises the uncertain, does not concentrate on rules which might drive CCTV operatives' behaviour and looks at the complex building of coherence. 'To make temporary, fragmentary and disjoint views of the world coherent and useful, relies on routine categorisations and discriminations made with respect to organisational purposes, of the human conduct they see before them' (1999: 3). Heath, Hindmarsh and Luff (1999) argue that tube drivers develop 'occupationally relevant ways of perceiving the scene' (1999: 561).

The interactions between tube drivers, platform conditions, specific stations and times of day are often diffuse and disjointed. However the decisions made by the drivers form a kind of coherence from the disparate elements and form these elements into something which is 'circumstantially sensitive', but which relies on 'background expectancies', to make a judgement about the scene (1999: 563). This may still appear to be very similar to the critical approach to CCTV outlined before. However, according to Heath, Hindmarsh and Luff (1999) the work of building accounts of activity 'is not simply a matter of contrasting some event or appearance with what might ordinarily be expected to happen, but rather learning to see particular events, activities, people or objects in particular ways' (1999: 4).

Ethnomethodology, visibility and representation

This fits closely with a broader ethnomethodological concern for questions of visibility and representation (see for example, Goodwin and Goodwin, 1996, 1995; Jordan and Lynch, 1998; Jasanoff, 1998; Suchman, 1993; see Chapter 3 for more discussion of visual witnessing and ethnomethodology). Goodwin and Goodwin (1996) suggest in their study of airport staff trying to pick out the correct aeroplane that a quick glance at activity is 'structured by larger organisational structures' (1996: 62). Goodwin and Goodwin argue that aeroplanes are not just seen by airport staff, but are noted within a web of activity involving the positioning of people, runways, aeroplanes and various other elements. Goodwin and Goodwin suggest that seeing is a socially organised activity sustained by a community of practice. In this sense, CCTV staff when glancing at monitors would do so within a structure of interactivity, demonstrating awareness of management prerogatives, the location of each camera, where the police on the beat are, what the police might want them to pick up on and so on. Furthermore, each interaction is part of an on-going series which over time build into a form of achieved coherence.

This approach signals a return to Garfinkel's (1967) work (particularly on coroners) and Sacks' (1972) work (particularly on police officers). Garfinkel's work suggested that coroners would actively constitute such totems of representation as cut marks on the wrists of dead bodies and make decisions as to whether they were marks of suicide or murder. That is, a suicide is not straightforwardly noticed by coroners, but is actively constituted by their processes of representation. Garfinkel suggests that when producing a representation: 'whatever is there is good enough in the sense that whatever is there not only will do, but does' (1967: 18). As Garfinkel is swift to point out, these representations as suicide are not based on any access to the original event, but what is particularly relevant for Garfinkel is that these decisions are made 'for all practical purposes' (1967: vii). The coroners, as those bestowed with authority, would say that 'for all practical purposes' it appeared to be suicide, that is, they appeared to be able to get the body to re-perform the act. Thus the suicide representation became an account that then moved with the body through any subsequent accountability activity, be that to the family or friends of the deceased who now 'knew' the body as a suicide case, or through any subsequent legal process where the body was similarly noted as a suicide case.

CCTV staff when looking at images of the High Street, then, would not simply notice the age of a person in an image, but would constantly orient accounts of images toward particular and regularly repeated forms of identification. 'Age' would not be an inevitable and accepted factual judgement but would rather occupy a performative position. The

CCTV staff could make a claim in interaction with the police that, for all practical purposes, a person in an image appeared to be a teenager and this suggested a series of potential subsequent activity which might need a police response. Although this appears laden with uncertainty, Sacks (1972) suggests groups such as the police, but also presumably CCTV staff, become expert in verbalising the observable. They orient towards a technique which elaborates on the observable with a form of discourse which situates and re-performs the observable as a verbalised reality.

Although Norris and Armstrong (1999) also draw on the work of Sacks, it is not clear that Sacks would recognise the pertinence of the 'rules' which Norris and Armstrong develop. Rather Sacks might have found it more appropriate to investigate notions of what a 'rule' might relate to, how a 'rule' came about and what provenance any particular 'rule' continued to have. While Norris and Armstrong (1999) suggest rules are relatively consistent and drive behaviour, Sacks would argue that rules are the achieved outcome of on-going activity which seeks to establish and consistently orient the interactional relevance of any 'rule' in the current interaction. And, while a range of claims would be made in an interaction, these would be made for all practical purposes. That is, claims about 'what is happening in the town centre' would be delivered with the proviso that the claims are, or may be, incomplete. These incomplete claims can still be powerful. Suggesting that 'there is a person walking through the town centre with what appears to be a knife and we don't know what he's doing' (see Chapter 5) almost guarantees a police response. Such a claim sets in motion a chain of accountability in which the police might later be called upon to explain any non-response. Just like the CCTV staff, the police must constantly orient their responses to claims through particular forms of discourse, awareness of their position within a range of immediate and future accountability interactions and the need to achieve a mutually recognised, on-going coherence.

Ethnomethodology and walking

While this sets out the basis for considering the ethnomethodological approach to the contingent accomplishment of accountability and introduces some initial considerations for analysing the activity of CCTV staff, the activity of people in the town centre is notably absent. Much ethnomethodological research, however, considers the ways in which people and space are involved in mutual interactive accomplishments. Ethnomethodological analyses of walking offer an initial entry point into these ideas. It might be said that in the example of kids standing still, there is not much walking. However, in order to engage with why standing still might form a matter of concern for CCTV staff, we need to consider the ways in which standing still forms a notable exception to expectations of walking.

The majority of people in Burbville town centre who feature on CCTV monitors are engaged in walking through the town centre. However, this section will engage with the suggestion that walking 'through' the town centre involves the on-going and active accomplishment of an accountable rendition of individuals, the activity of walking and the town centre space (specific difficulties of space will be discussed in more detail in Chapter 6). This form of accomplishment is made clear by Ryave and Schenkein (1974): 'We use the verb "doing" to underscore a conception of walking as the concerted accomplishment of members of the community involved as a matter of course in its production and recognition' (1974: 265). Livingston's (1987) study of walking suggests that people crossing roads towards each other are tied into a constant mutual accomplishment. They are involved in accomplishing the possibility of crossing the road and crossing the road in an ordered way, allowing for the possibility of many people to cross the road towards each other without colliding. This mutual accomplishment outlines how busy public areas both constrain people to mutually achieve and are dependent on that mutual achievement for some form of sensible continued existence. As Crabtree suggests 'space is not a worldly abstraction then, but embodied in, and integral to, the accomplishment of the activities that we do' (2000: 2).

The activity of CCTV staff appears in some sense removed from this accomplishment. If the town centre is accomplished through mutual interaction between people walking, what is it that the CCTV staff are doing? This notion of accomplishment can be expanded a little further and consideration given to Garfinkel's suggestion that accomplished accounts, 'do not have a sense that remains identical through the changing occasions of their use' (1972: 5). In this sense just as walking is a routine accomplishment for the people walking, producing an account of people walking in the town centre is a routine accomplishment for CCTV staff. Accounts of routine walking can be accomplished without the need to provide any further account. The accounts of routine walking fit into what Hester and Francis term the 'visually available mundane order' (2003: 36). The mundane as a concept features in a variety of social science work. This includes Brekhus' (1998) work on the unmarked, Pollner's (1987) work on mundane reasoning and Shove's

(2003, and with Southerton, 2000) work on mundane technology. For the purposes of this section, the 'mundane' will be used to emphasise that on-going accomplishments of walking can be talked of as everyday, routine phenomena. Those involved in doing walking are accounted for by CCTV staff while walking across monitors in CCTV control centres. The CCTV staff account for these activities of routine walking as not needing any further action. The CCTV staff accomplish the mundane through brief glances at the CCTV monitors, the linking together of talk of the space of the town centre, time of day and so on into suggestions that there is little that requires attention. In this way standing still is formulated as an unusual activity, as outside the routine of mundane walking.

To draw together this ethnomethodological approach to walking with previous ethnomethodological suggestions on visual representation, the CCTV staff can be said to actively constitute forms of interactivity (such as walking) as mundane routine and in need of no further scrutiny. This is achieved through claims relating the time of day, content of footage on monitors and interactions with the police, asking whether anything is going on. The CCTV staff thus render certain forms of visual activity as demonstrative of normal, everyday, mundane walking. However, at times they also render further actions necessary of attention by positioning them outside of these mundane routines. Constituting standing still as non-routine sets in motion a range of accountability relations in which both CCTV staff and police officers must produce accounts of 'what is going on', while also being aware of the possibility that such accounts could be held to future scrutiny. While kids standing still might appear not to pose a threat to the stability of the town centre, the articulation of these kids as non-mundane and non-routine means they must form the subject of further accountability relations between CCTV staff and police. It is only when both the latter parties have accomplished sufficiently robust accounts that the parties can be confident that their accounts will hold up to further scrutiny, that CCTV staff can return to producing mundane accounts of not much going on.

In sum an ethnomethodological approach to CCTV suggests that CCTV staff, police officers, CCTV managers and local residents are enmeshed in an on-going series of interactions. These are characterised by various parties producing and orienting claims about activity, through forms of discourse, verbalising practices of seeing and awareness of accountability relations, in order to achieve an on-going coherence. For CCTV staff these claims are often delivered in a partial or incomplete fashion. Completeness can be achieved through on-going interaction with other groups such as the police. For CCTV staff and the police particularly, these claims and occasional counter-claims (relating to walking, standing still or a broad range of other activities) are delivered with a protective 'for all practical purposes' clause. That is, any claim and response delivered is deemed suitable to the event at hand as best as that event at hand can be perceived at the particular time in question. The protective clause pays recognition to the further time frames when these interactions might be later called to account. The protective clause can form a responsibility 'get-out' in future accountability processes where the reliability of any claim regarding 'what was going on' in a set of images might be questioned (see Chapter 5).

What does this imply for the story of kids standing still? It is possible to retell the story as an ethnomethodological tale of High Street interactivity.

Friday evening and the interactive accomplishment of kids standing still

The CCTV staff actively constituted, and confirmed with local police officers, that nothing was happening. It was a Friday night and the pubs were full, there were kids standing outside McDonald's and no one was heading towards the one nightclub in town. 'Nothing happening' was a performative designation produced by the CCTV staff and occasionally mobilised to the local police. The 'nothing happening' account involved scanning the CCTV monitors, making claims for several years of experience of Friday night CCTV operation and what activity normally constituted a Friday, gaining confirmation from local police officers that they had no tip-offs about activity for them to follow and so on. 'Nothing happening' was not simply noticed, but was an actively constructed identification relying on particular practices of seeing, verbalising that practice and mobilising it to the police for corroboration. 'Nothing happening' formed a mundane routine for CCTV staff and police officers in Burbville.

The CCTV staff began to account for a particular set of images in the middle of the High Street. The CCTV staff began to build an account based around a set of claims relating to, or re-performing, a group of kids. The staff actively oriented their account of these kids to their regular interactions with the police. They suggested the kids were of an age when they might be likely to cause some unspecified trouble. The staff selected geographical location as potentially significant; these kids were not outside McDonald's. Yet there were few certain claims the CCTV staff could make to produce a police response; there were none of the usual things available which were likely to move an image into an event. There was little in the way of weaponry on show, there were no clear signs of illegal drugs and the kids were not showing any signs that they were likely to vandalise property. The CCTV staff mobilised an account, via the radio, that 'here are some kids standing still in the middle of the High Street and we don't know what they are doing'.

The 'we don't know what they are doing' aspect of the account delivered the uncertainty in interaction with the police which generated a response. Both police and CCTV staff had already interactively agreed that there was little else occurring in the High Street. The CCTV staff and police also regularly noted the frequency with which kids were involved in incidents. The CCTV staff were also aware that they needed a 'get-out' from any future accountability exercise which might look into the outcome of a possible event involving these kids. Having mobilised an uncertain account, it was now for the police to produce their own 'get-out' or actually constitute an event.

The police, once mobilised, attempted a variety of different exercises to constitute evidence that an event might occur. They called upon the kids to empty their pockets; was there anything which could form the cause of a future event? The police also asked the kids many questions; were there any verbal responses which suggested a likely future event? The police also had a range of options on further actions, such as taking the kids to the police station, which might have allowed them to constitute further evidence of a likely event. However, the police had amassed a sufficient account, an account which 'for all practical purposes' suggested nothing was likely to happen. An account which was a sufficient 'get-out' from any future accountability process which might question why they moved the kids along.

A Science and Technology Studies story

While the critical approach to CCTV was useful in highlighting the importance and consequence of distinctions and selective categorisations made by CCTV staff, ethnomethodology has provided a means to consider how such distinctions and categorisations can be made on a day to day basis. Even in the mundane, perhaps banal, example of the distinction between walking and standing still, ethnomethodology offers one means to capture the complexity of CCTV related interactivity. However, both the critical approach and the ethnomethodological approach can be questioned for the extent to which they offer a suitable vocabulary for talking of, about and for the technology of CCTV. While Norris and Armstrong (1999) advocate moving away from technological determinism and the idea that CCTV might produce the effects claimed for it, what might form a suitable means for engaging in developing an understanding of CCTV technology? Science and Technology Studies (STS) has provided a range of alternative means for engaging with technology from a non-deterministic viewpoint (see Mackenzie and Wajcman, 1985; Bijker, Hughes and Pinch, 1989; Woolgar, 1991; Bijker and Law, 1992; Mansell, 1994; Grint and Woolgar, 1997; amongst others). In this section, one area of STS – Actor-Network Theory (ANT) – will form the basis for initiating a suitable vocabulary for CCTV (further areas of STS will feature in each of the subsequent chapters).

Ball (2002) argues that 'the majority of empirical investigations into surveillance have been conducted using realist, microsociological approaches to observation' (2002: 586). Quoting Norris and Armstrong (1999) as an example of such an approach, she goes on to suggest a theoretical alternative 'largely founded upon Latourian (1987), post-structuralist conceptions of actor-networks' (2002: 586).

Actor-Network Theory (ANT) suggests treating human and non-human entities with a radical symmetry, allowing for no a priori distinctions of status to be carried into analysis. For Callon (1986) an actor-network is formed through the translation of entities via obligatory points of passage which go some way to stabilising entity identities. Via translation, 'the actor-world accumulates materials that render it durable' (1986: 28). For CCTV images, an obligatory passage point might be the CCTV control room where images would be accounted for in certain ways by police and CCTV staff. The identity of the images would not be dependent upon some set of assumptions about the town centre adopted by CCTV staff but would be actively translated into ANT entities by the actor-network of police, monitors, cameras, fibre-optic connections, CCTV staff and so on. Once translated into an ANT entity, the images would then be available for mobilisation through the network to other entities (such as the CCTV managers) and other areas of the network (such as the criminal justice system).

This notion of mobilisation is not straightforward however. Latour (1990) argues that a great deal of work goes into the construction of what he terms immutable mobiles. '[Y]ou have to invent objects which have the properties of being mobile but also immutable, presentable, readable and combinable with one another' (1990: 26). For example, scientists draw together a range of entities to act as faithful allies in the support of their account (say of a scientific discovery). These entities will be tied together in such a way that the account they form is understood in the same way in each location in which it is read, presented (etc.). According to Latour, if there are competing accounts, the strongest will be 'the one able to muster on the spot the largest number of well aligned and faithful allies' (1990: 23). In this way the CCTV staff would need to package image, verbal accounts that make claims about images, attempt to draw in a police corroboration of the account and tie in some suggestion of how the image has been filed, in order to produce an immutable mobile that travels to a court room, for example, in a stable manner. However, Latour makes no guarantees of immutability. There is no secret recipe for ensuring that a collection of entities will stay together and will be understood in the same way in each location to which they move.

Mol and Law (1994) talk of the instability of such ANT mobiles as fluid features of networks (for an alternative take on fluidity, see Haggerty and Ericson, 2000, discussed in 'An alternative theoretical approach' section). In Mol and Law's (1994) approach to fluidity, there is much less expectation of stability. In their study of anaemia diagnosis in Africa, Mol and Law highlight a range of fluidities in the way disease is talked of, accounted for and treated. Law and Mol (1998) ask 'what can be held and what by contrast escapes the grasp. Our object is to distinguish between that which is (ac)countable and that which is fluid' (1998: 23). Fluidity might provide a more appropriate argumentative strategy than immutable mobility for CCTV stories. The cameras, staff, police, managers, tapes, fibre-optic connections (etc.) could form an enrolled set of actor-network entities bound together by a series of fluid images. The images would be fluid in the twin sense that they flow between various entities and are not entirely or necessarily stable. That is, they are not necessarily understood in the same way in each location into which they flow. Fluidity, however, and the treatment of images particularly, may require further specification.

It could be argued that despite fluidity, CCTV staff still attempt to construct immutable mobiles from images and accounts of images. This could lead into the further argument that fluidity of the image/accounts, their mutability, is an unwelcome upshot of activity between actor-network entities that seek to challenge the image/account. For ANT approaches, however, such intentionality in constructing and challenging accounts is not greatly emphasised. Things either hold together or they do not. A CCTV image and account turn out to be immutably mobile or fluid or something else; little analysis would be given to any entities' active attempts to strategically construct an immutable mobile. Immutability and fluidity are post-hoc descriptions of things which have happened (or not).

Instability of CCTV images, though, could still be accommodated via a range of ANT's theoretical devices. First, there is the boundary object (Star and Griesemer, 1989). The boundary object is a locus for multiple representative practices that move through a more focussed passage point. Star and Griesemer (1989) argue that: 'Scientific work is heterogeneous, requiring many different actors and viewpoints. It also requires co-operation. The two create tension between divergent viewpoints and the need for generalizable findings ... Boundary objects are both adaptable to different viewpoints and robust enough to maintain identity across them' (1989: 387). In this sense, CCTV images and accounts could be seen as boundary objects, or organising focal points around which a range of entities are gathered, occasionally producing mutually incompatible renderings of the content of image/account.

A second alternative for representing this notion of dispute or disagreement about the content of the image/account would be to consider non-connectedness or a non-represented blank figure (Lee and Hetherington, 2000). The blank figure is not centred on an idea of the unknown, but rather on something which has the ability to trouble or retain a questioning status. Lee and Hetherington (2000) link this closely into an analysis of ordering. 'The blank figure ... is the "present absence" ' that allows 'for the possibility of ... otherness' (2000: 173). The CCTV staff in building uncertain image/accounts could be producing a disrupting flow for the CCTV actor-network. The various entities could come together around a particular account or begin to dissipate through uncertainty over how the image/account should be read.

Third, it is possible to draw further on Law and Mol's work (1998) on accountability. In ANT accountability is construed narrowly in comparison to ethnomethodology where it is considered as a pervasive feature of social life. Thus Law and Mol (1998) analyse mechanisms of accountability. They pursue a question of the work required to render fluid things available to accounting through 'a labour of division' (1998: 23). This labour of division, they suggest, is enabled through 'technologies of calculation' (1998: 27). Law (1996) argues that this shift between the fluid and the (ac)countable requires 'an active process of blocking, summarizing, simplifying and deleting ... [which decides] what is to count and what, therefore, becomes counted' (1996: 291). Within this view, CCTV images/accounts could be the subject of summarising, simplifying and deleting in order to shift the focus from fluidity to stability. Here fluidity is not an inevitable feature of actor-networks but is rather a characteristic which can be worked on.

To summarise, ANT can be used to look at ways in which a variety of entities are drawn together and, to some extent, hold together in a complex network such as a CCTV system. This is not a network in the (relatively) straightforward sense of a sewage system connecting various pipes. Instead it is a diverse and sometimes unstable range of entities held together by various mobile entities and flows. The content which binds the entities is not always treated in an immutably mobile fashion however and a range of theoretical devices are made available for reconsidering the instability of content (such as the boundary object, the bank figure and processes of accountability). ANT thereby stands in some contrast to the previous means of CCTV storytelling presented.

Unlike Norris and Armstrong (1999), the emphasis is placed on the complex range of entities tied into a diverse network. To return to Ball's critique, ANT does not depend upon a microsociological realist analysis. Also, though, unlike ethnomethodology, ANT does not focus greatly on interaction between entities, technological entities are given an equal status with social entities and little detail is offered on the deployment of particular strategies for producing accounts or developing forms of discourse.

What does this imply for the story of kids standing still? It would be possible to retell the story as an actor-network tale of socio-technical mobility.

Friday night's attempt to immutably mobilise kids standing still

The town centre represented a complex assembly of heterogeneous entities including people, benches, bus stops, lighting systems, cameras, shop signs and drainage covers. These were nodes; network entities which each represented further complex connections of entities. In order to appear in an account produced by CCTV staff, their node-ish qualities were important. A process of simplifying, blocking, deleting and summarising of entities as they passed through the obligatory passage point of the CCTV control room was necessary for enrollment. Without this, the High Street would remain a mass of complex entities for the CCTV system and there would be no mobilisation of images through the CCTV actor-network.

On a Friday night nothing was happening in the High Street. A range of images were comfortably enrolled into CCTV's actor-network connecting CCTV staff, police, monitors, fibre-optic cables, radio system and so on. Via the obligatory point of passage of the CCTV control room, images were immutably mobilised between various entities (mostly CCTV staff, through the radio system, to police officers). The connection of image and account of 'nothing happening' flowed through the network retaining a stability in each location into which it flowed.

A destabilising entity entered the network in the blank figure form of several kids standing still. They highlighted a particular presence of absence, a notable 'other' not easily incorporated into the network. What was it that they were doing in the middle of the High Street? Was this something or nothing? How could such a blank figure be comfortably enrolled into the actor-network to prolong the notion that 'nothing was happening'?

The kids formed a boundary object around which a range of entities were drawn in order to form particular accounts. The CCTV staff, cameras, monitors, radios and police were each connected in order to enroll the blank figure. What got counted and what was to count? Via emptying of pockets and a range of verbal questions, the presence of absence was gradually simplified, possibilities were deleted and most potentially troubling scenarios were blocked. Once simplified, the kids were enrolled into the network as part of the 'nothing happening' account which flowed between entities.

Continued

Continued

> The ability of the kids to act as a threatening presence of absence, an unsettling blank figure which required enrolment via a process of blocking, simplifying and deleting, highlighted the fragility of the flow of 'nothing happening'. When one kid pulled something from his pocket, all the uncertainty returned. What was this new blank figure? Was this something the police had failed to count? How could this be enrolled as part of the 'nothing happening' flow of image/accounts? The complex association of cameras, staff, police, fibre optic connections and radios designated the new blank figure as a sweet. At this point it became repackaged as a further entity in the node of kids who could now be immutably mobilised in the flow of 'nothing happening' once again.

An alternative theoretical approach?

Drawing critical approaches, ethnomethodology and ANT together

Thus far, four alternative versions of the 'same' story have been presented. The ethnographic version of the story should not be taken as an apolitical or neutral version of the story. It is laden with assumptions made by the researcher and formed into particular rhetorical devices and embedded textual renditions intended to configure readers into forming a particular relationship with the text (Atkinson, 1990; 1992; Grint and Woolgar, 1997). This relationship attempts to place the reader alongside the researcher as 'other,' as observer of these strange, textually re-performed CCTV relations. What the ethnographic rendition of the story offers is a particular and tight chronology of events, of image and account construction, of the role of technology in identity production. What it allows for in detail, it misses out in analysis (including the way in which the text itself is constructed). Hence to what extent could the ethnographic version allow researchers/readers to get at the key analytical questions? What are the key analytical questions? Or perhaps more pertinently, whose analytical questions are key?

For the critical approach to CCTV, for example the work of Norris and Armstrong (1999), the questions to ask relate to the discriminatory potential of CCTV, of the problematic impact of cameras and of relations between CCTV and the state. This is useful for highlighting the importance of distinctions produced by CCTV. The critical approach provides detail on a range of groups who may be targeted for extra attention by CCTV and provides some suggestions on why this selective targeting might occur. However, the questions asked by the critical approach to CCTV carry a set of distinct assumptions: that surveillance is or can be problematic; that we know what surveillance is; that building identities for images is relatively straightforward (and therefore should not form a detailed focus of study); and that 'things' (such as kids in the town centre, prolonged and targeted surveillance) are available for easy collection and analysis by CCTV staff and then by the researcher. It is not clear that any of these areas is as clear-cut as critical analysts suggest. Furthermore, the role of the researcher in deciding who is targeted/discriminated against and when and why are absent from analysis. It can be asked of critical analysts: from whose perspective are analytical categories drawn? Does the claimed relevance of a particular category (e.g. the claim that men are a category more likely to be targeted) provide a troublesome gloss for the complexity of interaction that might go into CCTV's process of target selection?

Although Norris and Armstrong (1999) usefully argue that surveillance technologies do not always work as claimed, they may have neglected to turn that sceptical attention to their own work. Such a sceptical approach is provided by the ethnomethodological rendition of the story. While there appears to be superficial similarities between the critical and ethnomethodological approaches (both draw on Sacks, both look at forms of categorisation, both focus on people primarily), in practice they are distinct. Ethnomethodologists such as Goodwin and Goodwin (1996) analyse looking/seeing as an on-going practice. They would not accept claims such as 'men are more likely to be targeted by CCTV' are easily available for straightforward observation. Goodwin and Goodwin focus more on the variety of different and possibly contested features of any social scene which are drawn together in producing a visual account of the scene. This sits alongside Heath *et al.*'s (1999) view of account production as the on-going achievement of mutual coherence. Furthermore, as Sacks (1972) suggests, things are not simply there to be noted, but are rather performed and re-performed through particular forms of discourse. As Garfinkel (1967) notes, these re-performances can include the production of accounts involving elaborate plays upon certainty and uncertainty, both of which can form powerful argumentative strategies.

Questions of accounts and accountability are a prominent feature of analysis in ethnomethodology. The interactional relations surrounding the CCTV system establish and maintain expectations that CCTV staff should produce accounts of images for the police and the police should respond to the images/accounts they are sent. This is not fixed and inevitable, however, and a great deal of interaction (including producing certain and uncertain claims in interaction in an attempt to produce a response) goes into establishing an event, that the police should and will react to an event and so on. The difficulty for CCTV staff and police lies in their awareness, frequently replayed through interaction, that a non-response or unusual response can later be recalled by CCTV managers and courts of law (see Chapter 3). The possibility of future accountability is drawn upon by CCTV staff and police in interactively establishing what an account/image represents. Ethnomethodology thereby allows CCTV analysis to deal with complexity, uncertainty and accountability in detailed studies of interaction, which are prominent features of the ethnography, but are absent from critical approaches.

However, relating ethnomethodology to CCTV also introduces some questions. First, it could be argued, that at least in comparison with ANT, there is a less detailed vocabulary for talking of/for technology. Second, while Garfinkel suggests that accounts are always reconstituted in each location into which they move, this might suggest that stability of accounts (immutable mobility) is unavailable. Hence a vocabulary for stable account mobilisation is also required.

A vocabulary for representing technology, mobilisation and complex uncertain forms of stability/instability is provided by the Actor-Network Theory rendition of the story. ANT allows for the technology to enter the story in a more prominent manner. Fluidity and the possibility of immutability allow for stability, instability and movement to be captured together in analysis. The boundary object, blank figure and ANT approach to accountability suggest means for dealing with the unrepresented and shifts of uncertainty to certainty.

It is not clear, however, that an ANT approach offers a useful vocabulary for getting to grips with the interactional detail that the ethnography provides. How to talk about the strategies and counter strategies deployed by CCTV staff and police officers using ANT terminology is unclear. The richness of interaction through CCTV, between CCTV staff and police particularly, appears a key point for analysis. It is in the interaction that a great deal of work is done to produce accounts for CCTV images, identities for CCTV staff and the police, the CCTV managers, the town centre and so on. Does this suggest some combined theoretical approach would be most appropriate?

While critical approaches, ethnomethodology and ANT have advantages, it is not clear that these can be easily combined. There has been research which considers drawing ANT and ethnomethodology together (see for example, Brown, 1999). However, the two are not always comfortable companions (see for example, Latour, 1986). One area where there has been an attempt to utilise features of STS research along with the concerns of critical analysts of surveillance technologies in a way which might still be compatible with ethnomethodological imperatives has been the literature on governance and governmentality (building on the work of Foucault, 1977). While Norris and Armstrong (1999) and Poster (1990) draw on versions of Foucault's (1977) work, a broader consideration of governance and governmentality can be useful for situating the forgoing debate in a rich history of studies of attempts to manage the activities of populations.

Governance and governmentality

Rose (1996) outlines a model of governmentality as 'a kind of intellectual machinery or apparatus for rendering reality thinkable in such a way that it is amenable to political programming' (1996: 42). Such programming of the activities of the population would not involve a straightforward imposition of power by, for example, a CCTV system, but rather a 'complex assemblage of diverse forces ... techniques ... devices that promise to regulate decisions and actions of individuals, groups and organizations in relation to authoritative criteria' (1996: 42). Rose utilises ANT (particularly the work of Latour, 1987), to consider the ways in which activity by specific parts of the population is rendered accountable, and draws on Foucault (1977) and ANT to consider the ways in which routines for action are translated from centres of calculation into a diversity of locales. The internalisation of these proposals into everyday actions is 'an outcome of the composition and assembling of actors, flows, buildings, relations of authority into relatively durable associations mobilized, to a greater or lesser extent, towards the achievement of particular objectives by common means' (Rose, 1996: 43). Through these processes individuals become 'enwrapped in webs of knowledge and circuits of communication through which their actions can be shaped and by means of which they can steer themselves' (Rose, 1999: 147). Thus members of the population are made aware of their own subjectivity and reflect on their actions accordingly. This approach is picked up by Miller, amongst others, in looking at the ways in which individuals come to regard themselves as measurable units of performance and as 'calculable' (Miller, 1992; Miller and O'Leary, 1994).

Similar ideas are drawn together in the work of Haggerty and Ericson (2000) when discussing what they term 'the surveillant assemblage' (2000: 605). In constituting this assemblage they shift focus a little from the work of Foucault (1977)[3] to the work of Deleuze and Guattari (1986), tying the practices of surveillance into broad social developments regarding informational flows (this idea of flows will be picked up in Closed-circuits of CCTV section). Using the work of Rose (1996) and Haggerty and Ericson (2000) in considering technological developments involved in holding parts of the population to account appears to offer opportunities to bring together critical analysts' questions of categorisation and discrimination with ANT's concerns with assemblages and flows. Ethnomethodology could then be utilised to consider the detail of interaction within and around these flows. However, this work on governance and accountability also raises questions. First, how can these ideas of centres of calculation, flows, assemblages and rationales be rendered appropriate to an analysis of CCTV? Second, in considering Rose's (1996) work, how might sections of the population pick up on rationales for action, or find themselves enwrapped in webs of knowledge and forms of communication? These are important questions for developing an approach to interrogating the day to day activities of privacy, surveillance and trust. A detailed consideration of the CCTV system of Burbville will suggest one way in which they can be addressed.

Closed-circuits of CCTV

Engaging with the technological details of CCTV can be suggestive of a useful way forward for analyses of CCTV. The closed-circuit of CCTV provides a powerful metaphor for thinking through alternative theoretical possibilities. It allows both development of a detailed picture of the social/technical relations which go into building and maintaining the circuit and a detailed analysis of the interactions that decide upon specific representations of image/account in the circuit. In this sense, insights from ANT on the construction and maintenance of heterogeneous networks and from ethnomethodology on account building can be drawn together along with considerations from critical analysts on the importance of categorisation.[4] This can then form the basis for a subsequent analysis of the utility of considering the population as enwrapped in webs of knowledge and communication (Rose, 1996).

It is possible to use ANT to look at the closed-circuit as a range of heterogeneous entities that are pulled together including CCTV staff, police officers, CCTV managers, cameras, cables, monitors and so on. Much work goes into maintaining the connections between these entities in terms of on-going immediate interactions between for example CCTV managers, log books, tape storage and CCTV staff, or CCTV staff, monitors, radios and police. Also efforts are made to maintain the possibility of connection (financially and politically) through further connections to local shop security (who help pay toward the system) and to the local political authority (whose offer of tax revenue is dependent upon at least notional representations of support from the police and local councilors; see Chapters 3 and 4). This on-going work helps to maintain the entities as a connected circuit. However, what holds the circuit together and provides the reason for connection, it could be argued, is the flow of image/accounts which move between the entities.

Drawing on ethnomethodology, it is possible to consider this flow of image/accounts which connect various socio-technical entities as a disputable, on-going, sometimes uncertain, collection of mobilised re-performances. The CCTV staff use monitors and radios to mobilise images and verbal accounts of kids standing still. That image/account flows to the police station, is transferred to police on the beat, gains a response from police station and town centre beat officers and flows back to the CCTV staff. This is not a smooth and linear flow, but an often bumpy, challenged, disputed collection of connections. Uncertainty is often played upon in the flow of images and accounts by CCTV staff, who demonstrate awareness of future accountability relations. The CCTV staff attempt to build sufficiently evidence-laden accounts (where the evidence itself can be uncertain or can involve the building of certainty, see Chapter 3) and attempt to mobilise these into the flow and gain corroboration from the police. Accounts mobilised as uncertain often act as an evidential get-out clause for possible later accountability exercises. Thus the 'there are some kids and we don't know what they are doing' account can seem quite uncertain and there is an expectation of mutability, but the accountability onus is placed on the police by the CCTV staff's account and acts as an accountability shift. The staff are no longer to be held responsible as they have effectively requested a police response (where requesting a response, in practice, is asking for police to take responsibility). It is now the police who are to be held to account. The police then call upon a range of devices in order to constitute various features of events as evidence or produce their own get-out clause – that as far as they can tell for all practical purposes, there doesn't appear to be anything happening. Maintaining mundane inconsequentiality in the High Street is an almost constant feature of the flow of images/accounts between police and CCTV staff. It is only occasionally interrupted by an event.

In this way CCTV staff build accounts with images which they mobilise to the police and by doing so also shift accountability expectations and thus responsibility onto the police. This activity occurs in and through CCTV's closed-circuit. The 'closure' of these interactions is an on-going achievement of CCTV's socio-technical assemblage. While images are drawn from the town centre, there are close(d) controls over who gets to see these images, how they are accounted for and so on. In this way a kid in the High Street can be a figure accounted for and mobilised through the closed-circuit, while the kid may remain unaware of any movement beyond their own action in the High Street (or in the case of the kids standing still, their inaction in the High Street). While images of the police in the town centre may also be accounted for, the police have greater access to these accounts. For groups such as the kids standing still, opportunities for access may only arise through those rare occasions when the closed-circuit is opened up for further inspection, such as in court cases (see Chapters 3 and 5).

This closed-circuit analysis can build towards questions of distinctions in and around the circuit. Who/what gets to be part of the circuit, accounting for, reading accounts and questioning accounts in the flow? Who/what is a part of the flow? Is there any stability in these positions? What work is done to maintain these positions? Are there occasions when these positions are threatened? These distinctions can help us to begin addressing broader questions of what gets to count as public and private in relation to CCTV (see Chapters 1 and 3). This might allow us to return to some of the questions, albeit from a different angle, asked by Norris and Armstrong (1999). It might be possible to investigate the discriminatory potential of issues of inclusion and exclusion. Such closed-circuitry also offers an opportunity to address the issues posed by research on governance and governmentality, for example, the work of Rose (1996). In considering the closed-circuit, and interactions between those deemed 'outside' and those deemed 'inside' the circuit, we might have the opportunity to consider in detail the extent to which local residents, shoppers and kids standing still are enwrapped in webs of knowledge and forms of communication (by CCTV) regarding how they should act. The extent to which those 'in' the town centre, and 'outside' the closed-circuit feel they have been made aware of their own subjectivity will form a focus for empirical investigation. This site for interactivity between the circuit and notable others is an important location for attempts at communication (see Chapter 3).

Thus questions are raised regarding the closed-circuit and issues of privacy and forms of communication between those 'inside' and 'outside' the closed-circuit (see Chapter 3). Further questions are also raised, such as how is CCTV dependent on making and maintaining connections (to retailers and politicians) and how do these connections open up the closed-circuit (Chapter 4)? What further circuits might CCTV's closed-circuit connect to (media, law courts) and how might these open up/ threaten the positions of various socio-technical entities whose position might depend on being closed (Chapter 5)? What questions does the closed-circuit raise about spatial issues: is the closed-circuit a space; how does the space of the town centre get reconfigured by the circuit and on the circuit (Chapter 6)? Is it possible to put together a model (or models) of account production for CCTV images (Chapter 7)?

Conclusion

This chapter has used a story of kids standing still in order to explore four ways in which CCTV stories can be told. Each means of story-telling has advantages in the argumentative strategy that it adopts and in the form of analysis achievable through each strategy. While the ethnographic rendition of the story incorporates much small-scale detail, the critical approach asks questions of governance and state apparatus. This differs from the ethnomethodological approach which details interactivity and accountability. This differs again from the ANT approach which opens up questions of the position of technology and issues of fluidity, uncertainty and connection. The chapter has argued, however, that it is not possible to simply collate these approaches into a single argumentative strategy or to run the strategies concurrently. Instead the chapter has suggested utilising the metaphor of the closed-circuit of CCTV and paying attention to the possibilities raised by research on governance as a means of detailing the role of technology and interactivity and asking questions of inclusion, exclusion, public, private and discrimination. The possibilities offered by the metaphor of the closed-circuit now require exploration in relation to the organising principles of privacy, surveillance and trust outlined in Chapter 1. In this way Chapter 1 and this chapter have asked more questions than they have answered, but through outlining privacy, surveillance and trust, four distinct analytic strategies and the closed-circuit metaphor as a means of engaging with CCTV, these chapters have also provided a basis for subsequent chapters to move forward. Questions on accountability, public, private and surveillance (Chapter 3), further connections and trust (Chapter 4), the media (Chapter 5) and notions of space (Chapter 6) will now be interrogated. This will build towards the construction of a model of CCTV interaction and accountability relations (Chapter 7).

3
CCTV Modes of Action: Accountability, Surveillance and Privacy

Introduction

Privacy and surveillance are approached in a variety of different ways in social science texts (see Chapter 1). The private, on occasions, is constituted in opposition to notions of the public (see for example, Fahey, 1995), privacy is approached as a field of rights (and wrongs) and legislation (see for example, Taylor, 2002), and privacy is considered as radically contingent (Hine and Eve, 1998). Furthermore surveillance can be construed broadly in relation to most practices of information collection (Lyon, 2001), narrowly in relation to forms of categorisation and demarcation in information collection (Bennett, 2005), or politically in power relations orchestrated through state apparatus (Norris and Armstrong, 1999). This chapter will now consider these approaches to privacy and surveillance in combination with the 'closed-circuit' of CCTV (presented in Chapter 2) in a detailed empirical analysis of the modes of action of Burbville CCTV system.

This chapter will focus analysis on CCTV's modes of action in accountability, surveillance and forms of privacy. Although these three modes may appear to be an imposition by the author, they are intended as organising principles for interrogating the data. The subsequent analysis will demonstrate that each of these modes is highly diverse and while the terms themselves are frequently called upon by participants to this research, there is an absence of consistency in what these terms are used to convey. First, this chapter will continue the themes of Chapter 2 in investigating accountability as a mode of action. It will argue that accountability activity renders a variety of publics available, combining accounting *of* the public as a form of surveillance with accountability of CCTV *in* public and accounting of CCTV *for* the public. Second, the chapter will consider this variety of accountable actions and forms of surveillance in relation to ideas of privacy and the public. This section will suggest these two areas are not as closely intertwined as may seem intuitive and are characterised by uncertainty. However, far from being a problem, it will be argued that such uncertainty may have utility for CCTV's modes of engagement.

The following sections will set up debates to be rejoined in subsequent chapters. Thus notions of public connectivity will be introduced here and will form a feature of Chapter 4. Producing a representation of CCTV for various public audiences via the media will also be introduced in this chapter and will return in Chapter 5. Furthermore, notions of public space will be analysed briefly here and form the central subject of Chapter 6. Finally, accountability relations played out through CCTV (and already discussed in Chapter 2) will feature once again in this chapter and form the subject of Chapter 7.

Accountability

Accountability forms an increasingly prevalent feature of discussions relating to technology development combined with approaches to information collection, analysis and management. In the United States, Enron rendered available a malfunctioning world of corporate accountability. In the United Kingdom, the Queen's speech of 2004 proposed a series of legislation unprecedented in the breadth and depth of the accountability mechanisms included to make available information on the population (from households' amount and positioning of waste through to the population's identities). With this rapid expansion in means and mechanisms of accountability has come an increase in social science attention. However, this attention is characterised by a further multitude of means for considering, conceptualising and engaging with accountability. In drawing these diverse analyses together one finds three fields of research which focus on accountability *of* the public, analysis of accountability *in* public and approaches which call for greater accountability *for* (and on behalf of) the public.

The first field of research considers accountability *of* the public, through Foucauldian inspired research which analyses social contingency in the production and use of, for example, accounting systems (Power, 1997; Baxter and Chua, 2002). A key argument is that social control is achieved through forms of discourse (Foucault, 1977), calculation

(Rose, 1996) and categorisation (Norris and Armstrong, 1999; Bowker and Star, 2000). When discussed in relation to systems of audit, Foucauldian inclined analyses suggest that social control occurs in virtue of a process of internalisation of categories and values (Miller, 1992; Miller and O'Leary, 1994; Rose, 1999; Ericson *et al.*, 2003; see also Chapter 2). A disadvantage of these Foucauldian approaches is that they tend not to provide detail about such questions as how internalisation works in practice (this will be taken up in the following section, 'Accountability of the public: in real time').

The second field of accountability research focuses in more detail on the contingent accomplishment of accountability, absent from Foucauldian approaches. This is found in the ethnomethodological tradition and equates to a form of accountability *in* public. The ethnomethodological tradition considers forms of mundane accountability (see Garfinkel, 1967; Luff and Heath, 1993; see Chapter 2). The claim here is that in making sense of the world each turn in a social interaction (e.g. a conversation) involves demonstrably holding to account the adequacy of the previous turn (by demonstrating in a conversation that the previous turn has been understood in a particular way, thus rendering that understanding available for scrutiny by other interactors). Accountability is a mundane, pervasive organising orientation for social action. In this sense interaction is constantly focused on making things accountably available in public. This does not rule out consideration of more formal mechanisms of accountability (e.g., in workplace studies of air traffic control centres, Suchman, 1993). Instead the claim is made that even formal mechanisms of accountability are dependent on routine, moment to moment interaction through which sense is made of the system and accountability accomplished. Of greatest relevance for this chapter will be ethnomethodological approaches to evidence (e.g. Lynch, 1998) through which courtrooms, for example, are considered as 'in public' mechanisms for assessments of accountability.

The third field of research focuses on forms of accountability *for* (and on behalf of) the public, looking at how, for example, organisations, scientific expertise and research should be governed and the adequacy of new methods of public consultation in the context of demands for greater accountability, transparency and value for money (for an overview see Irwin, 1995; Kleinman, 2000; Kitcher, 2001). In academia this has led to concerns regarding notions of research quality, accountable performance and possible restrictions imposed by the arranged production of information designed to succeed on the terms of the transparency or accountability regime (Strathern, 1999, 2000, 2002). In line with these arguments, publicly funded organisations (from CCTV systems to schools) are coming under increasing scrutiny to demonstrate, through the provision of accountable returns, successful accomplishment of accountability demands.

This section will use these three fields of accountability research to consider the ways in which a variety of publics are constituted through CCTV. This will begin with analysis of the means by which the public are accounted for through CCTV as a form of accountability *of* public, before looking at the ways in which CCTV is accounted for *in* public and held to account *for* the public.

Accountability of the public: in real time

The story of 'kids standing still' (Chapter 2) highlighted the work that went into the production and mobilisation of accounts from CCTV staff to police on the closed-circuit of CCTV. To what extent was the story of 'kids standing still' typical of such public account productions? Further ethnographic examples can highlight the continuity through which CCTV staff accounted for activity in the town centre in interaction with police officers.

For example, on a Saturday evening, police officers radioed the CCTV staff with a tip-off that a person in a denim jacket had been seen possibly carrying a knife. In Burbville for that particular evening, denim jackets were shifted from fashion choices to possible causes of crime. All denim jackets were selected out from other jackets and closely scrutinised. The police were informed of where denim jackets were in the town centre. The police were then directed to apprehend and question denim jackets. Despite this crackdown on denim, no offence was ever recorded. This accounting for 'what was going on' in the town centre was very similar to the story of 'kids standing still'. A claim was mobilised between police and CCTV staff and a series of accounts were produced and mobilised through CCTV's closed-circuit in response. This was not a form of prejudice (see Norris and Armstrong, 1999, and Chapter 2) against denim, but rather denim formed the observable to be articulated (Sacks, 1972). The mobilisation of denim as a sign of criminality may have been unusual, however the mode of accounting was routinised. What might explain this routinisation of accounting for town centre activity? A further example will prove useful.

Not a great deal occurred which appeared to be out of the ordinary on this Thursday afternoon to evening slot (2 p.m. to 10 p.m.) and the staff confirmed as much. In a similar manner to the story of 'kids standing still' (Chapter 2), the CCTV staff and police occasionally interacted to confirm that nothing was happening. Towards the end of the shift, however, a call came over the radio that seemed to be in code. It was from the police, it concerned a specific type of case and all eyes had to be on a local supermarket. The CCTV staff explained to me that this was a Mardi Gras alert. The Mardi Gras bomber was, in a similar vein to the Unabomber in the United States, a lone individual who targeted specific institutions (first a British High Street bank and then a chain of supermarkets) with small explosive devices. He was not known to have killed anyone, but the police suggested this was only a matter of time. A tip-off had been called in about a suspected Mardi Gras attack on a supermarket in Burbville. The CCTV staff went into action viewing all angles of the supermarket, looking out for anyone who appeared to be carrying anything not purchased from the supermarket or generally looking suspicious. A group of kids were followed out of the car-park, justified on the grounds that the kids had not made any purchases.

The real-time recorder was switched on and a full log was kept on the computer in the form of notes as to 'what was going on'. In this case, the CCTV staff did not produce any images that were reconstituted into an event. However, for a potential 'Mardi Gras' attack the protocol for viewing the town centre, collecting and compiling accounts had been set down in advance and this protocol was swiftly oriented towards by CCTV staff. At each step of activity, CCTV staff confirmed with police officers that the protocol was being followed. Various forms of interaction had been pre-planned; the staff were expected to perform tasks and report that those tasks had been completed. The Mardi Gras bomber was caught, charged and convicted in London several months later and no crime in Burbville was ever mentioned.

The protocol for the Mardi Gras bomber highlighted ways in which particular forms of CCTV activity could become routinised in the production of accounts of activity. Further to the insights of Chapter 2 on practises of seeing, the case of the Mardi Gras bomber highlights how the CCTV staff have developed a 'professional vision' in conjunction with local police for an organised and visual 'apprehension of the world' (Goodwin, 1994: 608). Organising and standardising practices, according to Cole (1998) and Jordan and Lynch (1998), further enable claims to evidence. Drawing on Jasanoff, this organised approach to seeing the world provides for a 'visual authority' (1998: 713) that provides for claims about 'what is going on' to be witnessed as factual accounts of 'what has happened'. The Mardi Gras bomber protocol involved following everyone in and out of the supermarket, the CCTV staff looked for bags, boxes or packages in the surrounding area and would have directed the police toward any claimed suspects. The 'event' was also recorded on 'real-time' video (These protocols and routines will feature later in the discussion of moving CCTV images into the court room).

The police produced a representation of what might happen (e.g. a bomb might be placed in a bag), transferred this to predictive paths of action the 'criminals' could take and also suggested routine activities the CCTV staff should complete. This complied with the CCTV managers' suggestion that CCTV staff were expected to record standardised types of images, gaining head and shoulder shots of each person in, for example, crowds in order to record a view of everyone present. However, despite this standardisation and routinisation in the story of 'kids standing still', the denim jacket and the Mardi Gras bomber, the CCTV staff still interactively oriented towards these predictions through their own actions and what they perceived to be occurring on the CCTV monitors at any time. Despite the development of a form of 'professional vision', the CCTV staff still had some opportunity for renegotiating the police procedures for producing an account. These account production processes were still dependent on orientations towards time of day, number of police officers available and so on.

Routinisation was not guaranteed to generate actions which always followed precisely the same process or rules. Neither did routinisation equate to prejudice (in the sense that any one group formed the target of CCTV scrutiny). Instead, routinisation led to broadly similar patterns of repetitive action within which a variety of claims were made and responses received as to 'what was going on' in the town centre. In terms of the literature on surveillance (see Chapter 2), this activity would appear to comply with the narrow definition of surveillance. That is, while a broad range of information was collected, CCTV staff and police officers only focused on an incredibly small number of real-time images in deciding what required a response. This fits in with the Information Commissioner's CCTV Code of Practice and the data protection principles of relevance and data processing. The code suggests data should be processed which is adequate, relevant and not excessive. In this sense the CCTV system's regular and routinised accounting *of* the public fed into the notional accounting of CCTV *for* the public (through the Code of Practice nominally holding CCTV systems to public account, see next section).

Complexity in holding the public to account does not end here: as the next section will show, images initially ignored, not seen or deemed irrelevant, were on occasions resurrected from CCTV's archive.

Accountability of the public: through retrospectively rendering history relevant

Alongside the CCTV staff's broadly repetitive activities, attempts to respond to police tip-offs and producing accounts of what was 'going on' in the town centre, the CCTV system also made available a history of CCTV footage. At the beginning of this research, CCTV tapes were kept in Burbville for eight weeks as a standard, but this could be expanded if necessary for tapes to be used for training purposes, criminal trials or to assess possible terrorist threats (following the CCTV Code of Practice (2000), tapes were stored for 31 days as a standard, although the same exemptions still applied). The following excerpt from the junior CCTV manager highlighted the importance of this history:

> Interview With Junior Manager:
> (For transcription notes see Appendix)
> JM: so you know cctv builds up <u>tremendous</u> histories of what goes on (.) >they haven't got <u>villains</u> written on their <u>backs</u> and they don't carry a *bag* marked <u>swag</u>< (.) um so you can see a crime <u>happen</u> and be totally <u>unaware</u> of it (.) so it's <u>not</u> generally a erm detecting crime as it <u>happens</u> although that <u>does</u> take place (.) but *that's* more infrequent than it is for the research (.) we're doing for the events which <u>haven't</u> been noticed

Thus what gets to count as a crime, for example, could be produced via a post-hoc reorientation of activity on tapes held in the CCTV system archive. Through the reconstitution of visual history, what was previously mundane videotape logged in the CCTV filing system could be resurrected and reconstituted as possibly containing relevant evidence of activity. On occasions in Burbville, police uncovered a crime or a crime was reported after it had occurred. The history made accessible through CCTV was not straightforward though. Tapes could be used to claim that a person was at least present in a particular space (e.g. Burbville High Street), but may not have contained shots of the particular incident (e.g. a crime) being focused upon. Alternatively, footage may have included a range of bodies, but confirming those bodies related to the identity of particular individuals and that subsequently those individuals were the cause of a specified event was not straightforward. In a repeat of events stated in Chapter 2, CCTV staff had to produce a range of claims about 'what was going on' and gain corroboration for those claims. Images required articulation (Sacks, 1972), orienting activity towards forms of professional vision (Goodwin, 1994) in order to produce accounts which attempted to perform 'what was going on' in any image. This retrospective reorientation of relevance involving the shift of CCTV footage from images of background, every-day, usual activity to (possible) images of crime set in motion a huge effort. Many hours work were required to go through many hours of footage in order to make claims (and gain corroboration for those claims) that any particular image was important, relevant or likely evidence. If a resident claimed their car had been stolen, CCTV man-agers would first have to decide if such theft was sufficiently important to devote resources in the form of CCTV staff trawling through hours of tape, before further claims could be made about the content of the tape.

One particularly well-known example of the use of CCTV's history, which did not occur in Burbville, was the Jamie Bulger case in which two children abducted and killed an even younger child. In this case the archives of several CCTV systems were searched for relevant shots that might fill in the missing history around the event. Young's (1996) analy-sis of these events highlights the importance of these spaces; 'The event is filled with spaces and blind spots. The mother who cannot see her child; the security cameras record but cannot "see"; the names of the two boys are not to be reported' (1996: 113). The discovery of a CCTV image of two young boys holding onto an even younger child formed the repeated backdrop to news stories about the case. The Bulger case became recognisable through the re-presentation of this image.

In these initial sections relating to the accountability of the public, we can see that the closed-circuit of Burbville CCTV system featured a form of 'professional vision' (Goodwin, 1994), to produce both accounts of activity in the town centre as it happened (real time) and retrospective reorientations of relevance via the system's archives. These sections have highlighted the partial routinisation of the account production processes of the closed-circuit. As these accounting activities only focus on a nar-row selection of images, Burbville CCTV appears to support the narrow definition of surveillance. In this sense, information collection proce-dures feature a range of ignored, unimportant or irrelevant information and specific moments of accounting might form an appropriate focus for surveillance concern. However, as CCTV's archive mean any tape still stored in the system can be scrutinised, even a narrow surveillance focus needs to pay attention to the possibility that huge amounts of taped data could potentially be deemed relevant for closer scrutiny at a future date. Hence even a narrow definition of surveillance needs to be situated within a range of possible moments of accountability scrutiny. This potential for future data scrutiny also pays attention to CCTV's public accountability with retrospective claims about particular images collected through trawls of tapes oriented towards data protection principles of adequate, relevant and not excessive data processing. Simultaneous to this accounting of the public, the CCTV system was involved in various accounting activities in public, in courtrooms and through the managers' attempts to promote a public identity for CCTV. The next section will engage with these forms of accountability in public.

Accountability in public: through tapes used in courtrooms

In legal proceedings, the CCTV managers, staff and police officers attempted to make available for scrutiny a particular identity for CCTV. In legal proceedings the police and CCTV managers placed emphasis on the regular, routinised activity of the CCTV staff as evidence of the 'professional vision', reliability and high standards of the CCTV system. These regularly routinised activities related to the ways CCTV images were accounted for by staff, the way images were passed onto the police, and the way tapes were stored and handled on their way to a legal trial (for more on the complexity of constituting court room credibility, see Daemmreich's (1998) analysis of attempts to establish the credibility of DNA). In the courtroom CCTV's accounting of public and the system's accountability in public were made available for scrutiny. The Crime Prevention Officer commented on the activity of police officers in these processes:

> Interview With Crime Prevention Officer:
> CPO: *accountability* their um tape storage and management of it all
> up there [IN THE CCTV SYSTEM] is all down the line as it
> should be which is <u>ideal</u> and also continuity is kept so that it's
> much better that they keep the tapes rather than hand them
> over say to the police because you've got another continuity
> link when you come to the court hearing it absolutely um. the
> person who puts the tape in and does the tour of duty and sees
> the <u>events</u> >or may or may not have seen the events< the
> statement will read that <u>that</u> individual has done this and this
> and this and this and there's a great deal of continuity where
> as if you started handing on tapes to all sorts. and it's gone all
> round the houses then you lose you can <u>lose</u>. the plot

Losing the plot in CCTV accounts that appear in court might have consequences for CCTV accountability. The account of the tape, what has happened to it, where it has been and its coherent retelling are as important as the claimed account of what is happening on the tape. Indeed the two are inseparable. Without a coherent account of what has happened to the tape and what is on the tape, the evidential strength of CCTV footage is questionable. As the likelihood of taped footage being later used in court is unpredictable (as we saw in the example of tape histories and the retrospective reorientation of relevance), all footage must be accounted for in broadly the same way. That is, the CCTV staff must be able to reproduce in court an account of their protocols for tape logging and filing and how they passed on comments to the police in more or less standard ways. The standard can then be held up as an exemplar of the evidential strength derived from accountability measures designed to be replayable alongside tapes. As Lynch's (1998) analysis of DNA profiling in the O. J. Simpson trial suggests, ' "links" in the chain of custody' (1998: 848) must be carefully reperformed as they can be attacked by defence in criminal trials. Lynch suggests that in the Simpson trial, 'no link in the chain of custody was too banal to be unworthy of intensive scrutiny' (1998: 848). The CCTV Code of Practice (2000) uses similar terms to emphasise the importance of the 'chain of evidence' (2000: 13). For Burbville CCTV system, the tape must remain as an observable (Sacks, 1972) and must be articulated. The articulation effectively acts as a reperformance (Garfinkel, 1967) of the tape's travel. The managers must produce a certain visible representation of CCTV for the courts by giving a complete (and untainted) account of tape travel. The CCTV managers, police, tape and CCTV system must perform an account which leaves little space for questioning in the court. Losing the plot involves leaving spaces for interrogation.

Questions of the evidential strength of CCTV relying on claims made about CCTV staff's routine and standardised interactivity with the police suggested that the CCTV staff were accountable alongside local residents walking through the town centre. The CCTV staff had to be able to re-produce accounts of their activity – why they were looking at particular things, how they noted this activity, how they passed the images on – in order that they could adequately re-perform the evidential strength of CCTV in court. While it might appear intuitive to assume that the subject of questioning in a CCTV related court trial would be the content of a video-tape, the CCTV managers suggested this had never been questioned (although see the arguments of Chapter 5). In court, the question would not be 'does the CCTV footage adequately reproduce what happened in an event', but rather 'does the reproduction of the mobilisation of evidence reproduce an adequate CCTV system' (i.e. was the closed-circuit adequately 'closed', and did the CCTV staff and police act correctly).

The particular representation made available in the court involved a combination of claims about the CCTV system (it was a reliable and good quality system), claims about CCTV staff (they had acted correctly and could re-perform that enactment), claims about the police (they had acted correctly[1]), claims about the passage of the tape (who had it, when and where) and finally claims about the content of the tape (claims as to what was going on). As a feature of these accountability relations, police officers had to be able to re-perform their particular courses of action – how they arrested a person, how many officers were present at the scene and so on. The Crime Prevention Officer reflected on this:

> Interview With Crime Prevention Officer:
> *CPO*:   if the police arrive and arrest (.) not only does it [CCTV] pro-
>   tect the member of the public in that the police will be doing
>   things properly and if not it's on film it also protects the
>   <police> if somebody makes allegation that the police men
>   hit them and they didn't it's all on video so it's protects the
>   public and the police and we love it

The Crime Prevention Officer claims the professional vision of CCTV (Goodwin, 1994) could account for police officers as much as local residents. However, Goold (2003) (also drawing on Norris and Armstrong, 1999) argues the police often utilise moments of CCTV accountability after events to perform their own retrospective retelling of what happened. Thus issues of accountability in relation to CCTV are complex, involving various modes of action and claims regarding that action. In the courtroom there is accountability *of* public (re-producing accounts of activity in the High Street), accountability of CCTV *in* public (with the integrity of the CCTV system rendered available for scrutiny) and accountability *for* (and on behalf of) public (involving claims that CCTV holds the police and CCTV staff to account for their actions and CCTV adheres to data protection principles). While this chapter has pursued a narrow focus on surveillance thus far, considering specific forms of accountability in relation to CCTV and the public, it appears that the number of distinct forms of accountability under scrutiny needs to be carefully considered. Specific moments of accountability scrutiny could involve accounting for residents, shoppers, police officers, the past, the present or the CCTV system itself. These accountability activities still result in much information never being scrutinised (the narrow surveillance focus) but the multiplicity of forms of scrutiny and the ways in which scrutiny is linked to broader concerns, such as the manager's suggestion that the public might be concerned with public funding (see next section), require consideration. Turning attention to the ways in which the managers attempt to make a version of CCTV publicly available, through forms of publicity, can help broaden this focus.

Accountability in public: making CCTV available through posters and signs

Making CCTV publicly available might at first glance appear to open up the closed-circuit of CCTV. However, the managers were aware that their task was to promote CCTV without allowing certain groups (criminals, those with criminal intent) too much information on the capabilities of the system. The CCTV managers were keen to get a message across of deterrence, protection and community benefits. The CCTV managers were aware that their version of a CCTV identity would not necessarily flow straightforwardly from their desks into the lives of local residents. However, the managers entered into a diverse array of attempts to communicate an identity for CCTV and this work (and the problems encountered) will prove illustrative of the managers' views on CCTV's public identity and accountability. The cameras were positioned very visibly, signs informed of their presence and publicity, in the form of local and national newspaper and television features (for more on media see Chapter 5), offered information about CCTV's successes. The senior manager discussed this issue:

Interview With Senior Manager:
SM: we talked to the local newspaper i was always conscious of the big brother approach to this and i think that was an issue which needed to be rehearsed in our <u>own</u> mind and i thought it was i didn't think it was sufficient to actually <u>accept</u> the old adage that if you're not doing anything wrong you've got nothing to worry about don't think that that is (.) sensible and viable
SM: i mean i <u>think</u> the (.) local media is very important (.) we've been fortunate to use and it's been quite supportive of what we've done so that's priority number one national media i think um comes second in priority (.) things like signs yeah they're <u>ok</u> i'm not sure there they >actually get a particularly successful message across< just saying it once again it's a bit <u>cold</u> you're not really telling people what you're <u>doing</u>

The manager suggests the purpose of the publicity was to reduce local people's concerns regarding CCTV. However, this also involved constituting a version of what those concerns might be (in this case 'big brother'). The CCTV managers were aware of the balance to be struck between claiming to address issues and the potential risk of causing alarm by associating CCTV with a particular issue (such as CCTV and 'big brother'). These concerns did appear to match frequently reiterated media stories linking the increasing number of CCTV cameras in the United Kingdom to 'Big Brother Britain' (Independent, 2004: 1). The second excerpt suggests differing types of publicity had differing levels of utility. The signs only informed people they were on CCTV and, to the managers, this was not useful in getting their message across as it said nothing about who the system was aimed at, what the system did and what it could offer to people in the town centre. The signs did not offer a very good account of CCTV (however, they were an obligation under the CCTV Code of Practice, 2000 and this maintained CCTV's public accountability).

For the managers, CCTV needed to do more than deter criminals. The system should be positioned as part of the community, which could look after the ill and the infirm, report accidents, alongside saving people from crime (or at least suggesting who committed the crime). Although the managers could blitz the town centre with signs, the managers suggested this might not make for a very pleasant town centre and may just tell the criminals where else to go to commit crime. The managers wanted to communicate a dual message of 'don't commit crime here' alongside 'Burbville is a great place to visit'. They openly acknowledged the difficulty of getting this across to people in the town centre (see Chapter 4 for more on connecting to local residents).

Burbville police Crime Prevention Officer worked with the CCTV managers to turn around what they perceived to be popular (negative) stories about CCTV. The CCTV managers and local police made claims that there were a range of popular negative stories in circulation about CCTV and constituted what they deemed an appropriate set of responses. (The CCTV managers expressed only mild concern that the response they produced might constitute evidence for residents that these popular negative stories should now be considered worthy of attention.) The Crime Prevention Officer and CCTV managers launched local newspaper stories of how CCTV freed police resources and did not reduce the number of High Street beat officers. Similarly, although covert CCTV could be seen to be secretive, it was rather, they asserted, community enhancing and neighbourly. Rather than crime being displaced, they suggested in a further story that there was no evidence of this claim. They asserted that outside the CCTV area, crime remained steady, it had not risen. Finally they asserted that although violent crime was a growing statistic, this was not a problem for most people as attacks on those not involved in fights were rare and mugging was almost non-existent in Burbville. Negative stories, reassuring counter stories and collectives who might need reassuring (e.g. newspaper readers who feared violent crime) were constituted through this publicity and identity work.

Did the local residents of Burbville take any note of these attempts to 'sell' them a positive CCTV identity? Local residents, in interview, frequently suggested that they had either never seen the CCTV system signs and publicity or had their own ideas of the CCTV system and deployed these ideas in a variety of settings, some well beyond the town centre (this lack of awareness was also demonstrated by the work of Ditton, 2000). Often local residents deployed various, mixed and somewhat contradictory representations of CCTV consecutively in interviews which were spaced by small clauses which accounted for the seeming incompatibility of the views expressed. For example, the system was identified as potentially an 'invasion of civil liberties' and the 'system protects my car in the car-park'. This kind of account was made coherent by the clause that it was 'others' who would have their civil liberties invaded as the interviewees were certain they were unlikely to be watched themselves. Most interviewees seemed assured that they would not be seen doing anything wrong and drew comfort from this, while, if prompted, could also express anxiety about privacy (this will be discussed further in the 'Private' section later). How did the views of local residents (as a public collective) tie into attempts to hold CCTV to account on behalf of residents?

Accounting for public through CCTV legislation and public funding

The literature on corporate accountability, transparency (e.g. Gray, 1992) and the accountability of science and technology (Brown and Michael, 2002) and academia (Strathern, 2002) highlights multiple methods and effects of organisational accountability for (and on behalf of) the public. However, it should not be assumed that such accountability is straightforwardly achieved (see Neyland and Woolgar, 2002). Problems are encountered with both the mechanisms for making information available and multiple translations of information once made available. Although efforts are made to render CCTV accountable for the public through forms of legislation and guidelines on public funding, CCTV is not free from these complex accounting orders and associated problems.

Given the number of expanding, new and emerging technologies involved in the collection, categorisation, storage and analysis of information on the UK population (see Chapter 1), it is perhaps not surprising that there has been a range of relevant legislation enacted in recent years (such as the Freedom of Information Act, 2000; Data Protection Act, Regulation of Investigatory Powers Act, European Human Rights Act, all 1998). Although this might suggest legislative and accounting confusion, the relevance of this legislation for CCTV has been given greater focus by the Information Commissioner's (2000) CCTV Code of Practice. The Information Commissioner's Office is a UK body which reports to parliament and attempts to enforce the Data Protection Act (1998) and Freedom of Information Act (2000). The eight Data Protection Act principles[2] have been translated into the CCTV Code of Practice which particularly focuses on issues of initial assessment regarding the purpose of a CCTV system, the siting of cameras, quality of images, processing of images and access and disclosure procedures. To an extent this puts in place criteria for rendering CCTV publicly accountable. However, as this chapter, Chapter 5 and the Information Commissioner's Office (2004) research shows, exactly how these principles should be interpreted and enforced is a matter of debate. Although detailed consideration of legislation will form the focus for Chapter 5, it should be noted here that the interpretability of these principles suggests that a national and standardised CCTV response to the code is unlikely. Within Burbville the likelihood of each image being accounted for in exactly the same way is also unlikely. However, such flexibility is within the spirit (at least) of the code. This suggests that although the code might be promoted as a means to standardise CCTV and assess CCTV's standards, in practice the code is used and interpreted fluidly.

Legislation does not provide the limits for forms of accountability for the public. Burbville CCTV system is also subject to the constraints of local and national government funding. This public funding from tax revenues required that the CCTV managers maintained the support (or at least did not provoke any particular opposition) amongst a range of local and national groups. The CCTV managers had to work a way through the demands of county level police guidelines, local police officers' demands, police suggestions on camera locations, engineers' suggestions on technical issues (such as camera locations), suggestions from local retailers (see Chapter 4), the views of local councillors and financiers and guidance provided through national government funding initiatives (see McCahill, 2002, for a detailed analysis of the latter). This involved further promotional activity relating to CCTV crime reduction and community enhancement. The CCTV managers suggested they would use meetings with local groups to emphasise promotional activities occurring in Burbville and the successes of the system (mostly relating to arrest rates and reductions in crime). However, alongside these attempts to mobilise putative support to a further set of audiences (such as the local political authority), the CCTV managers were also aware that the demands of these groups were incommensurate. The junior CCTV manager reflected on this:

Interview With Junior Manager:

JM: when we started off the *design* of the system was an <u>engineering</u> design the design of that system was we'll put the cameras **here here and there** and that seemed like the best <engineering> places to put them but the police come along and say yeah but the crime occur s **here here and here** (.) so we need to <u>compromise</u> if it's <u>going</u> to be a partnership between us and the police then the engineering measures versus the crime measures (.) um needed to come a bit closer obviously you can't <u>always</u> put a camera in the right place

Thus the job of CCTV managers was to move between and connect groups and shift forms of publicity about CCTV from group to group while also trying to reach a compromise over the incommensurate demands made by each group (for more on competing rationales for camera placement, see Martinais and Betin, 2004). Retaining public funding was a concern for CCTV managers and was utilised in CCTV publicity as one of the areas where local people might be concerned. Although this initially seems to suggest that moments of surveillance scrutiny need to be considered in relation to a broader range of concerns, it is not clear that these concerns of public funding attributed to local residents go far beyond the CCTV managers own concerns. In this sense the extent to which any local resident felt they required the CCTV system to be held to account for the way it spent money was negligible. Of greater concern for residents was CCTV's closed-circuit of interactivity. This will be taken up in the 'Private' section given later. What this section demonstrates is that although calls are made for CCTV to be accountable, the mechanisms designed for this purpose, their limited scope and fluid interpretability make them less than relevant to interests expressed by local residents. This raises the question: to what extent was this accountability for the public? Furthermore, who (if not the local residents) were the public on whose behalf accountability was maintained? (This will be taken up in the 'Private' section).[3]

Forms of public, surveillance and accountability

While this section has outlined the complexity of issues implicated in considering CCTV, accountability, surveillance and the public (including the constitution of identity for members of the public in real-time and through tape archives, constituting publicity for CCTV, making CCTV publicly available in court and considerations of legislation and public funding), it has also raised questions for considering surveillance. Initially it was suggested that Burbville CCTV system appeared to fit the narrow conception of surveillance with huge amounts of information collected and only small amounts ever scrutinised. While this does appear to be the case, the range of different forms of scrutiny in which CCTV is involved (in real-time, through post-hoc reconstructions of relevance through archives and in CCTV being held to account in court) suggests that surveillance needs to be considered in relation to a range of accountability actions. Thus while a version of the narrow definition of surveillance still appears applicable (only certain information is selected), the variety of moments of scrutiny and close accountability (which form the actions of surveillance) also need to be considered. Furthermore moments of scrutiny need to be considered along with broader concerns, which CCTV managers and the police suggest local residents have (such as concerns over public finance and fear of crime) and the concerns which local residents actually discuss (see section entitled Private and Chapter 4). These place moments of surveillance scrutiny in a broader context of concerns. Hence surveillance can be construed narrowly as those moments where decisions are made to select very particular forms of information for particular forms of scrutiny, but such moments need to be considered in terms of the contents of these moments of activity (from kids standing still to bomb alerts), the outcomes which result from such activities (from CCTV producing accounts in real-time and through tape storage, to CCTV being held to account by courts and by residents) and the broader concerns of accountability in and for the public with which they might fit.

This chapter will conclude with an outline theory of the concept of surveillance and how this is tied to a number of versions of the public. The Conclusion section in this chapter will also raise a range of questions that subsequent chapters will have to answer in relation to this theory. However, prior to such theorising, the variety of publics made available through accountability needs to be understood in relation to (and as distinct from) issues of the private.

Private

In the same way that a range of views were articulated in relation to accountability, surveillance and the public, the private and privacy were also fluid terms in this research. In Chapter 1 it was suggested surveillance can be thought of as a field of action and privacy as a field of rights (and wrongs) and legislation. However, as Hine and Eve (1998) suggest, privacy is not a fixed concept. In Burbville, privacy and the private were contested terms that shifted between various accounts of what it meant to have privacy, what activities should be private, when privacy should be guaranteed and what forms of space should connote privacy. However, it should not be assumed that all talk or activities or claims regarding such activity could neatly fit into a binary division of (an understanding of) public on the one hand and private on the other. While various claims were made in 'Accountability' section about the term public, made available through forms of accountability, it did not necessarily follow that everything else was then private. This section will begin by looking at local residents' concern with ideas of privacy in relation to CCTV. Then, the CCTV managers and police approach to privacy will be considered. Third, the section will engage with the times, spaces and actions of privacy. Fourth, uncertainty in CCTV, privacy and accountability will be analysed.

Local residents' concerns about CCTV and privacy

Local residents offered accounts of the benefits of CCTV, for example purse protection, being looked out for in the town centre and so on. These arguments were a close match for the rhetoric of the CCTV managers that the system increased people's sense of safety and deterred criminals. However, local residents also highlighted several areas of concern. First, residents made claims about who should worry about CCTV:

> Interview With Resident Of Burbville:
> *F2:*   *uh i mean* <u>cameras</u> i'm not really bothered about <particularly> (.) because if you're in a public place you can be <u>seen</u> by anybody *anyway* can't you (.) <u>and</u> i don't really think feel they're obtrusive because i'm <u>99.9%</u> of the time not doing anything i <u>shouldn't</u> be doing (.)

Local residents frequently suggested, as in the above excerpt, that they were not a group likely to be targeted by CCTV. Instead 'kids,' 'criminals' and various 'others' were 'observables' likely to be articulated (Sacks, 1972).

These claims of who should worry about CCTV were linked in to specific times and places. Indeed, some respondents made arguments suggesting they may well have once been in the group that should worry, or suggested that they did worry about threats posed by these groups ('kids' and 'criminals') at night and in certain parts of Burbville (see Chapters 4 and 6 for more).

Second, local residents, on occasions made claims that they were worried about CCTV:

Interview With Resident Of Burbville:
Int: do you think [CCTV] has any <u>other</u> implications ?
M6:   <u>erm</u> you've got the old <u>you know</u> the fact that you've got no
       <privacy> haven't you when you're out at all
Int: does that <u>bother</u> you when you're out in the high street ?
M6:   <u>yeah</u> er don't <like> the idea of people being able to see what
       you're doing the whole time to be <u>honest</u> (.) that's really <u>bad</u>.
       but er <u>don't know</u> (.) you can't really <u>like</u> have a um you either
       have like . the . television security there or you <u>don't</u> have it
       there i don't think >like even having one there< i still think
       it's an <u>invasion</u> of like your your well it's not <u>privacy</u> is it
       because you're out in the street but you know
Int: yeah
M6:   the idea that people can <u>record</u> what you do and keep tabs on
       you that's <awful> really innit

In the above excerpt, the interviewee struggles to come to terms with the idea that he does not like to be seen, but is not (in his view) in a private space. He appears to settle on the notion that the problem is to be recorded. These claims fitted a range of suggestions made by local residents that they had some problems with the idea of being seen and more problems with the idea of tape storage. Not having access to CCTV's closed-circuit was an issue for local residents. The concern for local residents was that visibility in particular spaces might lead to the production of specific accounts of activity in the town centre, to which they would never have access. In this sense local residents articulated a concern with privacy and lack of access to tapes rather than the possibility of surveillance and forms of accountability or invasion of their privacy. Local residents, as the following account suggests, wanted the CCTV system to be available as an observable (Sacks, 1972) for the system to be accountable to a degree which the system's management would not readily agree.

Interview With Resident Of Burbville:

M6: it's just you don't know what other people's responses <u>are</u> to seeing you and that makes you feel really <uncomfortable> um (.) it's like i don't like using the phone very much and <u>i'd rather</u> given the choice >of going round to see them and ringing them< i'll go and <u>see</u> them because you know when you talk to them they're not <u>pulling</u> faces and i think it's a *similar idea to that video type thing*

This interviewee wanted to be able to see how he was being seen, articulated, accounted for and re-performed (see Chapter 2 and the work of Sacks, 1972 and Garfinkel, 1967). Local people, then, had some concerns over how they were seen, and more pronounced concern over how that visibility was stored and replayed, and their lack of access to this visibility, storage and replayability. Local residents broadly construed privacy as relating to access and wanted the opportunity to reverse forms of surveillance so that they might have an opportunity to hold CCTV to account through forms of access. However, access as a term shifted between accounts. There were problems raised regarding CCTV's visual access to the town centre and to local residents, and there were issues raised about local residents' lack of access to tapes stored somewhere by CCTV. Local residents were also unsure how they might ever access more information about CCTV. Their views of the CCTV system involving a control centre, a store of tapes that recorded almost everything, stored indefinitely, were apparently based more on media representations (particularly James Bond films) than access to Burbville's CCTV system. This apparent concern should not be emphasised too strongly however. While local residents suggested they did not know exactly what the CCTV system did or could do, they did not make great efforts to find out more (see 'CCTV, privacy, accountability and uncertainty' section given later).

Thus residents related privacy to ideas of access and had concerns regarding what happened to their image once recorded by CCTV. Local residents were unsure they liked the idea of being accessible on tape once they were no longer in the town centre. If public meant being visibly accessible by others, then CCTV meant that residents no longer had to be in a public space to be this visible. Even after they had left that space, they may still be retrospectively accessible on tape. Yet perhaps this was not public space at all, as the tape remained within the closed-off confines of CCTV's closed-circuit. CCTV might have formed a change in the private, rather than the public, with the public (as people in the town centre) whisked off from the public space (of the town centre) into an altogether private arena to which people in the town centre had no access. Indeed, if the Mardi Gras bomber had been caught in Burbville, his image would have been removed from public space into CCTV, and he would have (presumably) also been removed physically into a police cell. Also his image on CCTV would no longer have been treated as a member of public, but as a potential killer/crazy psychopathic bomber.

Local residents expressed concerns about privacy, then, particularly with regard to access and linked these concerns to forms of surveillance, regarding being seen and recorded and accounted for in particular ways. Privacy here could still be regarded as a 'rights' issue in considering the possibility of rights to access what CCTV records, how the system produces accounts and so on (although as Taylor (2002) points out, rights in relation to CCTV are complex; also see Chapter 5). What some residents seemed to want, on some occasions, was a form of privacy protection that opened up the private surveillance sphere of CCTV – its closed-circuit – to greater accountability. However, alongside these concerns, residents also did not try to find out more about CCTV and articulated a range of benefits CCTV could offer (there is more on these benefits in Chapter 4). How did the CCTV managers and local police respond to this variety of issues relating to privacy?

Knowledge as privacy

The CCTV managers were aware that local residents might have particular privacy concerns in relation to the CCTV system. However, while the CCTV managers' previous constitution of likely public concerns (such as the possible reduction of beat police officers, possible displacement of crime, etc.) had led to local newspaper stories that attempted to persuade local residents otherwise, concerns about privacy were treated differently. The following exchange comes from a discussion relating to the possibility of CCTV cameras peering in to residential flats above shops in the High Street:

Interview With Junior Manager:
Int: i mean >the people that kind of< live in the houses that are potentially within your cctv are aware of the cameras
JM: on *yeah* i'm sure they are i mean they're town centre people they must i mean they can see the cameras >from their own windows< so clearly it doesn't take much …

This excerpt follows on from a discussion of the possibility of using digital cameras to 'block' intrusive views into, for example, residences in the town centre. This interview was conducted immediately prior to the introduction of the Information Commissioner's CCTV Code of Practice (2000) which states that local residents whose properties can be seen by CCTV should be consulted. The question of blocking poses a question for the Code. If the camera is digital and can be programmed so that black squares appear in certain locations (e.g. people's windows), does that mean consultation is still required as the camera cannot 'see' into the residence? Alongside problems with the interpretability of the Code, are issues regarding the data subject built into the Code. The subject is called upon to take an active interest in their privacy protection and sets out the means through which subjects can make a complaint regarding the CCTV system. However, this results in privacy protection being dependent upon the subject. Subjects are required to be aware to some extent of CCTV's existence, possible capabilities and how a complaint should be put together. The assumption that 'town centre people' or data subjects can easily elaborate such views of CCTV is problematic.

In 'Local residents' concerns about CCTV and privacy' section, we saw how local residents' ideas about what the CCTV system 'could do' were based on a range of ideas (often taken from the media). The assumption of knowledge, that residents would be aware of the premises outlined above, is predicated on what may be misplaced assumptions about the degrees to which local residents were informed about CCTV (see also Ditton, 2000, Information Commissioner's Office research, 2004). Making claims about residents' knowledge as the basis for claims about CCTV's non-invasion of privacy partially shifts responsibility for residents' privacy away from CCTV managers to residents. Just as the residents made a variety of claims as to 'what they knew about CCTV', there may also have been a varying knowledge amongst residents as to who was responsible for their privacy. Not knowing how cameras worked, not knowing how to make a complaint and not knowing that they were responsible for noticing any possible invasion of privacy might mean the forms of privacy residents talked about would remain out of reach. Counter to the popular view of CCTV that cameras invade privacy and privately store information, this view of privacy suggests CCTV shifts responsibility and the burden of knowledge on to local residents. CCTV in this view does not necessarily invade privacy, but instead the private spaces of CCTV are not rendered accountable in ways the local residents' desire or in some cases expect.

The local police made a similar set of assumptions regarding local populations. The Crime Prevention Officer discussed the possible problems that local residents might have with cameras:

> Interview With Crime Prevention Officer:
> CPO: i <u>think</u> . i think the residents forget the cameras are there
> CPO: they're just not bothered but the people that are going to
>   come into to commit <u>crime</u> those sort of warnings are things
>   they're going to be on the ball to look for

This excerpt makes assumptions about residents and criminals. This division appeared to separate those who should worry about CCTV from those who should not. These claims as to what people 'knew' were performative (Garfinkel, 1967) of individual's identity as criminals and thus concerned, or alternatively, non-criminals and thus 'not bothered'. The problem in the above excerpt, linking back to the managers' talk of CCTV's public identity was that this was exactly what the managers wanted to avoid. For the managers, CCTV disappearing into the background was the worst thing that could happen. Just being another scarcely recognised feature of the town centre was not sufficient to justify Burbville's annual investment in the system. According to the managers, the CCTV system needed to be seen to be protecting the community, enhancing the community and offering a great deal more to the community than a frequently forgotten background presence. Lack of awareness, then, was not a way out of the difficulties of CCTV promotion for the managers. This lack of awareness was adequate for the police it seems, who were more concerned that fear of crime did not rise and that 'smart' criminals would be on the look out for (and be deterred by) the system anyway.

The Crime Prevention Officer did not try to shift responsibility for privacy away from CCTV, but instead assumed that local residents did not (and need not) have any concerns about CCTV. For the managers this was insufficient in that their work to promote CCTV as caring and community enhancing would be lost if the cameras were ignored. However, the shifting of responsibility for privacy away from the CCTV system to local residents provided the means for CCTV managers to not engage with potentially problematic issues and still adhere to the CCTV Code of Practice (2000). While the CCTV managers did not want CCTV to form merely a background presence in the town centre, neither did they want CCTV to become a prominent system linked to privacy concerns. Publicising CCTV as a prominent and non-problematic system seemed a difficult task for CCTV managers as so much of their activity involved responding to 'problems' that they themselves thought local residents had with CCTV. The managers had to consider: How to engage with privacy without raising concerns of privacy? Local residents meanwhile may not have been aware of their responsibility for privacy, may not have cared all the time about CCTV and when residents did voice a concern, they asked questions of what could be seen by CCTV and how tapes were stored. These shifting grounds for concern and shifting claims about issues of public and private will be drawn together in the next section.

Privacy according to time, space or action

A variety of issues relating to accountability, the public and private have been presented thus far in this chapter. Participants talked of public funding and legislation as accounting for the public, talked of CCTV's public image as available for accounting in public and talked of their own accountability as members of public. Talk of privacy and the private related to issues of rights of access to being seen and being recorded. This talk sat alongside privacy being something of little concern on occasion, being the responsibility of local residents and being something only criminals should worry about. Privacy and the private were fluid terms (Mol and Law, 1994) that shifted between times, spaces and actions.

On occasions, accounts of privacy were strongly worded. These strong accounts were quite definite that on particular occasions privacy should be a concern. Examples of this included: a resident who was worried about being taped using a toilet in a fast food restaurant, a resident who was worried about being taped falling over in the High Street, a person who was against the taping and use of the tape of his suicide attempt in the High Street (see Chapter 5). Although each of these examples was claimed by the particular resident as proof that on some occasions certain times, spaces and actions were 'obviously' private, there was no broad agreement. For every account of a particular time, space or action that should be seen as recognisably private, there were a range of further accounts of non-concern or non-interest in privacy issues.

Although Chapters 5 and 7 will form the focus for discussing policy and legislation, it seems reasonable to suggest that attempts to legislate for these shifting grounds of privacy would be difficult (this point is considered by Gallagher, 2004). What was private for one resident, in relation to one activity, in one time and space, may not have been a privacy concern for another resident. Although the CCTV Code of Practice (2000) could be seen as a set of flexible fair information principles (Bennett and Raab, 2003) for handling this diversity, no resident in this research had any awareness of the code. Residents' varied concerns and the content of the Code suggest that the CCTV managers' claim that residents should take the responsibility for making a complaint if they had a privacy issue was reasonable. How else to accommodate the shifting concept of privacy than to allow residents to produce their own complaints based on their own definitions or concerns? However, perhaps it should be reiterated that the CCTV managers' claim that residents had responsibility for privacy was bound up with claims relating to residents' knowledge of CCTV, of how the system worked, how a complaint could be made and so on. This was not an area where the public and private of CCTV came together. Local residents were unaware of opportunities to complain about CCTV and assumed that there existed a notable authority to hold the private spaces of CCTV to account. However, as the next section on uncertainty will show, it was not clear that residents (given the chance) would necessarily have made many complaints about privacy issues.

CCTV, privacy, accountability and uncertainty

A range of questions have been posed by the participants to this research. Residents asked questions of CCTV (e.g. what is it? what can it do?), CCTV staff and police officers asked questions of people in the town centre (e.g. why are these kids standing still?), CCTV managers raised questions about publicity (e.g. how to publicise CCTV without increasing concern?), and courts of law were used to interrogate CCTV (questions were asked, for example, is CCTV reliable? who has had access to the tapes?). Furthermore there is no certainty in how many CCTV cameras there are in the United Kingdom (see Chapter 1) and CCTV legislation is fluidly interpretable. STS research (such as Woolgar and Cooper, 1999) suggests that questions of technologies and what they can do, can be subject to on-going challenges. Rappert (2001) argues that these challenges can be steps toward ambiguity resolution while Lee (1999) suggests (in relation to legislation) that questioning can act as a form of managed deferral of certainty. In accounting of the public, the CCTV staff and police are tied into a regularly repetitive system which produces more or less certain accounts of what is going on, for all practical purposes, through a few turns in interaction. For local residents, CCTV's capability is the subject of on-going deferral, characterised by moments of apparent certainty over CCTV, what it can do and how (often based on stories from friends and media sources). CCTV managers utilise publicity in order to reduce concerns with CCTV held by (what they imagine to be) very specific populations, but simultaneously defer pronouncements of certainty regarding CCTV's capabilities in order to avoid giving those with criminal intent access to information on how CCTV works. These forms of uncertainty resolution and managed deferral of certainty produce questions regarding issues of accountability and surveillance, the public and privacy. How can surveillance, linked in this chapter to talk of the public and forms of accountability, be adequately theorised as a field of action? How can privacy and the various concerns grouped under the term private be approached as a field of rights (and wrongs) and legislation? How do uncertainty, ambiguity resolution and managed deferral of technological capability play out in these two areas of privacy and legislation? The Conclusion section in this chapter will engage with these questions and use this initial theorisation to underscore questions that will form the content of subsequent chapters.

Conclusion

This chapter has begun to highlight the complexity of issues relating to surveillance and accountability (particularly focused here on rendering available various publics), privacy and the private. Participants in this research talked of the public image of CCTV, of how CCTV accounted for the public (in real-time and through tape archives), of public funding and of public space. The insights from Chapter 2 on the closed-circuit of CCTV were utilised to consider the professional vision (Goodwin, 1994) of CCTV staff and their regular and routinised activity (Jasanoff, 1998; Jordan and Lynch, 1998), which could be replayed through, for example, courts of law. It was suggested that in accounting for activity (in real-time and retrospectively) and in being held to account CCTV activity conformed to a narrow definition of surveillance where specific areas of information collection were subjected to greater scrutiny and accountability and thus formed the focus of concern. Privacy was then talked of in relation to access, and particular times, spaces and actions. Here we can see that the closed-circuit of Chapter 2 forms a useful means for CCTV management and police to control access to who sees CCTV. The closed-circuit of staff, police, managers, cameras, monitors, notepads, accounts and so on can be a means of directing access and instituting or stabilising distinctions between those connected to the CCTV system and those outside the system. This distinction broadly maps onto those (usually) able to produce accounts in the flow of data travelling through the closed-circuit and those who are accounted for in the closed-circuit. When residents chose to articulate concerns over privacy, these were not always about being seen, but more often focused on being recorded and held in the closed-circuit of CCTV. Privacy then can be conceptualised as a concern of those not in the closed-circuit who do not have access to the surveillance (accounting scrutiny) activities of CCTV and more notably, the storage and further use of accounts in the closed-circuit. It was suggested, though, that this narrow focus on particular moments of accountability scrutiny needs to be augmented by a consideration of the position of the narrow surveillance focus in relation to broader concerns (such as CCTV managers' views that residents might be concerned about, for example, public funding of CCTV or violent crime in Burbville). The provenance and relevance of these concerns will be analysed further in Chapter 4.

However, the preceding focus on uncertainty emphasised that moments of accountability involving members of the public in forms of surveillance, the public image of CCTV, what should count as CCTV and what should count as privacy were not fixed. The fluidity (Mol and Law, 1994) and uncertainty of these concepts was utilised by some of the participants to this research who aimed to shift responsibility for surveillance and accounting activity or avoid establishing definite capabilities for the CCTV system. Under conditions of uncertainty there was resolution of ambiguity (Rappert, 2001) in accounts of local residents and deferral of decisions (Lee, 1999) particularly in relation to accounts of the CCTV system itself (except in courts of law). This section will now begin to outline how distinctions between public and private were made and maintained through specific surveillance moments of accountability, accomplished via the closed-circuit. This will look at the ways in which the closed-circuit operated to produce and mobilise accounts of who was public and who was not and how this circuit could disrupt conventional relationships of public membership and space.

In Burbville town centre, a person could simultaneously be a member of 'the public' and a person 'in public'. The two concepts were difficult to separate; being of 'the public' formed a membership category, being 'in public' formed a spatial descriptive tag. In this sense, a person could not easily be 'in public' without being categorised as a member 'of public' and could not be a member 'of public', easily, without being 'in' a 'public' space. However, since the introduction of CCTV to Burbville, the system has disrupted this relationship. Post-installation of CCTV, a resident could be held to account by CCTV and that account could be mobilised around the circuits of the CCTV system on tape. This could happen when an individual was no longer in a public space and the person could become separated from the 'general public' by specific performative designations (e.g. as the Mardi Gras bomber). These performative designations were a form of surveillance and the upshot of interactions between CCTV staff and police who might deem that any particular person required close scrutiny. This scrutiny was not of the 'general public' but of specific individuals, still 'in' a 'public' space, but not being considered in the same way as the rest of the 'members of public'. This accounting occurred through CCTV's closed-circuit, where access was strictly controlled and towards which claims to privacy were oriented by local residents. Thus the closed-circuit was the location for a mode of action – surveillance – which focused on particular features of a mass of information for further scrutiny and it was a lack of access to this mode of action and subsequent tape storage and mobilisation to which residents articulated concerns – a form of privacy rights discourse.

However, being visible as a person in the town centre, perhaps being seen as a member 'of public', was not entirely straightforward. Different interviewees elaborated a variety of concerns; occasionally that CCTV could see them, more often that CCTV could store images of them, and now and again that it was others who should worry about CCTV. Local residents demonstrated an awareness of the possibility of being held to account (surveillance) and made suggestions of a variety of likely targets for surveillance accountability (criminals, kids, etc.). Local residents' accounts existed simultaneously with CCTV staff and police negotiations of accounts for people in the town centre. A complex and disjointed set of interactions seemed to be occurring in and around Burbville town centre between those in, and those outside, the closed-circuit. However, it would be too simplistic to assume that those in the closed-circuit always produced accounts and those outside were the subject of accounts. In the court, CCTV was held to account (made publicly accountable) and police officers, although not members 'of public', still operated 'in' a public space and so could also be held to account. As we shall see in Chapter 5, although it was unusual for the police and the CCTV system to be held to detailed accounting scrutiny, when their location 'in public' *was* held to account numerous questions followed.

This chapter serves as an introduction to these issues. The following chapters will now pick up on these initial ideas of surveillance and accountability, the public and private. Chapter 4 will begin elaborating the identity work involved in questions of trust by investigating connections between CCTV and local retailers (including an analysis of public funding and a search for connections between town centre systems) and connections between local residents and CCTV (investigating how and whether CCTV can form trust relationships with local residents). Chapter 5 will engage further with the CCTV managers' attempts to promote a particular identity for CCTV as caring and community enhancing 'in public', in the media (and the problems this instigated). Chapter 6 will engage further with notions of public space, investigating Burbville town centre and how it was accounted for by CCTV and local residents. Chapter 7 will then draw together the themes of accountability introduced in this chapter (accountability *of* public, accountability *in* public and accountability *for* public) in producing a model of privacy, surveillance and trust.

4
Trust and Informational Mobility: CCTV, Local Retailers and Local Residents

Introduction

The opening chapters of this book have offered much detail on issues of privacy and surveillance. This chapter will now pick up on trust as the third organising principle for interrogating the data in this study. Trust will be used to analyse the work that goes into the production of a CCTV identity by the CCTV system and by local residents and local retailers. This analysis will be achieved through a consideration of the processes of information mobilisation in Burbville. Such mobility has become a recent reference point for studies of emerging and developing technologies. There have been conferences dedicated to notions of mobility (Oxford, 2003; Surrey, 2004) alongside special issues of journals (Surveillance and Society, 2004), there are research centres and projects set up to investigate issues relating to mobility (CeMoRe, University of Lancaster; RIS:OME, University of Surrey) and there has been a diverse range of publications on questions of mobility. We are told bodies have never been more mobile (Urry, 2000; 2001; Sheller and Urry, 2003), and information has never flowed so rapidly and in such large quantities (Castells, 1996).[1] It is suggested that these forms of physical and informational mobility raise questions for everyday forms of co-ordination, interaction and social exclusion (Shove, 2002) and the ways in which we capture, account for and think of the social (Thrift, 2004).

As the number and diversity of information collection, categorisation and analysis systems, from biometrics to cameras, have increased, these themes of mobilisation have been picked up in order to suggest that these technologies are involved in 'an automatic functioning of

voyeuristic power' (Smith, 2004: 379). With increasing numbers of technologies tied together with (apparently) increasing sophistication and
information flowing over greater distances, in ever larger amounts, it
may appear as no surprise that surveillance technologies would work
with increasing efficiency, speed and effect. At a glance, the closed-
circuit of CCTV (introduced in Chapter 2) may appear to form an
example of this automated functioning of power with a variety of technical (monitors, fibre optic connections, computers, radios, etc.) and
social components (CCTV staff and managers, and police officers) tied
into a mechanism which holds a flow of images to account. However, as
emphasised in Chapters 2 and 3, much detailed, messy and moment to
moment activity went into a variety of identity work in Burbville CCTV
system (from producing identities of members of the public to producing identities for CCTV for various public audiences). This chapter will
argue that such interactivity questions the notion that CCTV is involved
in the automated functioning of power and suggests CCTV is not characterised by a straightforward series of interconnected information
flows. The chapter will also suggest this closed-circuit interactivity raises
a series of questions for understanding trust.

The chapter will be organised in three sections in order to perform this
analysis. First, a comparison will be made between Burbville CCTV
system and a town centre retailer (a bank). This section will explore
information flows, how these are achieved by a bank and the ways in
which CCTV stands distinct from such flows. Second, the chapter will
investigate how interactivity between the CCTV system and local retailers
can lead to a variety of identity conflicts and much identity work to
establish who CCTV is for, who should pay and how trust should be
assessed. Third, local residents will be drawn into the analysis in considering their views on local retailers, CCTV and informational mobility,
alongside a consideration of the ways in which they constitute trust
relations in the town centre.

Comparing CCTV and a bank[2]

Talk of information and physical bodies flowing ever faster, in greater
quantities, over longer distances (Urry, 2000; Castells, 1996) is often
associated with the automated functioning of technology (Smith, 2004).
While Burbville CCTV system's closed-circuit may not have operated in
such a way, local retailers in the town centre did position themselves in
relation to such automated flows. The local bank manager articulated
the position of his bank branch as a single connection in a global

network of branches, call centres, offices and data processing centres. The bank manager's articulation of networks will be utilised initially to construct a comparison between CCTV and the bank. This comparison will engage with three areas of bank and CCTV activity: data-flow, the production of identities and (what could be termed) 'customer' relations.

CCTV and bank data-flow

The bank manager and CCTV managers expressed a variety of concerns regarding the information which flowed through and connected the different parts of the organisations in which they worked. The bank manager talked of the recent completion of the bank's call centre and data-processing centre (in a neighbouring town) which now dealt with all the paperwork and telephone enquiries of the bank's local branches. This system for telephony and paperwork may seem initially to provide a comparator for CCTV's Closed-circuit (see Chapter 2). Utilising ANT (Latour, 1987; Callon, 1986; Mol and Law, 1994), it could be said that a range of social and technical entities (bank staff, computers, branches, offices) were translated via obligatory points of passage (bank head office) into a connected network for the stable mobilisation of an information flow (customer details, enquiries, bank statements, etc.). This informational flow connected the various entities and helped to constitute the connected entities (at least in providing their reason for being connected to the flow). The bank manager's talk of call centres and data-processing centres highlighted how the flow connected parties, how the data was initially produced for travel and how the robustness of such production processes allowed for the maintenance of connections. These connections and robust data production processes, the bank manager suggested, allowed the bank to continue operating as an apparently smooth, automated system.

The bank manager suggested that the flow of customer information was made robust for travel through the deployment of a Burbville identity tag (bank paperwork was stamped Burbville, there was a Burbville courier to carry paperwork, etc.) and the flow was maintained by paperwork, couriers and data inputers (who entered the paperwork as Burbville customers into the bank's database). The database then allowed for telephonists in phone banking to complete the flow of customer data by talking to Burbville customers, offering them a return on the data entered into the data flow in transactions those customers had previously completed. In the call centre, data was produced for travel and deployed in interaction between bank telephonists and customers to forge a sense of closeness between call centre telephonists and customers. This 'closeness' could take the form of using first names, asking how the customer was and so on. Although telephonists were trained to deploy a regularly repeated script in interaction with customers, this training incorporated a notional closeness between customer and bank telephonist and between customer and bank branch (through continuity between telephone scripts and branch scripts). Through robust data production, reliable connections and notional continuity, customers formed an immutably mobile (Latour, 1990) flow of information, enabling the bank to continue as a local and international series of recognisable, functioning, financial connections.

In comparison, the CCTV system's flow of data was less clear, was the subject of a great deal of scrutiny and provoked many questions. Although a great deal of work in Burbville went into the production of CCTV's closed-circuit, many questions were still asked in the circuit of what an image represented, what constituted an adequate response to an image and what future accountability mechanisms might be utilised to hold the closed-circuit to account (effectively opening the closed-circuit). Furthermore, local residents raised questions of the closed-circuit itself and asked what return they might receive from CCTV's informational flow (see next section). While the bank aimed to operate a flow of data as secure as CCTV's closed-circuit, the bank's contact points with local residents were oriented toward constituting closeness and continuity. CCTV did not present the same opportunities for relationship building (although the CCTV managers were keen to try, see 'The bank, CCTV and "customer" relations' section). However, as the next section will demonstrate, it should not be assumed that CCTV interactivity was always messy and disjointed and bank activity smooth and effortlessly automated.

CCTV and bank identity production processes

Both the bank and the CCTV system were involved in processes of identity production and verification. Initially it seemed that the bank's system for identification could be characterised by swiftness and certainty and the CCTV system by uncertainty, leading to forms of ambiguity resolution, for all practical purposes (see Chapter 3 and Garfinkel, 1967). The following excerpt from an interview with the bank manager can illustrate this:

> Interview with bank manager:
> (For transcription notes, see Appendix)
> *BM*: if a different customer from a different branch of this bank
>   comes in and seeks to cash a cheque we would have to previous

to the technology we have now we would have some difficulty first of all establishing their identity cause we wouldn't have papers in our office which showed his signatures or any other form *of identity* we would've er had to find out if they've got the funds available to spend and all that sort of thing so from our point of view there's the security problem and er a time problem a are they okay to pay the money to *b* (.) can we spend the time finding it out and from the customers' point of view there was a . significant time convenience problem now we can <er> on any pc within the network get a copy of their signature on the screen um and er details of their the er balance of their accounts

According to the bank manager, the bank could achieve a level of satisfactory identity production and verification by producing data on a screen from their database (which retained sufficient information in order to re-produce an account of how the identity was produced and verified by bank staff). Despite the professional vision (Goodwin, 1994) of CCTV staff, their ability to articulate chains of custody for evidence (Lynch, 1998) and their expertise in account production processes, they did not have a database suggesting who was who in the town centre.[3] The bank staff on telephones in the call centre or in face to face interaction in the branch, could make swift judgements about who the person was in front of them, if they perceived they had the correct information to continue an interaction. The bank staff utilised the bank database and the physical characteristics of the body and signature presented to them, and decided if they could be entered with continuity into the banks' data-flow. The CCTV staff had to do a great deal of work to establish any form of account of 'what was going on' (see Chapter 2), to establish reasons behind what appeared to be the activity taking place (e.g. 'who are these kids and why are they standing still?') and then had to work to get a response from the appropriate source, be that the police, ambulance service, their own managers and so on. The CCTV staff had to produce this account of town centre activity while paying attention to the possible need to re-produce an account of how they produced their initial account, depending on the deployment of sets of claims regarding CCTV staff activity that were far less categorised than the bank's database.

This suggests a dichotomy between the automated and smooth data-flow of the bank and the bumpy and uncertain connection of accounting activities characteristic of CCTV's closed-circuit. However, the bank manager made it clear that the bank factored into its accounts that occasionally money may be fraudulently obtained and that, on occasions, the production and verification of identity might later turn out to be incorrect. In this sense the bank's data-flow was not always smooth, customers made complaints, some genuine customers were turned away and on occasions money was taken out of customers' accounts illegally. The manager suggested that often complaints and possible problems with identity verification that arose after a transaction had taken place were referred to him. In these instances there was no clear and definite database screen to orient interaction. Instead the manager would produce a decision articulating his own experience with regard to (what appeared to be ambiguous) head office guidelines. He offered the example of customers who claim to have deposited more in the ATM (which allows for customers to deposit cash in envelopes, through the machine, when the branch is not open) than appeared in the envelope retrieved by bank staff from the ATM. Rather than automatically accept the ATM's version of events, the manager would look at how long the customer had held an account, how much money was in the account and whether or not he knew the customer. On these grounds, the manager would assess whether to accept the ATM or customer version of events. Although this situation may appear incongruent (that the bank would have an apparently automated system and the manager would make decisions on whether or not to accept the decisions of the system), it fits a broader research concern with the ways in which automated, quantifying systems are imprecise (Thrift, 2004), lack neutrality (Strathern, 2004) and can be involved in forms of exclusion (Shove, 2002).

An important point to emphasise here is that the bank 'factors in' to its activities the possibility of future problems with identity production and verification and financial transactions. This is a form of what Thrift calls 'working with ambiguity' (2004: 584). Thrift argues that 'what we are seeing is a new form of seeing, one which tracks and can cope with uncertainty' (2004: 584). Such uncertainty is characteristic of both the bank and CCTV. However this uncertainty plays out in different forms. For the bank, 'factoring in' allowed for potential future problems to be a pre-articulated expectation, translating a possible systemic inadequacy or failure into an anticipated, occasional, delivery problem. For the CCTV system, the 'for all practical purposes' clause in accounting for town centre activity paid recognition to possible future occasions when further evidence might be constituted which questioned the currently articulated account. Ambiguity in 'what was going on' was incorporated via the clause in order that decisions could be made in real-time to respond to apparent events in the town centre. However, while 'factoring in' the likelihood of future problems in customer identity provided the bank with a means to resolve or defer problematic questions and maintain a smooth and apparently automated system, the same could not be said for CCTV. For the CCTV system, multiple interactors were called upon to take part in identity production and corroboration processes, these were called to account, the CCTV system was liable to be the subject of questioning and exactly how CCTV staff made identity decisions formed a focus of concern. Thus both systems had distinct mechanisms for dealing with questions of identity and for CCTV these questions were not always easily resolved (see Chapter 5).

In sum, the bank system was designed to allow staff to base decisions on their close connections to customers and computers, the connection allowing the production of identity to be swift and robust and easily re-performable (using stable, coherent, redeployable categories from the database). The bank staff could generate a robust identity (one deemed sufficient by the parameters of the system) through their close connection to the computer system that had been set up to allow for swift identifications to be made. The CCTV staff meanwhile could not produce an account of town centre interaction without interacting with other sources (managers, police, the ambulance service) to confirm or refute the account, and thus were connected to a series of groups who observed and decided upon possible corroboration of the CCTV staff's accounts. The CCTV staff oriented toward a less definite, coherent or stable series of (more or less) repetitive activities, displayed recognition of the possibility of being held to future account and were connected to a series of groups who could question (rather than contribute to) these accounts. While both systems recognised the possibility of identification uncertainty, the bank 'factored in' uncertainty (rendering uncertainty acceptable within limits) while the CCTV staff either worked hard to negate uncertainty (by making claims about the evidential strength of their account of what was going on) or utilised uncertainty to shift responsibility for completing an account of what was going on. Bank data was trusted (treated as reliable) within the bank's system to the extent that a certain amount of future problems were factored in to organisational activity. CCTV accounts of activity were considered with far greater initial uncertainty and even when resolved were liable to potential future questions (such as in courts of law). Trust that a CCTV account provided an accurate rendition of 'what had happened' in the town centre always contained the proviso that such accuracy could be further scrutinised.

While it could be argued that the bank maintained a (more or less) smooth and automated system, Burbville CCTV activity appeared some distance from the automated functioning of power as noted by some analysts (for a discussion, see Smith, 2004). This raises questions for the governance literature (introduced in 'An alternative theoretical approach' section of Chapter 2). When Rose (1999), for example, talks of individuals becoming 'enwrapped in webs of knowledge and circuits of communication through which their actions can be shaped and by means of which they can steer themselves' (1999: 147) and Haggerty and Ericson (2000) talk of the surveillant assemblage, it appears that the activities of collecting, categorising and analysing information on the population are assumed to run more like the bank system than the CCTV system. These questions of governance can be considered with regard to CCTV and bank 'customer' relations.

The bank, CCTV and 'customer' relations

The bank manager was keen to talk of the close connections the bank forges with its customers. In the governance literature (such as the work of Rose, 1996) it would appear that such closeness would form a prerequisite for communicating and accounting for activity. However, for Burbville's CCTV system, such closeness and the opportunity for fostering closeness appeared notably absent. The bank manager articulated his view of customer relations as follows:

> Interview with bank manager:
> BM: i think if you're to have a relationship and to talk to a customer having a glass screen between you is not ideal and . i think it's a er <u>pity</u> that still we have that glass screen between people handling the cash and the customers i'd like to think that er some <technological> solution might er might eventually er be sorted out i mean i think various ones *have been tried and decided they don't entirely* work i think it's (.) er got to be the way forward to (.) having people sitting face to face with no barriers

For the bank manager there was a dual impetus for the bank to get 'close' to customers: first, making the customers aware of what was on offer, making the bank's products available in some form (that customers may orient toward in future interactions); and second, gaining connection to the customers, getting a greater idea of their problems with the bank. This stood in some contrast to CCTV's closed-circuit where 'barriers' to access 'what was going on' in the circuit appeared to make it more difficult for residents to assess what might be going on. The following excerpt can illustrate this:

> Interview with bank manager:
> BM: we are trying at branch level er to *try and contact* as many of our
>   customers just on the telephone on a service basis just to <u>phone</u>
>   them up and ask them what they think of the service and is
>   there anything they're <u>not</u> particularly happy with and try and
>   build some relationships and <u>kill</u> off any er issues where they
>   feel the bank has let them down

The bank manager was interested in 'attempting to build some relationships' and '*kill* off any er issues' that were problematic. This connection
to the customer effectively aided the bank's data-flow. The connections
formed opportunities to maintain the relevance and robustness of data
on the flow. The CCTV system did not seek to get in face to face contact
with residents of Burbville, it had no means set up to do so and it was
very unclear what it would offer to people if it could contact them (aside
from newspaper stories and signs saying you are on CCTV). How CCTV
could ever take in local residents' images as part of a data-flow that
would return information to those people without generating problems
(see Chapter 5), remained unclear (this will be taken up in 'Trust, the
bank, local residents and CCTV' section of this chapter). However, for
the governance literature, rendering individuals aware of their own
observability and accountability, rendering them as calculable entities
(Miller, 1992) and using connections as forms of communication to
enwrap them (Rose, 1999) in rationales for action are central features of
governmentality. The failure or absence of such connectivity, forms of
communication and rationales for action suggest the CCTV system is not
characterised by smooth, automated functioning of the surveillant
assemblage and does not incorporate many of the features of governance
mechanisms highlighted by the literature.

In this opening section to the chapter a comparison between Burbville
CCTV and a local bank has been utilised to contrast the data-flow,
identification production processes and 'customer' relations of both organisations. This comparison has been utilised to highlight how the detailed
and moment to moment interaction of CCTV's closed-circuit is quite distinct from another organisation's forms of data-flow. It has also been used
to suggest that CCTV's identity production processes can be characterised
by greater uncertainty than displayed by other organisations. Finally this
comparison has also been utilised to highlight the CCTV system's absence

of close connection to any specific group of local residents or shoppers. It has been suggested that these distinctions raise questions for the governance literature which appears more appropriate for studying the bank than CCTV. However, the bank does not just provide a comparator for CCTV in Burbville. As 'Interaction between CCTV and a bank' section will show, the CCTV managers were keen on articulating the bank as a beneficiary or user of CCTV, instigating further questions of informational flow.

Interaction between CCTV and a bank

Although 'Comparing CCTV and a bank' section suggested that for the bank manager, forms of interaction were important between bank branch and customers, for the CCTV managers, interaction between CCTV and the bank were equally important. The CCTV managers put in a significant amount of work to, first, sell CCTV as part of an 'overall package' of investments in Burbville town centre that could make the town as a whole worth investing in, and second, sell CCTV as worth investing in as it could protect retailers' customers, and encourage customers to spend longer in the town centre. The suggestion made by CCTV managers was that CCTV could look out for retailers' customers and could be used to promote the town centre as an area where investments had been made. The CCTV managers did not find in retailers a close match for the bank's customers and they did not seek to enwrap retailers in webs of communication providing rationales for action. Instead the retailers formed an audience who could be sold a positive account of CCTV. The following talk from the senior CCTV manager outlined the first of these issues:

Interview With Senior Manager:

SM: >[CCTV] was part of a strategy< came at the time what we were
     <u>trying</u> to do >y'gotta remember that this was at a time< when the
     town had felt the effects of [A MAJOR OUT-OF-TOWN RETAIL
     DEVELOPMENT] (.) it was struggling sort of within a regional
     shopping context. trying to find where it's place in the <u>hierarchy</u>
     was and at that time it was <u>losing</u>. this was at a time when you
     know improvements in the town centre were coming aboard and
     <u>we we</u> put it in cctv was seen as <u>part</u> of an overall town centre
     improvements <u>package</u> but part of it that we <u>hoped</u> had marriage
     value so as a whole

Int: yeah

SM: we're moving the town in the right <u>direction</u>. so it <u>wasn't</u>. seen
     as (.) a stand alone issue

This excerpt suggests the town was 'struggling', perhaps 'losing' as a retail environment, and yet had to be seen to be doing something. Perhaps the high quality, account that the CCTV system could produce was a revamp of the town centre's image (rather than a full colour, clear and precise image of a criminal on a screen). This talk is characteristic of much of the managers' approach to CCTV's identity, where only infrequent connections were made between CCTV and crime control (see Chapter 3). Thus the impetus behind the system was directed towards the perceived retail (not crime) problems that the town was having. In the above excerpt the claim is articulated that if investment in CCTV is made, the value of the town itself is enhanced. The CCTV managers outlined part of their job as convincing existing and potential retail investors of the value of Burbville, which was a safe place, where money had been spent to make sure that Burbville was a place where people wanted to come and shop. To quote Street: 'The way things look or seem may be as important as what they do' (1992: 12). If the CCTV managers could offer an account of an enhanced town, this might be taken on by existing retailers (such as the bank and the bank manager) and encourage them to stay in the town and might also effectively improve the town by encouraging in new retailers.

The existing retailers, such as the bank, were a group the CCTV managers attempted to articulate as users of the system. As such, the CCTV managers suggested they could appeal to retailers for financial assistance in the running of the system; they were a group who could be 'sold' the revamped account of the town centre. However the retailers identified themselves as beneficiaries, rather than users, of the system.

Interview With Senior Manager:
SM: are those that benefit from it [CCTV] you know should they be
       contributing more
Int: yeah
SM: than they are now you know they're contributing <u>nothing</u> at
       the moment
Int: mmm
SM: well they feel they give us enough money now that <u>may</u> be the
       case but the fact is that they may well be <u>benefiting</u> from this in
       ways that they can't really see

In this talk the CCTV manager recognised that local retail contributions to CCTV were a contentious issue. He suggested that local businesses should pay a little more towards the system. The CCTV managers perceived that it was within their role to enlighten these groups who could not 'see' the benefits they were receiving. These groups should be persuaded to align with the particular accounts the CCTV managers built of CCTV and the town centre (see Chapter 3 for more detail). However, as the CCTV manager suggests above, local retailers were quite adept at resisting, reformulating or rebutting this sale of the positive role of CCTV. The bank did not want to buy into the CCTV managers' account of CCTV. The bank manager suggested he would make nothing more than a small contribution to the on-going costs of CCTV as the bank had its own CCTV system and he did not think the bank's customers, or the bank's head office, would look favourably on linking up 'his' system with the town centre technology. The bank manager put this reticence down to unelaborated privacy concerns. The bank manager resisted the CCTV managers' vision of Burbville. The CCTV managers were caught in a complex interactive position. The CCTV managers could not insist retailers paid toward the system and did not want to encourage any negative comments about CCTV that might be fed back to the local authority (who made decisions on system funding) through the local traders' association. Instead the CCTV managers aimed to gently promote a particular version of CCTV, of Burbville and of retailers' position in relation to both.

While much is made of the ever increasing flow of information and bodies over ever greater distances (Urry, 2000; Castells, 1996), the sites of resistance to ever greater connectivity need to be considered.[4] Burbville is characterised by partial connections (Strathern, 1991). The CCTV system is connected to local retailers' security via a radio system. However, CCTV does not have access to retailers' data-flows, retailers are resistant to connecting more closely with CCTV (partly for financial reasons and partly due to privacy concerns) and retailers resist the accounts of town centre improvement and investment offered by the CCTV system. This attempt at, and resistance to, connectivity occasionally touched on issues of privacy and surveillance, with CCTV managers suggesting customers could be protected by CCTV and retailers expressing vague privacy concerns. However, unlike the governance literature, connectivity was more frequently the site for practical, financial discussions (how much CCTV cost to run and how much the bank could possibly contribute) than attempts to govern activity and render individuals or retailers governable. Comparisons can be drawn, then, between CCTV and the bank, but interactivity between the two is not so easily elaborated. Yet, as 'Trust, the bank, local residents and CCTV' section will highlight, this did not always result in the CCTV system and bank remaining unconnected.

Trust, the bank, local residents and CCTV

This chapter has suggested that the technological systems of Burbville did not straightforwardly map onto any form of network society (Castells, 1996). The town centre was not characterised by dynamic and connected information flows which carried ever greater amounts of bodies and information over greater distances with greater certainty (Urry, 2000). Instead the bank had a reasonably robust data-flow which factored in likely failure, and CCTV's closed-circuit contained multiple forms of sometimes connected and sometimes disjointed forms of accountability interactivity. While some effort was made to connect these systems, these efforts did not involve connecting systemic data-flows but instead involved negotiations over financial contributions. Even these connections were disputed and partial. This appeared to leave CCTV some distance from the automated functioning of power as discussed by Smith (2004). In developing an understanding of privacy and surveillance, this work to resist connection equated to work to control access. Just as the CCTV system operated to closely control access to CCTV's closed-circuit of interaction (particularly in terms of what could be seen and who was allowed to account for what could be seen), the bank system was established and maintained to carefully control distributed forms of access (through branches, call centres and data-processing centres). In returning to the discussion of Chapter 3, here privacy responsibility is taken on by the bank and articulated on behalf of customers (the bank will not offer access to customer data-flow), while the bank manager also articulated financial concerns (he worried that closer connection to CCTV would necessitate larger financial contributions to CCTV). If the narrow focus of surveillance (analysing those forms of interactivity designed to closely scrutinise forms of information collection and categorisation) is retained here, thus far this chapter does not offer many further insights beyond a comparison between the bank's apparently smoother and CCTV's apparently messier activities of information scrutiny.

This questions the appropriateness of governance for understanding these forms of privacy and surveillance. While Rose (1999), for example, talks of individuals becoming enwrapped in webs of communication through which rationales for action are communicated and internalised, making individuals aware of their individual calculability (Miller, 1992), such communicative connections appear absent here. However, turning attention to local residents can reveal an alternative set of disparate, temporary and ad hoc connections which did not necessarily enwrap

individuals in webs of communication, but did form sites for the negotiation of trust. Although cash-points and other elements of banking
technology were not a central focus of interviews with local residents of
Burbville, the interviewees frequently talked of these technologies.

In discussions relating either to the main features or most frequently
noted technologies of the town centre, cash-points were most often
mentioned. While other technologies such as street-lighting, credit card
machines in shops and electronic doors were discussed in interviews,
these technologies were not articulated as consistently as cash-points.
There were three consistent features of residents' accounts of cash-
points. First, the time that cash-points had spent present in the town
centre was noted. Second, the perceived direct usefulness of the cash-
point was discussed. Third, the direct connection people suggested they
had to the bank system, allowing them to produce a straightforward
account of themselves, was emphasised. These articulations rendered
cash-points obvious. Residents of Burbville only seemed to have difficulties in further elaborating on certain aspects of cash-points because
they suggested my questions were unnecessary. These were questions to
which everyone knew the answers. That is not to say everyone had
exactly the same view of cash-points existing across all discussions, but
to each individual resident there seemed to be a relatively coherent set
of claims they could make about cash-points.

For local residents this 'obviousness' about cash-points relating to
their apparent utility, identity and connectivity raises questions for
CCTV. Could CCTV match such utility, identity or connectivity? These
points are neatly brought together in the following exchange.

> Interview With Resident of Burbville:
> *Int*:   yeah yeah would you say that um cctv is seen as a conv<u>enience</u>
>   in the same way as cash-points ?
> *M8*:   i wouldn't have said that the <u>awareness</u> was <u>that</u> high and it's
>   also a <passive er convenience> in that with a cash-point you
>   actually there's your bit of plastic and you use it whereas
>   with cctv is there much in the same way as you'd like to see a
>   policeman standing on the corner and um taking on much of
>   the same role to <u>some</u> extent (.)
> *Int*:   yeah yeah

In this excerpt issues are raised regarding passivity, awareness and direct
connection. The suggestion is made that with cash-points a person owns
and holds their own card that they insert, entering an extension of

themselves into the system (the data-flow in 'Interaction between CCTV and a bank' section). The system demonstrates awareness of the customer and this facilitates their withdrawal of money. With CCTV a person's image may be whisked off from the town centre into CCTV's closed-circuit, but not necessarily through choice. Furthermore, there would not necessarily be any immediate benefit to the individual or perhaps the kind of benefit only noticeable through presence and not absence (e.g. in interviews residents suggested that if followed by a strange person, people might be glad of a camera's presence, but no residents suggested that if there was not one around, people would start to think where is a camera when you need one). Unlike the bank system, this entry into data-flow was not contactable again. There was no CCTV equivalent of the phone-banking system, bank clerks or managers in branches who could be contacted about entries made in the data-flow (although there is notification on signs for who runs the system, this was not noted by residents as an opportunity to get in touch with CCTV or the system's managers).

While local residents articulated the identity, utility and connectivity of cash-points, they also raised concerns in relation to the times and spaces in which they might use cash-points.

Interview With Resident of Burbville:

M3: **i mean the only time it would** <u>bother</u> me would be at <u>night</u>. >i'd be very wary about< where i drew money out at night . i mean it wouldn't bother me during . the . day

Int: mmhmm so would that be . the . number of people that are there *during the day that would be better or* ( )

M3: um (.) no ( ) i mean just think statistically i think it's proven just sort of safer to <u>do</u> <u>it</u> during the day

Interview With Resident of Burbville:

Int: yeah how would feel about withdrawing money from a cash-point in a public place ?

F4: um (.) <u>again</u> >i think um i mean< the actual <u>act</u> <u>itself</u> i'm quite <comfortable> with but then it's >referring back to what you said before about cctv< you know should it be a dark high street late at <u>night</u> i would feel threatened (.) but then that's more to do with the sort of <u>context</u> which i'm doing it in than the actual act itself (.)

Int: what is it about the <u>night</u> <u>time</u> situation that's really scary i mean less <u>people</u> or ?

F4:   yeah i mean all the <traditional> reasons why <u>really</u> yeah because it <u>is</u> dark yeah because there <u>are</u> less people around less people to <u>call</u> if you <u>did</u> get in trouble . because it's sort of *i don't know if it's proven* but it's felt that you know criminals hang around <u>at</u> <u>that</u> <u>time</u> <u>of</u> <u>night</u>

Interview With Resident of Burbville:

Int: yeah (.) um (.) how do you <u>feel</u> (.) for example about . withdrawing money from a <cash-point> in a public place ?

F2:   mmm ? (.)

Int: do you feel quite <u>comfortable</u> with that ?

F2:   i probably feel more <comfortable> the more <u>people</u> are around (.) somehow i think if it was <u>quiet</u> (.) i think i'd probably feel slightly more <wary> about it don't quite know <u>why</u> i think but um >i'd feel safer in a crowd< (.) may not be quite <u>right</u> actually but . er . it's (.) *i feel like that*

This set of responses (there are others which followed a similar pattern) suggests that articulating concerns over cash-point use achieves a consistency. These articulations can be considered as issues of trust involving judgements as to whether or not it was safe to act. However, the use of 'trust' as a term (see Szerszynski, 1999; and also Chapter 1) can risk simplifying a complex set of processes. In Chapter 1 the work of Garfinkel (1963; 1967), Barber (1983) and Shapin (1994) was used to consider the social accomplishment of trust. Garfinkel's (1963) experimental ethnomethodology suggested that although trust could be considered as underpinning social relations and the social order, it receives most attention and is most clearly articulated in relation to apparent breaches and potential breaches of the social order. On such occasions of breach and potential breach 'trust' forms the focus for articulations of 'what has happened,' how this action might breach a convention or expectation and how the interaction in focus might get back on track (or be repaired). Questions of trust focus on both the routines which we expected (trusted) to happen and the fall back on (trusted) conventions required to carry on. Szerszynski (1999) considers such concepts of trust in relation to forms of responsibility and particular social relationships (1999: 239). In considering the excerpts on cash-point use, residents focused on three areas of breach or potential breach of their social conventions in articulating trust.

First, concerns of trust were articulated temporally: night-time was a significant focus for assessment. Second, concerns of trust were articulated spatially: if there appeared to be an open space with few people in it, this was a further consideration. Third, concerns of trust were articulated in relation to ideas local residents made a claim for: criminals hang around at night, the dark is where evil dwells and so on. Thus the focus for forms of assessment in using cash-points involved a variety of concerns regarding attracting attention. However, using Garfinkel's work, who or what would form the focus for repairing breached social conventions or preventing such a breach in these situations? In the following excerpt, a local resident articulates whether or not CCTV would be welcome when using a cash-point:

Interview With Resident of Burbville:

F1: um (.) i'd probably . be (.) indifferent to <u>pleased</u> . <u>because</u> i sometimes feel (.) um not particularly <u>safe</u> drawing money >out of
cash-points at night< if i'm on my own or going somewhere (.)
<u>specially</u> if i'm in london >that's where people hang around<
outside <u>cash-machines</u> and um i don't feel <suspicious> drawing money out of a cash-point (.) it's quite a you know <u>simple</u>
>thing to do< so i think i'd be quite <u>glad</u> *if i felt anything at all*

On this occasion a local resident had little problem in producing an account of CCTV. The presence of fear and absence of surety suggested CCTV's ability to produce accounts of local people was justified at times when local residents wanted to be accounted for and wanted their unac-countable surrounds (the mysteries of the dark) to be accounted by CCTV (which they assumed could see in the dark, could see them and could dissuade criminals from acting). Local residents produced an account of CCTV as useful and offered an account of themselves to CCTV as needing assistance. In the above excerpt CCTV is considered as a potential site for forming relations of trust and a focus for constituting the repair of breached, normal and ordinary social relations or such social relations perceived to be at risk of breach. The possibility of being articulated as an observable (see Sacks, 1972), a notable presence made available for accountability scrutiny on the CCTV monitors, was wel-comed. Responsibility for the safe and normal transaction of withdraw-ing money from a cash-point without running into trouble was shifted from an individual matter to a focus for building a relationship with the CCTV system. In this sense trust does not exist as a good or service to be carried or exchanged, but instead trustworthiness is constituted and assessed in the building of potential connectivity between individuals and CCTV.

While previous sections suggested that the CCTV system and bank remained unconnected, questioning the relevance of ideas of governance (Rose, 1996; 1999) or the network society (Castells, 1996), people in the town centre do provide a form of connectivity. However, rather than forming an automated and globalised information flow, local residents had the opportunity to act a little like Hirsch's (1992 and see Chapter 1) multi-site ethnographer, making connections and links that crossed conventional boundaries. These connections provided potential moments for CCTV to match the connectivity of bank and customers previously elaborated by the bank manager.

The bank manager aimed to make a constant connection to customers to gain awareness of customers and to offer an account of the bank to customers. In the town centre at night, though, the bank could not make such a connection, could not make customers aware they were safe, and CCTV, despite its problems of connectivity, of ever defining a set of users or a use, could step in to encourage cash-point use. Connections could be made by CCTV through drawing on the bank's customers. By engaging with these customers, CCTV had a reasonably defined group to form a connection with and was articulated as a beneficial presence. However, it was local residents who made this connection themselves. Local residents noted this occasion of utility for CCTV and entered into assessments of the potential for forming relations of trust with CCTV. CCTV publicity (see Chapter 3) did not pick up on the opportunity presented by these forms of connectivity. However, this connectivity is complex. Local residents did produce an account emphasising the usefulness of CCTV, but this account was still tied into numerous, complex, simultaneous interactions and was inconsistent; local people still feared, ignored or questioned CCTV on occasions. Also, although people in the town centre formed a connection between CCTV and the bank, this did not result in the two systems operating together. The bank and the CCTV system remained geographically linked, but financially and informationally separated.

This series of uncertain, ad hoc and temporary connections did not result in local residents becoming enwrapped in webs of knowledge and forms of communication (Rose, 1999), neither were they rendered calculable (Miller, 1992). Instead it was residents who occasionally drew together the bank and CCTV system. However, the CCTV managers did pick up on the potential for connectivity with local residents at moments where residents might enter into assessments of the likely safety and trustworthiness of a particular situation. The CCTV manager's aimed to install panic buttons in the town centre. These panic buttons would be situated (if the money could be found) in positions decreed potential trouble spots by both the police and CCTV managers. If a person in the town centre was worried that they were in trouble or required the attention of the CCTV staff, pressing one of these buttons would alert the CCTV staff in the control room to which button had been pressed. The staff could then locate the button presser on the nearest camera to the pressed button. The managers perceived that this was a service they could advertise widely as fear of crime in the town centre at night already appeared to be high and this service may reduce rather than encourage fear. The service may induce a sense of 'public' connectivity to the CCTV system, it may increase local residents' awareness of the system and it may increase their sense of CCTV's presence making up for significant absences. The panic buttons may demonstrate to local residents that they have the opportunity to place their trust (i.e. hand over responsibility for paying attention to their concerns) in CCTV.

This form of (potential) connectivity operated in a broadly similar fashion to the bank's connection to its customers. The connection formed an opportunity to try and gain data from particular individuals and inform those individuals of services available. Perhaps this tactile connectivity was a signal that the CCTV management was paying recognition to people's fears of being in (un)certain spaces at (un)certain times and was trying to carve out a presence for CCTV in those spaces. This might form a minimal return on the data-flow local people offered to the system. The CCTV system may have been able to offer a useful service that residents might have been keen to make use of, unlike much CCTV publicity which was frequently ignored (e.g. local residents were not familiar with the local newspaper stories run by the CCTV managers and police, see Chapter 3). The buttons also offered the CCTV staff an opportunity for a neatly categorised informational input that almost matched the bank staff's data screens (the CCTV staff would be informed that a person was in trouble and would be told which camera and monitor to look towards). Whether the panic button and its associated publicity would provide a sufficient presence to make up for CCTV's many absences (what could CCTV see? what happened to tapes stored?) and could forge a matching closeness to that of the bank and its customers will remain a feature of the on-going questioning of Burbville CCTV.

Conclusion

This chapter has utilised data on local retailers to establish a three part analysis of informational mobilisation and issues of trust. First a local bank was drawn into the analysis. It was suggested that the bank's practices of identity production were apparently swifter and operated more smoothly than CCTV's closed-circuit. It was suggested that this rapidity was realised through the fixed categories of the bank database, the robustness of information prepared for the bank's data-flow and factoring into the flow areas of possible uncertainty. This was utilised to suggest that CCTV's closed-circuit was characterised by less certain and multiple practices of accountability which always left open the possibility for further questions to be asked of CCTV staff's accounts. This chapter suggested that the appropriateness of metaphors relating to the network society and forms of governance require careful consideration in analysing CCTV. These metaphors could well be more appropriate for relations between the bank and its customers, where closeness and connectivity was more apparent. Second, the chapter looked at sites of potential connection between the bank and CCTV system. It was suggested that these sites did not form a focus for consistent articulations of privacy and surveillance. Instead the latter formed a secondary concern to financial considerations. Third, the chapter suggested that this apparent absence of connectivity between the bank and CCTV was not always absolute. On occasions, particularly when entering into assessments of trust (focused on questions of the breach, potential breach and possible repair of the social order), local residents did make connections between such technological systems as the bank and CCTV. Rather than forming a network society, these occasions of connection were temporary, ad hoc and unstable. It was finally suggested that the CCTV managers' attempt to install panic buttons in the town centre might encourage a broadly similar sense of connection to that noted between the bank and its customers.

While previous chapters have focused on privacy as an area of rights (and wrongs) and legislation negotiation, and surveillance has been construed narrowly in relation to specific moments of informational accountability and scrutiny, this chapter has begun to consider empirically the identity work involved in trust. In this chapter, investments in trust were made by local people in handing over responsibility to CCTV to look out for their concerns about the dark, criminal activity and so on. Just as CCTV staff watched cash-points as potential trouble-spots, so people in the town centre were aware of the criminal attention they could attract and called on the CCTV staff to account for local people (who may be able to use the panic buttons, if and when installed). Thus the CCTV system was called on to adopt the bank's customers to protect and the customers treated the CCTV system as somewhat of an extension to the security they implied cash-point use necessitated. This suggested people in the town centre might both constitute the content of CCTV's closed-circuit (the images to be articulated) and be an important factor in maintaining the connection of the parties to that flow (see also Chapters 6 and 7). If CCTV could not offer a useful service to local residents, but remained funded by a local political authority, the (at least) notional public support required to maintain system funding might be absent.

This chapter has incorporated into the analysis of privacy, surveillance and trust issues of connectivity and informational flows, both within CCTV's closed-circuit and beyond. To consider in more detail the ways in which CCTV's closed-circuit can connect to other circuits and can be challenged by forms of connectivity, Chapter 5 looks at a single incident which drew together CCTV, local residents, local and national media, UK and European courts of law.

5

'We Sold Pictures of a Man Cutting His Hands Off For Entertainment Purposes': The Story of Mr. B and CCTV

Introduction

Chapter 4 suggested that CCTV systems do not form part of a growing network society (Castells, 1996) of ever more connected information flows, rendering bodies and information more mobile, in greater quantities, over greater distances (Urry, 2000). It also suggested that town centre CCTV systems did not involve the automated functioning of power (Smith, 2004). Instead it was suggested that accounts of town centre activity flowing through CCTV's data-flow were messy and contingent, while much work went into the continued separation of the information flows of CCTV and a local bank. It was argued that greater connectivity between town centre systems was resisted, rebutted and reformulated in line with financial and privacy concerns. While local people did make connections between such technological systems as CCTV and the bank (e.g., when calling for CCTV attention during the use of cash-points), did not form a network society, but a series of temporary, ad hoc and uncertain (or partial, Strathern, 1991) connections. Through paying attention to the closed-circuit of CCTV and the bank's attempts to avoid further town centre connectivity, it could be argued that in place of ever greater connectivity, there was continuity in system separation which only altered slightly with the introduction of new technologies.

In this line of argument, rather than a globalised series of interconnecting information flows, there was a series of carefully separated and robustly bounded closed-circuits. However, these circuits were not hermetically sealed. The bank needed to retain existing customers and required new customers, and this led to further forms of engagement which risked opening up new forms of access beyond their conventional and closely guarded routines for handling information (see for example, internet banking and concerns over security risks, Guardian, 2000). Similarly, CCTV required on-going local political support, needed to retain local retailers' interest and had to garner at least notional public support in Burbville (see Chapter 3). In order to achieve this support, attempts were made to engage with media sources to gain positive publicity regarding CCTV. This chapter will argue that while such engagement did not signal CCTV's entry into globalised data-flows, the media did allow for forms of access to CCTV which raised a series of troubling questions for the surveillance activities of the closed-circuit, and for local residents' understanding of privacy and trust.

This chapter will analyse the details of a particular case – the story of Mr. B – as reported by the various participants to this research. The story will be used to explore questions of CCTV connectivity to the media. This will strengthen previous assertions that CCTV images are not left to speak for themselves,[1] that much work goes into the production of accounts of what is going on in the town centre (see Chapter 2) and that a great deal of work goes into the production of an identity for CCTV (see Chapter 3). A three stage re-enactment of the Mr. B story will ask: How are identities for CCTV images made 'clear', accounted for and mobilised? What work is done through the media to promote the notion that we have nothing to worry about with CCTV? How does connectivity between CCTV and the media raise questions of privacy, surveillance and trust? This re-enactment will be followed by the Analysis section which considers the complex closing and opening of CCTV's closed-circuit.

In August 1995, Mr. B (not his real name) entered Burbville town centre with a knife. This much has not been disputed by any party. However, what followed this is, and has been, a matter of some contention. The story has been split into stages for ease of analysis and to highlight the temporal development of the story (see 'Analysis' section for further discussion of these stages).

The Mr. B Story

Stage one

In August 1995 Mr. B walked into Burbville High Street carrying a large kitchen knife. Was this a sufficiently striking image that it spoke for itself? No; the CCTV staff began articulating the observable (Sacks, 1972, and Chapter 2), producing an account which situated the image of the person, knife, time of day, geographical position and lack of other people in the town centre in making a claim that the images presented evidence of what might happen next. The uncertainty over what might happen next was communicated to police officers in the police station and on the High Street beat, effectively shifting responsibility for the resolution of this ambiguity (Rappert, 2001) from CCTV staff to police officers. The police officers agreed that the account and images presented sufficient evidence to be constituted as an event to which they should respond. The CCTV staff began the real-time recorder to capture further images and made notes to later update their logbook, aware that their managers expected them to be in a position to offer accounts of their activity at future dates should they be called to account. The CCTV staff and police worked together to produce a corroborated account of 'what was going on' in the town centre. In the police station, officers were talked through the image of Mr. B by CCTV staff on the radio and agreed on the presence of a knife that this was a police event that required a police response. Police in the High Street were directed, via the radio, to Mr. B by CCTV staff switching from camera to camera as Mr. B moved through Burbville.

On arriving at the scene, police officers did not discover a potential attacker, but a confused and upset man who claimed he was planning to commit suicide. The police decided that Mr. B's account was sufficiently compelling that the future likely course of events required a response from the health service. Mr. B was taken to the police station initially, and was subsequently offered medical attention by the health service (the police officers called a doctor who inspected him prior to releasing him without charge). This no longer appeared to be a police story. It was no longer a CCTV story either as Mr. B was removed from the visible range of the cameras. However, Mr. B's image was retained on tape in the filing system operated by the CCTV system.

In this stage of the story there were several different accounts of 'what was going on'. The CCTV staff produced an indefinite account – 'there is a man with a knife and we don't know what he is doing' – which shifted responsibility for ambiguity resolution to the police. Police officers and CCTV staff between them then worked to resolve 'what was going on' by confirming the presence of a knife, tracking and then locating Mr. B. There were notes taken by the CCTV staff to meet their own accountability requirements, images on time-lapse tapes and images recorded on the real-time recorder. The resolution of ambiguity regarding 'what was going on', accomplished in interaction between CCTV staff, police officers and Mr. B, called into question the initial account offered by CCTV staff. The future events they had articulated appeared mistaken. The initial 'knife threat' account was replaced by a 'health assistance required' account. It was still an event, however, and the CCTV staff could be confident they had acted in ways which, if held to account, would uphold their guidelines. The images did not speak for themselves but were mobilised with accounts through a particular socio-technical configuration involving radios, cameras, verbal accounts, monitors, fibre-optic connections, police officers both in the station and in the High Street, CCTV staff, their guidelines and logbooks.

These social and technical entities completed the closed-circuit of closed-circuit television (see Chapter 2 for an introduction to 'closed-circuits'). Images and accounts were mobilised as an ambiguous flow of information, access to which was strictly limited. Although a person (Mr. B) featured in images, he was not initially given the opportunity to offer an account of his actions. Rather his image was accounted for in the closed-circuit, in negotiation between CCTV staff and the police. These accounts were not fixed or stable (what Latour (1990) would term immutable mobiles). Instead, as Garfinkel's (1967) work suggested, these accounts were contingent products of on-going activity which were produced according to what appeared to be available to hand and could be redirected and renegotiated in moment to moment interactivity. However, accounts and images were not independent, they were co-articulated. The CCTV staff demonstrated expertise in gaining a police response by deploying accounts such as 'potential knife threat'. The prominence of the knife in the CCTV staff's account acted as an attempt to gain recognition for the presence of a knife in the image. The image did not get to speak for itself, but was an important feature of the mobilised account. Yet the account did not guarantee a shift of the initial account into an event and corroboration by the police was an important feature of interaction on the closed-circuit. In this particular story, contact with Mr. B eventually challenged the account produced by CCTV staff which had previously been corroborated by the police. Mr. B's account of events was fed into the information flow – the content that connected the various social and technical elements of the closed-circuit – by the police on the radio and remained as a feature of the notes and tapes stored in the CCTV system. The logbook offered the chance for tapes and accounts to be filed together in the CCTV system's organised and recollectable history.[2] This activity appears to fit with the narrow definition of surveillance with CCTV staff and police officers closely scrutinising one set of images amongst the mass of data available. It also connects to the privacy concerns articulated in previous chapters. In a similar vein to Chapter 3 where it was argued that knowledge of CCTV's activity formed an important component of privacy, here questions could be asked: did Mr. B know he had been on CCTV and that tapes and notes of his activity had been recorded?

Stage two

This was not the end of the Mr. B story. Thus far we have seen the mobilisation of accounts in the information flow of the closed-circuit of closed-circuit television. This circuit involved police officers, CCTV staff, cameras and monitors, occasionally incorporating the health service, also available for connection through the CCTV control room. The Mr. B story represented a rare occasion on which the circuit incorporated the account of the subject of the image. However, alongside this activity inside the closed-circuit, the managers had a remit to mobilise images and accounts beyond the confines of the closed-circuit to promote the benefits of the CCTV system (see Chapter 3). A few months after the Mr. B incident, a real-crime documentary team got in touch with the CCTV managers and asked if they might have any suitable footage for the promotion of CCTV. The managers asked the makers of Crimesearch if they would include stories not solely featuring crime (despite the series title) in order to promote the community beneficial aspects of CCTV. The Mr. B story, the managers suggested, was a good example of the way CCTV could help out in the community, saving lives (moving CCTV away from its usual associations with cutting crime, see Chapter 3).[3] The senior CCTV manager outlined his view on the importance of this connectivity:

> Interview With Senior Manager:
> (For transcription notes see Appendix)
> SM: we didn't discourage people like *crimesearch* to come to us *and* talk to us about erm talk to us about the system and we were *more* than happy at that point to
> Int: yeah
> SM: actually take the offers that came in and you know i've said it before that that is actually the right thing to do *in my mind* because er if we publicise what we do >if we go about it in the right way< if we <u>publicise</u> what we do we <u>are</u> being open and we are being <u>honest</u> to people and we show in training what we do there's nothing <u>covert</u> or <u>secretive</u> about we do which i think is

> where this can end up being a pretty <u>difficult</u> area yeah. ours is that we are as open as we *can* be and there what we do i <u>see</u> <u>publicity</u> as being a key part of that informing people what we do

Schlesinger and Tumber's (1994) account of crime reporting argues that official sources such as the police use the media to publicise a certain 'visual identity' (1994: 109). This operates, they argue, within a 'culture of promotionalism' (1994: 13). They suggest that questions can be asked of this culture 'about the tactics and strategies pursued by sources seeking media attention, about their perceptions of other, competing, actors in the fields over which they are trying to exert influence, the resources at their disposal, the organizational contexts in which they operate, their publicity goals and how they assess their own effectiveness in using the media' (1994: 13). Using Schlesinger and Tumber's (1994) terms, the 'tactics and strategies' of such groups as CCTV managers and police officers are centred on immediate 'publicity goals' designed, for example, to promote a community beneficial version of CCTV (see Chapters 3 and 4) and the 'resources at their disposal' (1994: 13) for publicity would include videotapes, local newspapers and also occasionally TV companies. In Burbville, this promotional activity involved mobilising CCTV video-tapes while also mobilising an identity for CCTV. These attempts to publicise a particular identity for CCTV also involved promotion of the CCTV system's account production processes. Just as CCTV account production processes were made available for scrutiny in courtrooms (see Chapter 3), the CCTV managers wanted to suggest via Crimesearch that the ways in which images were collected were trouble free and hence CCTV was trouble free. However, civil liberties groups, part of the growing industry of protest (see Chapter 1), wanted to argue that such image collection practices raised profound and worrying questions regarding privacy and hence suggested we should be worried about CCTV (see 'Stage Three' section).

Drawing on Schlesinger and Tumber's (1994) analysis of the promotion of visual identity, it can be argued that the CCTV managers deployed specific tactics and strategies of information management. The managers asked the TV company to only use the footage of Mr. B in an appropriately educational and informative manner and to obscure Mr. B's face. The managers also checked and made sure their actions adhered to their own system guidelines. The managers attempted to extend some of the boundaries of the closed-circuit into national television. They did not simply hand the tape over, but hoped to mobilise the taped images and a particular account of those images (that CCTV could save lives and benefit the community) within a set of usage boundaries. They hoped to connect the closed-circuit to national TV in such a way as to use their account of a CCTV image to promote their version of CCTV as open, caring and community benefiting. The managers did not want to fully open the closed-circuit, but instead sought to carefully control access to the closed-circuit by making attempts to control what could be seen and by providing a way in which the CCTV images should be articulated. As demonstrated in Chapter 3, the CCTV managers did not have many opportunities for publicising a positive account of CCTV without threatening to open up CCTV's closed-circuit to, what the managers' claimed, would be the wrong kind of access (i.e. negative publicity or access to those with criminal intent).

While Crimesearch stuck to the agreed boundaries for use of the images and included the community beneficial account of CCTV in the programme, the adverts for that week's Crimesearch contained a different account. Rather than promoting CCTV as community beneficial, the adverts showed pictures of Mr. B and asked cliffhanger questions of whether or not this man (Mr. B) could be saved by CCTV and the emergency services. To find out, viewers were implored to see Crimesearch tonight. The account of the images was changed again. The story of Mr. B had shifted from ambiguity, to resolution, back to ambiguity again. This might suggest a radical 'inconcludability' (Woolgar and Cooper, 1999: 5, and see Chapter 3) to the Mr. B story. Further to this, while the images of Mr. B's face were supposed to be obscured in all footage, the attempts made were not entirely successful. According to Mr. B at a later date, this resulted in close friends and family, who had not known the extent of his troubles, recognising his image. Mr. B also saw some of the images and was surprised to find himself on prime-time TV without his prior knowledge.

Once again there were images and accounts being mobilised into information flows connecting various people and technologies. There was Mr. B and the police as TV image, the CCTV system and National TV company as provider of the image, televisions in people's homes and a range of viewers including Mr. B and his family and friends. The images of Mr. B were important, but not independent of the accounts produced of Mr. B. There was an account of impending doom and an account of community benefit, alongside a shocked account from Mr. B and his family and friends. Although the Mr. B story had previously been linked in local newspapers to CCTV as community-beneficial, these were not viewed by 9.2 million people – there was a suggestion in Mr. B's initial complaints that it was the size of circulation that most concerned him. The narrow definition of surveillance, with CCTV staff applying scrutiny to a small range of images amongst the many available to them, is still relevant here, however allowing access to those images and accounts beyond the closed-circuit opened up questions of privacy (such as: did CCTV have the right to show these images?) and trust (such as: in what ways did the Mr. B story breach apprehensions of the normal social order and how should local residents reorient their understanding of CCTV in terms of its reliability, benefits and decision-making in tape storage in line with any apparent breach?).

Stage three

Mr. B and Freedom, the civil liberty group, joined forces to get a High Court injunction against Burbville CCTV system to stop them from acting in the same way in the future. Simultaneously, the Daily Monograph began a series of strongly anti-CCTV articles, that referred to the Mr. B story and a complaint was made to the National TV company who agreed to broadcast an apology. The CCTV managers attempted to mount a defence of their actions, but gained little publicity for their account of events. The mobilisation of Mr. B from the closed-circuit of CCTV to the broader arena of national television encouraged the production of a range of accounts as to what Mr. B's image represented. The extended boundaries that the CCTV managers had attempted to construct were swept away in this wide range of accounts. The CCTV managers responded in the following way:

Interview With Senior Manager:
SM: you know but of course i've got copies of the monograph article but i mean basically they're saying is here's an authority who knowingly issued a picture of a man effectively cutting his hands off at [TOWN CENTRE] and then sold it for entertainment purposes nothing could be further from the truth that wasn't what happened at all and yet there is in the public domain *talking* about us rather than *that* sort of bloke reporting as interesting as it might be is hugely damaging as far as we're concerned hugely damaging and i think they've knocked the confidence of a lot of people i've sensed that there's a lot of people looking and wanting to know what happened (.)

This differed from Freedom's viewpoint:

As B's story shows, the uncontrolled use of CCTV means that none of us has the right to privacy – and that is profoundly worrying.

Imagine a country where … someone who is filmed – whatever they are doing – has no right to say what happens to the film, or even to stop it being broadcast.

It is through Freedom's campaign that Mr. B's name and details of his medical history became appended to the stories. As each party attempted to articulate *the* convincing version of events, it appears each party attempted to make a claim for ever greater certainty in their evidence and placed questions by the evidential practices of other parties (for more on evidence, see Lynch, 1998, and Chapter 3). As a result, accounts now regularly referred not just to Mr. B's anonymous image but to his name and background too. The Daily Monograph, National TV, CCTV managers and Freedom campaign were not the only accounts of Mr. B's story. The local residents also expressed a range of views:

Interview With Resident Of Burbville:
Int: if you were involved in some kind of incident and then it got shown on <u>crimesearch</u> or something like that
F4: yeah <i suppose putting it in a you know personal perspective> (.) again it's er the same reaction (.) it er would <u>anger</u> me and it would er feel like an <invasion> of my privacy yeah but by the same <u>token</u> i sort of also see the <value> in <u>capturing</u> the criminal and (.)
Int: so you think there's some kind of <balance> there?
F4: i think there <u>is</u> **yeah**. but i er <u>once again</u> i would sort of say you know sixty percent towards invasion of privacy and. you know. you know *there are other other ways and means of capturing criminals*

Interview With Resident Of Burbville:
F1: i'd say obviously there um (.) aren't enough strict <u>controls</u> and maybe there hasn't been enough <u>legislation</u> there <hasn't been> enough <u>legislation</u> <u>created</u> yet maybe because it's a <u>new</u> <u>thing</u> um and (.) i <u>think</u> it could become a <u>problem</u> >you know if it's going to become widespread< (.) you know with cctv cameras in <u>all</u> the major high streets *you know* <u>all</u> <u>over</u> the place i think it would have to be regulated

For local residents, the Mr. B story was an event they could recall and talk about. Burbville did not frequently receive national media coverage and residents deployed a variety of claims in response to this story. However, these excerpts still reflect the complexity of accounting for CCTV's identity. The residents produced accounts highlighting issues of a balance between threats to privacy protection (in the form of lack of controls over what might happen to tapes) and capturing criminals, while also expressing concerns over an absence of legislation (someone else to take responsibility for issues of control, access, etc.). Rather than a series of accounts travelling around a closed-circuit and either achieving corroboration or being disputed, the Mr. B story became dispersed. This fluidity (Mol and Law, 1994, see also Chapter 2) of accounts did not find a focus in the same way that a boundary object (Star and Griesemer, 1989, Chapter 2) organises a focal point for divergent viewpoints. Instead the various Mr. B stories became amorphous and partially disconnected. The CCTV managers ceased their promotional activity, worried that anything they said might get misinterpreted. The local police also appeared to stop actively promoting their connections to the CCTV system. To some extent the CCTV system began to withdraw its visible identity (although cameras and signs of their presence still remained in Burbville High Street), the system attempted to become less available as an observable for articulation.

One forum through which the stories were at least partially reconnected was in the High Court. Freedom launched a High Court action against Burbville CCTV system in an attempt to prevent further 'misuse' (use that contravened Freedom's version of correct usage) of CCTV footage by getting an injunction stopping Burbville council from acting in the same way in the future. The CCTV managers attempted a defence of their actions and of the boundaries they had attempted to construct for the movement and use of the tape. Freedom and Mr. B argued that his privacy was invaded. The High Court ruling took two years to deliver, by which time the media, particularly the Daily Monograph, had seemingly lost interest in the story. The High Court judge ruled that Mr. B's actions had been in a public place and so no invasion of privacy under English law could have taken place. However, the judge tempered this somewhat by saying there were few legal grounds in Britain (at that time) for granting a right to privacy in a public place. The judge also suggested that in the absence of a right to privacy, his decision had to be based purely on whether the local authority in Burbville had acted rationally or irrationally.

The CCTV managers were delighted with this outcome, which they took as the ultimate corroboration of their account of the Mr. B story and their version of the CCTV system's identity.

Interview With Senior Manager:

SM:　we have been in somewhat of a <u>difficult</u> <u>situation</u> because of the high court case with er mr. b and *er freedom* that's been unfortunate and it's been *not* unfortunate because it hasn't been an issue we didn't want dealt with we're quite happy to deal with that and there's no argument the judgements proved that's proved us to be right. there's nothing in the judges er in the (.) judgement that (.) came to us to say er that *we were wrong* more that what we did was absolutely right but it's stopped us from moving on it's stopped us moving forward

SM: there is absolutely nothing wrong with what went on there is nothing wrong i was really pleased with the [CRIMESEARCH] program which was excellent it did all the work and it's just it's just the way that it's been translated by others to their own advantages

The managers once again began publicising CCTV's presence in the town and the local police returned to promoting their connections with the system. The CCTV managers also had to get this account circulated amongst groups which CCTV depended on for political or financial support (the criminal justice system, national government finance groups, local councillors, local retail groups and so on, see Chapters 3 and 4). However, as much as the CCTV managers may have wished the Mr. B story was now complete and had now returned to the closed-circuit of CCTV, not everyone was as convinced of the judge's ruling. The local residents of Burbville expressed a range of views about the High Court ruling:

Interview With Resident Of Burbville:
Int: yeah i mean like the <legal> side of that is that (.) if you're in a public place anyway like a high street (.) then you're in the public eye and that cctv is just an extension of that

M5:   mmmm i disagree (.) i think that that's wrong <completely> the street was there before the cameras so that's rubbish i think (.)

Interview With Resident Of Burbville:
Int: *i mean the <legal precedent>* is that if you're in a high street then you're in a public place and so it's not invasion of privacy (.) how'd you feel about that?

F1:   mmm well um i don't mind being watched >because i don't particularly think about it< but . if . for example a new television series about like you know >people making fools of themselves< caught purely on cctv i think that would be a bit you know i think i'd have a problem with that and **i think a lot of other**

people would it would raise public <u>consciousness</u> awareness of cctv in a very negative light

Once again local residents provided a range of alternative accounts as to 'what was going on'. The Mr. B story did not provide the basis for an entirely negative account of CCTV. While some of the local residents' accounts were strongly worded ('that's rubbish') others talked of a balance between being watched by CCTV (construed as reasonable) and being shown on TV (construed as not reasonable). Although local residents had previously (see Chapter 4) actively engaged in articulations of trust (e.g. judging CCTV to be a system worth connecting to in particular situations where there appeared to be potential for a breach of the ordinary social order such as using a cash-point at night), in relation to the Mr. B story on occasion calls were made for some other notable authority to enhance CCTV's trustworthiness by taking responsibility for decisions over, for example, tape handling and use. However, such calls were inconsistent and not all local residents suggested the Mr. B story represented a problem for CCTV. While there were few signs of ambiguity resolution (Rappert, 2001) in discussions of how to characterise CCTV, this was not a sign of organised, managed deferral of resolution (Lee, 1999). The mutually incompatible arguments sought resolution on the terms of each argument, but effectively maintained a lack of resolution through the continued push for incompatibility.

The range of responses offered in relation to the Mr. B story continued as Freedom refused to accept the validity of the High Court ruling and, even after being turned down for a High Court appeal, went to the European Court of Human Rights. At the end of January 2003, the Strasbourg court ruled that Mr. B's right to respect for his private life had been violated. The court suggested that the CCTV system was in the wrong as it could have sought Mr. B's consent, could have masked his identity effectively before passing the footage on or had written contracts with the TV companies ensuring his identity was masked. The court also decided there had been a breach of article 13 of the Human Rights Convention in that Mr. B had no right to an effective remedy. A privacy complaint to Burbville CCTV would only have been possible after the broadcast when Mr. B became aware of events. Although in Chapter 3 the responsibility for privacy was shifted from the CCTV system to local residents, in Strasbourg this responsibility is shifted back toward CCTV. The ruling appears to be a call to open up the closed-circuit, at least in the sense of informing residents 'what is going on' in the closed-circuit and what might happen to tapes of local residents' activities. This may prove difficult for Burbville CCTV, as Chapter 4 emphasised there is little communicative connectivity between CCTV and residents.

Freedom responded rapidly to this judgement:

> The court has confirmed something that should be glaringly obvious to people operating CCTV systems ... they can't pass on footage of people without any regard for those people's right to privacy. Sadly, that's too often ignored. CCTV is still very poorly controlled by UK law – it's high time proper regulation was put in place. (Freedom, 2003)

The UK Home Office accepted the ruling of the European Court.[4]

Analysis

The images of Mr. B did not speak for themselves. They were accounted for in a variety of different ways and the accounts produced were either corroborated or disputed by a range of further parties. Each stage of the story can further inform an understanding of privacy, surveillance and trust in relation to CCTV.

Stage one of the Mr. B story highlighted how the closed-circuit of closed-circuit television was maintained as a means for allowing or denying access, as a means for assessing mobilised accounts of images and for assessing what counted as a reasonable response to an account. The reasonable response provided further accounts on the closed-circuit which could be used to corroborate or dispute previous accounts, which could be the subject of further accounts and so on. Opening this closed-circuit, even partially as in Stage two of the story, was very rare. The local residents of Burbville highlighted this as a possible problem with CCTV (see Chapter 3). If surveillance is taken narrowly (see, for example, Bennett, 2005) to refer to those moments of close accountability scrutiny carried out by CCTV staff and privacy is related to rights (and wrongs) and legislative discussions (see Chapters 1 and 2), then in Stage one of the story residents were not concerned primarily with surveillance but with privacy. The local residents were not concerned that CCTV could see them or account for their actions, but that the tapes might be stored and reused in various ways to which they would not have access. That is, local residents were concerned they would not have access to the mechanisms that would make tapes available beyond the closed-circuit (at least not prior to them appearing in public on TV, for

example). Rather than CCTV invading privacy and rather than a concern with the private accounting of images taken from public spaces, it
was the potential for that private accounting to invade the public (via,
for example, prime-time TV) that proved more troubling (although see
later and Chapter 3 for difficulties with notions of 'private' and 'public').

Stage two of the Mr. B story highlighted the messiness and uncertainty
of questions surrounding rights and responsibilities involved in producing accounts for images. The CCTV managers suggested that their aim
was to promote the community beneficial aspects of CCTV, what
Schlesinger and Tumber (1994) term 'visual identity' (1994: 109), that
the system was open and caring. However, they did this by using an
image without consent. The National TV agreed to use the images in line
with a particular account of what those images portrayed and in line
with a set of usage boundaries. However, they did not manage to
entirely obscure the face of Mr. B and the adverts for their programme
used an alternative account of events. Freedom attempted to gain a High
Court injunction against Burbville CCTV in order to prevent them from
misusing footage. However, this was dependent upon Freedom's own
definition of misusage, Freedom used Mr. B's real name and continued
to use Mr. B's story to promote what they believed to be the evils of
CCTV. As the author of this chapter, my account should not be excused
such scrutiny. I put together a particular account of the Mr. B story in
order to highlight issues surrounding the ambiguity of CCTV images,
how CCTV accounts were corroborated and disputed. Although I made
efforts to provide anonymity for various parties in the chapter, I may
have only inspired attempts to guess their 'true' identities. In Stage two
of the story it was not just CCTV staff producing accounts of 'what was
going on' in moments of accountability scrutiny (a form of surveillance).
In place of a single plot, there were multiple account mobilisations, each
intended to promote a specific identity for CCTV systems. These multiple accounts engaged in a rights (and wrongs) debate regarding CCTV
and issues of privacy. The accounts mobilised by the CCTV managers and
Freedom attempted to articulate that their actions were right(eous) and
that their version of CCTV was correct (this could be approached as
a form of contingently achieved ethics).

Stage three of the Mr. B story raised further questions of 'public' and
'private' (see Chapters 1 and 3 for an introduction to the complexities of
'public' and 'private' and see Sheller and Urry, 2003). There have been
two regularly recurring conceptions of public as membership criteria
and/or a spatial relation in this research. People walking through
Burbville town centre could be said to be in public (as a space) and

members of the public (as a membership category). In the ethnography these two conceptions of public were usually tied together so a person was usually considered a member of the public while in a public space. However, police officers for example, were often in a public space, but were not considered members of the public. Furthermore, with the introduction of CCTV, people could be singled out for close attention as not just any member of the public but perhaps instead as a potential criminal, someone in need of help and so on, or images of people could be stored on tape and viewed as members of the public, in the private space of the CCTV control room, when those people were no longer in the public space of the town centre.

Returning to the work of Garfinkel (1967) and Sacks (1972), with the introduction of CCTV it could be said that membership of the public became a performative criterion. All those accounted for as performing adequately in a way that could be considered within the criterion 'members of the general public' by the CCTV staff would be constituted as 'public'. Those selected out according to police tip-offs or through accounts of visible activity such as carrying a knife would be accounted for in a variety of other membership categories (potential killer, etc.). Adequately being a member of the public involved different actions at different times of day. Looking in a shop window on a Saturday afternoon could permissibly be categorised 'member of the public' activity. Looking in a shop window at night, when the shops were closed, however, might involve entirely different membership categories. Indeed the CCTV staff suggested in conversation that anyone walking through the town centre at night would be followed by the nightshift CCTV operatives due to the small number of people about at that time in Burbville. Mr. B's presence in the town centre at night and his knife carrying might then mean that he was never in public, at least not in the membership sense.

However, such a claim ignores the spatial understanding of 'public'. In the Mr. B story the spatial understanding of public did not depend on any categorisation of activity, but rather on the notion that particular spaces allowed for visual access. Access to someone's image denoted they were in a public space. In this sense, police officers who were not accorded the category 'member of the public' could still be accounted for by the CCTV system as operating in a public space and could be prosecuted if, for example, they used excessive force in arresting someone (see Goodwin, 1994, for an analysis of these issues through the Rodney King videotape). In the same way, people carrying knives, although not considered as members of the public by CCTV staff, could still be accounted for in a public space. However, this understanding of public space as visually accessible ignores the opposite: the visually inaccessible. Visual access by local residents to *what* CCTV could see was strictly limited. Also, however, and in line with the argument that the visual images of CCTV did not speak for themselves, access to *how* CCTV sees was strictly limited. Access to both the activity (how CCTV sees) and the images (what CCTV sees) of the closed-circuit were carefully controlled. In this sense CCTV was only nominally in public (with visually available cameras and signs), was not considered to have public membership and was perceived by residents to operate mostly in private (in the closed-confines of CCTV's closed-circuit).

The High Court judge's ruling that Mr. B's actions were in public thereby depended upon the notion that the images spoke for themselves, as if the key location for events was in the town centre. The initial account of Mr. B as a threat was not produced in public (in terms of action or space) and the further account of his personal problems was partially available for an instant (when Mr. B spoke to the police in the town centre), but was stored in the closed-circuit. The rewriting of Mr. B's story as a promotional tool for CCTV also occurred away from visual access. It only became available on National TV, and then CCTV was suddenly subjected to an account of itself (the production of which it had no access to) in the adverts for that week's show. This led the CCTV managers to partially withdraw the CCTV system's visual identity. It was only in the High Court that any of the activity that went into the production of these accounts was made available and publicly accountable. None of the CCTV accounts of Mr. B treated him as a member of the general public and none of these accounts was produced in a publicly visible space. A concern for most residents was that Mr. B's story then invaded the public through National TV without consent. In this sense the High Court judge's references to private and public did not cover the range of issues raised by participants to this research.

Although the High Court judge talked of the public space of Mr. B's actions, it was not clear that the location for his original actions was ever the central point of contention, particularly for local residents. Instead it was the opening of the closed-circuit, the repackaging and mobilisation of Mr. B's image from CCTV to National TV (and other media forums) that was identified by residents, Freedom and the European Court as problematic. The latter suggested that the problematic public location was National Television and that people's image should only appear there if consent had been granted and/or if their image had been masked. It was not being a member of public, in the public space of the town centre which was a focus for concern, but being an image accessible on National TV. This was still a very image-focused ruling and did not get close to discussing the way images were delivered in conjunction with particular accounts which attempted to act as instructions for the reading of the image. Under this ruling it would appear that the subject of the image should be able to grant consent to use or not use the image, but the extent to which the subject can question the story told through the image is unclear. The images were never left to speak for themselves. Instead each group attempted to get the images to speak for them and then claimed the account they offered lay in the images themselves (i.e. their account was an indisputable property of the image), irrespective of their own particular interests. And each party claimed to have done the right thing – to have acted 'correctly'. Thus attempts to gain corroboration for image and account also involved attempts to promote an account of the image, an identity for CCTV and a particular course of action as 'correct'.

Discussions of consent and masking of the image by the European Court and Freedom did not draw attention to the activity that went into the production of accounts for images produced on the closed-circuit of CCTV. Looking at the masking of Mr. B and the issue of consent, it is possible to say that the local authority made an attempt to mask the image of Mr. B and mobilised the footage without consent; the civil liberty group revealed many of Mr. B's personal details with no masking, but with consent; and in this chapter I have attempted some masking of the story (no name, no image and no medical history) but like the local authority, I had no consent from Mr. B. At the moment, Freedom and Mr. B hold the corroborated account of the Mr. B story and so hold some claim to have acted 'correctly'. However, as local residents continue to make up their own minds the Mr. B story remains, to some extent, unresolved. This form of 'inconcludability' (Woolgar and Cooper, 1999: 5, also highlighted in Chapter 3) is likely to continue[5] for as long as each party argues for mutually incompatible resolution to the story.[6]

Stage three of the Mr. B story highlights the range of different privacy concerns articulated by local residents and Freedom. That the closed-circuit could see and account for activities in the town centre (the narrow conception of surveillance) was not deemed problematic. That the closed-circuit could form an inaccessible series of bounded interactions that could store tapes, further account for images on tapes and use connections to external groups (such as the media) for the further mobilisation of tapes was considered very problematic by Freedom and an occasional concern by residents. The High Court and European Court privacy debate over rights (and wrongs) and legislation involved calls for protection to cover such closed-circuit interactivity. However, the ruling regarding consent and masking did little to consider the variety of ways in which images could be accounted for and what would count as adequate masking and consent. These discussions raised questions for consent: would adequate consent relate to passing on videotapes or also include the content of the account to travel with the tape, would it also relate to the storage of the tape or just the re-emergence of tapes from the closed-circuit? The discussions also raised questions for masking: what counts as adequate masking, who gets to decide, should those involved in images grant consent for the adequacy of masking? These questions amounted to on-going assessments of what should constitute adequate privacy. With a range of distinct views regarding privacy articulated in discussions (in opposition to public, as a right, as relating to a particular space or action or source of information; also see Chapter 1), these questions may only find resolution in each occasion of the concept's use (Hine and Eve, 1998). Articulations of CCTV's identity in relation to these questions formed one focal point for residents' assessment of trust in relation to CCTV (this will be taken up in Chapter 6).

Conclusion

In this chapter particular groups (CCTV staff, police, CCTV managers and civil liberties groups) attempted to get the images of Mr. B to speak for them and claimed that their account of the images was a feature of the images, not representative of their own interests. In these claims it was always the group juxtaposed in opposition who was doing a great deal of work to 'misrepresent' the image. The making and possible corroboration of these claims about images in the Mr. B story worked in tandem with attempts to represent the 'correct' course of action. The CCTV managers and Freedom were particularly keen to emphasise that their version of the Mr. B story was correct and that they had acted correctly. Arbitration in these claims about images and CCTV identity was complex, uncertain and on-going. It was difficult to see a final and just settling of accounts (Lee and Stenner, 1999), or even a settling which everyone would agree was *the* authoritative statement of events. The various parties involved in the Mr. B story had problems in deciding what the questions were that required answers. Each party attempted to use a particular account of the images to promote a particular version of CCTV (as community beneficial, as invading privacy). The uncertainty surrounding the Mr. B story was likely to remain for as long as each party argued, more or less equally, for a mutually incompatible resolution to the story and made claims for authority which were, more or less equally, unrecognised.

This on-going debate has been used in this chapter to continue discussions (see Chapter 4) regarding CCTV and connectivity. Chapter 4 suggested careful consideration was required in assessing appropriate metaphors for the analysis of CCTV, with concepts of the network society (Castells, 1996), super-panopticon (Poster, 1990) and forms of governance through circuits of communication and webs of knowledge (Rose, 1996), each engaged. Chapter 4 suggested that Burbville CCTV system was insufficiently engaged in the automated functioning of power to form a super-panopticon, was insufficiently connected to broader information flows to be considered part of the network society and insufficiently connected to local residents and shoppers to operate as a Foucauldian mode of governance. Although this chapter has high-lighted a distinct form of connectivity (to the media and to courts of law), it is not clear these metaphors have gained any greater relevance. The Mr. B story has initiated further discussion of the complexity of accounting for images on the closed-circuit and the range of different accountability activities to which CCTV is subjected (from local resi-dents, to TV audiences, to newspaper stories, civil liberties groups and courts of law). The production of an account of 'what is going on' in any set of images and the production of accounts as to 'what is going on' in CCTV's closed-circuit still appeared messy, partially connected and dis-tributed amongst CCTV staff and managers, police officers, local resi-dents and various media. Connectivity in the Mr. B story, although initiated by the CCTV managers in order to promote a positive identity for CCTV, only served to increase the number of accounts of what CCTV could do and why various groups should be concerned about CCTV.

These concerns involved further elaboration of the concepts of privacy, surveillance and trust. A narrow focus on surveillance relating to moments of accountability scrutiny entered into by CCTV staff was retained and appeared unproblematic to the research participants. However, privacy issues regarding what happened to tapes and accounts of tapes and how these could be mobilised instigated a range of con-cerns. While some local residents regarded the Mr. B story as unprob-lematic for CCTV, other residents and a civil liberties group thought the story had significant implications for notions of public and private activities, spaces and forms of information. Although the European Court eventually ruled in Mr. B's favour, suggesting adequate masking and consent was required for the mobilisation of images, questions remained as to who would assess the adequacy of, and what form adequacy would take in relation to, masking and consent. For some local residents the Mr. B story formed a focal point for considerations of what CCTV might be able to do and whether or not CCTV should be considered trustworthy (i.e. consideration was given of the extent to which CCTV was a system able to repair apparent breaches or potential breaches to the ordinary social order). Although in Chapter 4 connectivity between local residents, CCTV and a bank formed the site for negotiations of trust, in the Mr. B story connectivity to the media and courts of law formed a site for asking (mostly negative) questions of CCTV.

This chapter suggested that both the High Court and European Court ruling did not regard issues of privacy with the same complexity elaborated by the participants to this research. While privacy has been regarded in relation to rights (and wrong), forms of legislation, space, action, sources of information, forms of knowledge and membership criteria, the European Court focused on masking and consent only. Chapter 6 will engage with notions of privacy, private and public through engagement with the space of Burbville town centre. This engagement will be utilised in order to consider when, where and how local residents raise concerns over privacy and trust.

6

Constituting the Town Centre: Space, Trust and Accountability

Introduction

Chapter 5 suggested that a detailed understanding of privacy, surveillance and trust requires detailed engagement with the space in which technologies of information collection, storage and analysis operate. Given the rising number of such technologies, it is not surprising that increasing analytic attention is targeted toward spatial issues. Borders, biometrics (Collier, Lakoff and Rabinow, 2004), airports (Adey, 2004), workplaces (Mason, Button, Lankshear and Coates, 2002), and restaurants (Crang, 1996), form just a few of the spaces analysed in relation to surveillance activities. However, these studies utilise a variety of analytical and methodological approaches. In analysing the space of Burbville town centre, its CCTV system and issues of privacy, surveillance and trust, what would form the most appropriate analytic and methodological strategy? While Gallagher (2004) suggests that privacy rights and legislation should not relate to spaces but to people, CCTV staff and local residents still produced spatially oriented accounts of 'what is going on'. In the story of kids standing still (see Chapter 2), CCTV staff constituted accounts of specific locations (the kids were not by McDonald's, but in the middle of the High Street) while also making a variety of claims about time of day (late evening), the people in a particular location (kids) and the actions of those people (standing still). Police officers responded by mobilising resources into that location, they questioned the kids in situ and made decisions about whether or not to move the kids to another location (the police station). This chapter will argue that although conceptualising the space of the town centre is complex, involving many people, technologies and forms of interaction, it is through producing accounts of the town centre space that CCTV

116

staff engaged in surveillance action and local residents most clearly articulated concerns of privacy and trust. Decisions regarding how to act in the town centre (e.g. when and where to withdraw money from a cash-point, see Chapter 4) depended on the complex interweaving of a variety of issues, utilised to assess whether or not to trust assemblages of technology, people and space. Particular times, actions and claims to knowledge were oriented by residents toward producing accounts of the space of Burbville.

In order to engage with the space of Burbville town centre, a method was required which could directly operate in, and reproduce accounts of, the town centre. Given the research focus on analysing CCTV interactivity involved in constituting accounts, storing and categorising videotapes, making a short video of the town centre seemed an appropriate way forward. This allowed some capture of spatial interaction on tape, which could be replayed to local residents and enabled discussions amongst local residents about the town centre. Discussions were important for capturing collective action amongst residents (in place of relying solely on individual interviews). A video also enabled the analyst to engage with questions relating to the nature of video capture. However, making a video, as this chapter will demonstrate, did not prove to be a straightforward process, raising questions of space, accountability and technology. To engage with these spatial issues, this chapter will first offer a brief theoretical reorientation toward notions of space. It will draw together the insights of visual anthropologists' use of film, ideas from Science and Technology Studies (STS) research on technology and space, and ethnomethodological studies of interaction. Second, the chapter will concentrate on the author's experience of making a video of the town centre, analysing the usefulness of video as a methodological tool in producing analyses of space in relation to CCTV. Third, the chapter will analyse responses to the video offered by local residents in discussion groups. Fourth, the chapter will draw these sections together in order to produce an analysis of space, trust and accountability.

Theoretical reorientation

While there is a growing body of research on CCTV (e.g., Webster and Hood, 2000; Fyfe and Bannister, 1996; McGrail, 2002; Norris, Moran and Armstrong, 1998; Norris and Armstrong, 1999; see Chapter 2) specific questions of space and video-taping have been hitherto somewhat marginalised. While there is a small number of studies which feature questions of CCTV and space (Koeskela, 2000, 2003; Levin, Frohne and

Weibel, 2003), and there are also studies not focused on CCTV which consider issues of surveillance and space (see for example Crang, 1996; Graham, 1998), these do not focus on the complexity of spatial accounting, how space might be captured for analysis or issues regarding space and trust. In order to analyse space, trust and accountability, this chapter will first consider ethnomethodological analyses of the accomplishment of walking and accountability, and second STS analyses of technologies of accountability. These insights will be augmented in the following sections through insights from visual anthropologists' use of film.

Ethnomethodology and the town centre

Chapter 2 introduced ethnomethodolgical studies of accountability. It was suggested that the work of Garfinkel (1967) and Sacks (1972) can be utilised in considering the ways in which CCTV staff articulate observable images of activity in the town centre. Rather than accept that information is made straightforwardly available for CCTV staff to draw from video images, this approach suggested accounts of 'what was going on' in any set of images that were actively constituted. It was argued that the CCTV staff relied on forms of professional vision (Goodwin, 1994) to produce accounts which articulated initial versions of 'what was going on' in order to initiate interaction with, for example, police officers to gain corroboration for accounts. It was suggested that the professional vision of CCTV staff could also be considered in relation to Lynch's (1998) work on chains of custody to analyse the ways in which CCTV staff displayed awareness of their own potential to be held to account when producing accounts. The work of ethnnomethodologists studying control centres (see, for example, Heath and Luff, 1999; Goodwin and Goodwin, 1996; Suchman, 1993) was also drawn into the analysis in order to emphasise that the forms of activity CCTV staff entered into were one aspect of on-going routine, repetitive and accountable actions.

In preceding chapters this analytical framework has been used to consider the mass of detailed and close accountability scrutiny CCTV staff enter into when accounting for images on CCTV's closed-circuit. Such activity has been organised under a narrow definition of surveillance. This has shifted emphasis away from any expectation that the CCTV system was engaged in the smooth and automated functioning of power (Smith, 2004) and placed questions by the relevance of existing notions of governance (e.g. the work of Rose, 1996; or Haggerty and Ericson, 2000) for analysing CCTV. These contingent and on-going accountability interactions can be usefully conceptualised as processes for the production of corroborated accounts of space. In this approach, space would not be restricted to the physical geography of the town centre, but instead a spatial account would form the accountable product of interactions (between say CCTV staff and police officers) which articulated claims regarding times, actions, identities and movements (this will be analysed further in 'Science and Technology Studies in space' section). While this approach has utility for considering the ways in which CCTV staff might produce accounts of the town centre it somewhat neglects local residents' understanding of space. However, the ways in which local residents account for the town centre space appear to be important for developing an understanding of privacy and trust issues (see Chapter 5).

Chapter 2 drew on the work of Ryave and Schenkein (1974) and Livingston (1987) to consider the ways in which forms of walking are tied into the regular and adequate accomplishment of routine space. Drawing on Crabtree (2000) these accounts of space can be considered as mundane and everyday (they are something people produce all the time), yet also complex and intricate achievements (they involve the careful articulation of multiple entities in a variety of forms of interactivity). Thus, in a similar fashion to CCTV staff, local residents may have regular routines for accounting for town centre space. However, these accounts are not tied into a closed-circuit or subject to the same forms of accountability as CCTV staff. For example, local residents may be questioned in a conversation about how they consider the town centre, but do not produce accounts with the constant awareness of the possibility that their account may be held to account at a later date in, say, courts of law.

Utilising these ideas, it could be said accounts of space are achieved and thereby space is accomplished through each occasion of interactive accounting. We could then attempt to distinguish further between characteristics of the 'professional vision' of CCTV staff in control centres and details of their interaction with police officers, and 'everyday' accounts of space produced by, for example, local residents while walking through and interacting in town centres. One way of accomplishing these distinctions would be to draw further on Sacks' (1974) work and also Lee's (1984) work on Membership Categorisation Devices (MCDs). Lee points out 'Harvey Sacks has suggested that we can refer to the collections which members use to bracket categories together as Membership Categorization Devices' (1984: 70).[1] MCDs are positioned as recognisable ways to categorise events, incidents, interactions and so on and are made recognisable in such interactions. If we drew distinctions between the forms of membership made recognisable in interactions involving MCDs, we might get somewhere in accomplishing distinctions between the way town centre space is categorised by CCTV staff ('professional vision') and by local residents ('everyday accounts'). The forms of membership implicated ('professional' 'everyday') and the means of accomplishing the form of membership might provide for a location in which distinctions of spatial accounting are made available.

This chapter will attempt to analyse these everyday forms of spatial accounting in order to assess the ways in which the adequate accomplishment of space for local residents is tied into questions regarding the adequacy with which technology, privacy and trust can be understood. STS can augment these studies of accountability with insights into technology and space.

Science and Technology Studies in space

A focus on accountability and space suggests claims made in interaction and the on-going production of mutual understanding are important features of spatial interaction and that neither claims, mutual understanding nor space are simple, pre-determined concepts. Chapter 2 highlighted the useful insights STS can provide in analysing people's understanding of, and relation to, technology, where both 'people' and 'technology' are disputable terms (see for example, Bijker, Hughes and Pinch, 1989; Mackenzie and Wajcman, 1999; Woolgar, 1991). Such analyses can be spatially oriented. Mol and Law (1994) suggest that the 'social inhabits multiple topologies' with 'no clear boundaries' (1994: 659). They argue, in their comparative analysis of anaemia diagnoses in Africa and the Netherlands, that fluidity connects spaces and is engaged in the constitution of space, but neither sticks to (what might be termed) conventional geographical boundaries nor pays explicit recognition to those boundaries. This approach to fluidity (Mol and Law, 1994; de Laet and Mol, 2000; Law, 2002) suggests that space can be considered in relation to conventional physical geography and in relation to network space – the connections with which any particular object or person is engaged. For example in de Laet and Mol's (2000) work on the bush pump, the technology moves through physical space (e.g. from the development company to the village where it will be installed) and through network space (e.g. the connections with which the pump is engaged shift from designers and engineers to villagers).

In considering CCTV and space, it would be possible to draw together this fluidity with Latour's notion of immutable mobility (1990). Latour suggests that in a convincing account 'the "things" you gathered and displaced have to be presentable all at once to those you want to convince ... In sum you have to invent objects which have the properties of being mobile but also immutable, presentable, readable and combinable with one another' (1990: 26). It might be said that the CCTV staff work hard to produce a sufficiently durable association of account and image, an aggregation of visual, textual, verbal and material that travels in a stable manner from CCTV staff, to police, to town centre, back to CCTV staff (and perhaps further in courts of law, in the media and so on as required). The account would need to prove durable through physical and network space. However, could it be argued that local residents' accounts are a matter of greater fluidity as they are subject to lesser accountability pressures?

One way to address this question is provided by turning to the work of Hetherington on museums (1997; 2002). Hetherington (1997) (who draws on STS research in combination with ideas from Derrida, 1976; Foucault, 1970; Serres, 1991) argues in his study of the space of museums, that museums are classifying machines, separating, cataloguing and suggesting readings for space. He looks at an example of a museum exhibition that is based around objects placed in chronological order, the chronology establishing a means to read the space and to read it as some thing quite specific. The space appears to be a conventional, linear representation of history. Yet it is more complex than this; in the centre of the chronology is the museum's key and most popular exhibit (an ornamental owl) that is placed in the centre due to its popularity, but effectively disrupts the spatial identification the museum has previously elaborated. Its central location is chronologically out of place. Hetherington suggests that this creates a fold in the chronological space, the past and the future totems linked together in a disrupting relationship. Effectively the conventional linear reading of the physical space is disrupted by folds in the network space as connections are made between a past, a future and then a different future.[2]

Hetherington suggests these readings of space are not limited to aspects of vision; 'to see is not to understand. Understanding, rather, is performed through the material semiotics through which such arrangements of things come to be performed' (2002: 191). Latour (2002) suggests 'The folding ... mingles beings into an heterogeneous existence and inaugurates an unexpected history by multiplications of aliens which henceforth intervene between two sequences of action' (2002: 254). Thus Latour and Hetherington both position the fold as a drawing together or aggregation *and* a disruption or tension. In this sense, folds could be utilised to consider the ways CCTV staff, for example, fold the verbal, textual, visual and material together in accomplished spatial aggregations. That is, the verbal, textual, visual, material might both be drawn into an aggregation and form a focus of tension or disruption. For example, with kids standing still, the CCTV staff articulated a conventional reading of the physical geography of the town centre and gained corroboration for the account that nothing much was happening. However, the articulation of the kids' inactivity involved the constitution of a tense and disruptive fold, rendering irrelevant the smooth and linear reading of 'nothing happening' in the town centre. Focus was turned to the unaccounted kids, with times, texts, talk, claims about identity and likely future action folded together into an account which could be the source of further disruption depending on the response offered by police officers. The conventional reading of the geography of the town centre was disrupted and the network connections of the kids were placed under scrutiny. Police questions effectively smoothed out this disruption and the conventional reading of nothing much happening was reinstated.

Although Chapter 2 highlighted the difficulties involved in drawing features of ethnomethodology and STS together, the fold might be utilised to consider the tense and (potentially) disruptive process of utilising distinct theoretical insights. Thus for ethnomethodology it might be said that such talk of folds, topologies and heterogeneity is some distance from members' methods for making sense of the world. What is the utility of such tension? While folds and fluidity might be useful for capturing the ways in which CCTV staff consider different accounts of 'what is going on' in the town centre and tension derives from expectations that every account is potentially to be held to further account, what can this tell us about the spatial views and activities of local residents? Can such an approach further inform understanding of privacy and trust in relation to the town centre? 'Making a video' section will begin to engage with these questions through consideration of the process of recording a video of Burbville town centre. However, as 'Making a video' section will demonstrate, making a video proved a problematic theoretical and practical task.

Making a video

Ethnomethodology provides for a history of studies accomplished using video-based analyses (for a summary, see Mondada, 2003). However, Livingston warns that those making videos are often too focused on 'pre-requisites for producing an adequate analysis' (1987: 60). He suggests that analysts often assume a video is strong grounds for claiming that their account is the correct account because (the analyst claims) their account can be seen in the video (a similar claim to that made by CCTV managers and Freedom in Chapter 5). The purposes of this video-making exercise, however, and particularly the way in which questions of adequacy will be asked, are somewhat different. The purpose in this section is to explore, through a textual rendition of the process of making a video of Burbville, the ways in which an adequate 'everyday' (rather than professional CCTV) videoed spatial account of Burbville can be accomplished. This video was not intended as a visually available record of Burbville, but framed an attempt to fold together a tense and possibly disruptive spatial accomplishment which could then be shown to local residents. In this sense the video was not informed by, for example, conversation analysts' attempts to videotape interactions in order to claim access to the 'way things happened' (for a discussion, see Livingston, 1987), but instead drew on visual anthropology (Rory, 1996; Grimshaw, 2001; Ruby, 2000) as a methodology for exploring and engaging with the on-going accomplishment of space.

Visual anthropology has a history of attempting to problematically 'tell the world as it is' (for a discussion, see Grimshaw, 1997), as if anthropological films simply picked up parts of the world and replayed them elsewhere. However, visual anthropologists have more recently moved to actively discuss exactly what films do tell. Pinney (1992), for example, suggests that film can be an overpowering medium, with the combination of visuals, image selection and commentary forming a difficult source to counter. On a similar cautionary note, Martinez (1992) suggests that fairly open films that present a range of ideas rather than a fixed narrative can 'empower viewers by allowing them spaces to negotiate meanings in a more dialogic, interactive way' (1992: 134). It should not be assumed that a move to engage with 'visual' anthropology is a move to engage with the visual at the expense of the textual, material, verbal and so on. Pink (2001) suggests, making a video is not simply about the visual, but about 'ambiguity and expressivity' (2001: 3). Pink goes on to suggest that 'video is not simply a "data collecting tool" but a technology that participates in the negotiation of social relationships' (2001: 138). By making a video I hoped to participate in and consider the accomplishment of an adequate, everyday account of town centre space.[3]

How difficult can it be to video Burbville?

To reiterate: this is a textual rendition of the video. It is designed as an engagement with 'everyday' accomplishments of demonstrable adequacy in spatial accounting.[4] The videotaping of Burbville was split over two weekends. There were few people in Burbville Town Centre on Sundays and we (myself and the assistant director) were able to video cash-points, street signs, benches, bus-stops, lighting, furniture, shops, drain covers, phone-boxes, cars, telephone wires, television aerials and the few people who happened to be wandering through the town centre. On the first day of taping we parked in Burbville's multi-storey car-park and set about taping a few shots of the interior. The first shot of the car-park lighting system was progressing smoothly until we were interrupted by shouting. It became clear this was the car-park assistant, drawing our attention to the fact that permission to video was required in the car park and needed to be obtained in advance from the council. The car-park assistant suggested that through the council and his attachment to the council, he had the authority to say who could and could not video the car-park. This was access problem number one: the invocation of a rights (and wrongs) discourse situated within a demonstrable attachment to an employment position that further positioned our spatial manoeuvres as inadequate. The council, through the assistant, accomplished a position in interaction as the granters of permission to video. The council were also happy to video us through their CCTV system, not taping them. This, it could be argued, was access problem number two. Somewhere there might have been a CCTV video of our videotaping activities, which we could not access.

The CCTV cameras that followed our movement through the town centre swiftly became witness to access problem number three, involving the local cinema situated on a concrete balcony overlooking a parade of shops. Access problem number three arrived in the form of a slightly overweight, middle-aged man in a tatty t-shirt and paint-splattered jeans. He shouted at us to take our camera away, that the balcony was private property and that we had no right to video there. My assistant director suggested that we did have every right to video there, that it was a 'public' place, that we were intending to make no money from the video, that it was not a commercial enterprise, that the footage was for private use and that there were no signs up saying that we could not video. My directorial assistant asked what any of this had to do with the man, allowing me enough time to pack the camera away. The man made it very clear that he was the manager of the cinema. The invocation of this recognisable MCD (Lee, 1984) 'manager' ran counter to my attempts of accomplishing demonstrable adequacy in interaction. He said he was the manager, yet he had no shirt or tie or suit, he had no name badge, he wore nothing that connected him to his official capacity or even to the cinema and he relied upon a discourse that was not, as far as I was concerned, managerial. The verbal invocation 'manager', however, provided sufficient dispute to our previous visual-material account of the scruffy/threatening man that in order to continue accomplishing adequacy in our spatial manoeuvres we felt we were required to leave the balcony.

Our final access problem, access problem number four, became apparent on our return to the car-park to retrieve our car. We arrived at five to five, aware that the car-park shut on Sundays at five, only to find that access problem number one, the car-park assistant, had shut the gates early and gone home. There were pull down metal shutters across the entry and exit points, the doors to the lifts were shut and the information office was empty and locked. Again this raised questions of demonstrable adequacy in our spatial interactions in the town centre. Had five o'clock been the correct time, were our watches correct, had the car-park assistant known our car was the only one left and deliberately shut early?

We decided we needed to find someone who could operate the car-park and had the requisite authority to grant us access to our car, and to access this notable figure we needed to find a telephone. To gain access to the telephone number of the authority holders who may or may not have granted us access to the car, we had to gain access to a further notable authority who may have the number through which we could gain access to those who controlled access to the local car-park (there was no obviously advertised information number to phone). We decided we must telephone the police as the most notable authority in the local area. They may have the requisite information, the authority to hold and dispense that information and the ability to give us access to the holders of access to the car-park. This indeed turned out to be the case and through the facilitation of two telephone calls (one to the police, one to the council number given by the police), my holding of a credit card and being able to demonstrate adequately the information they required me to have of the card, a further telephone call by the council to the car-park assistant (otherwise known as access problem number one), his access to a council van, his ability to drive the van and his performative demonstration of knowledge of how the car-park barriers worked and his willingness to grant us access allowed us to get back to the car. Accomplishing adequacy in this spatial manoeuvre took a number of interactions, some time and (almost) some money; I was supposed to be charged ten pounds for this access, but the bill never arrived.

A brief consideration of these access problems can provide a means to analyse the features of an adequate accomplishment of a spatial account of Burbville town centre. Access problems one to three highlighted differential articulations of space rendered available through the interaction of socio-technical systems (a car park and council staff, a CCTV system and the staff who might be watching, and a cinema and its manager) and people wandering through the town centre. Access problem number four highlighted the complexity of town centre connectivity (see also Chapter 4), with people in the town centre forming the focus for connections to be drawn between a variety of socio-technical systems (phone lines, police, council staff, car parks) and themselves (and in this example, their car). These forms of socio-technical interaction and connectivity can be useful for considering distinctions in the spatial accounting activities of CCTV staff's professional vision and people's everyday accounts of the town centre.

CCTV accounts featured folded aggregations that stabilised in control room interactivity in such ways that they were no longer mobilised but stored in/by CCTV, and formed aspects of what Brown and Lightfoot term organisational memory (2003). CCTV logbooks and notes on the CCTV computer, tapes in storage and police officers' notes acted as mechanisms of storage that helped to maintain the immutability of CCTV accounts, as if all the questions of a particular account had been asked (for the time being). It was only in further movements that questions were asked again or even asked for the first time (e.g., when images and accounts were played in court). Thus the CCTV system in Burbville was demonstrably set up to maintain a mechanism for accomplishing adequate, temporary certainty in spatial accounting. The CCTV staff produced accounts featuring 'foldings' of times (such as 'Saturday night'), locations (such as 'taxi rank'), material (such as 'denim' or 'knives'), visuals (the selection of a series of images to show the police) and talk (a set of putative instructions in 'what was going on'). As Hetherington (1997) and Latour (2002) suggest, these folds are about aggregation, but also about tension or disruption. Police officers located their disputation of accounts in these folds. In this way, police officers made suggestions such as 'we can't respond to parking offences on a Saturday night' or 'that is not the suspect we are looking for'. Each of these police accounts folded together a range of demonstrable features relating to the regularity of CCTV staff-police interactions. Folding acted as a form of editing procedure that constituted a feature of the production of temporary certainty in CCTV accounts of space. The CCTV staff folded together the textual, material, visual and verbal in producing an account of what they claimed 'was going on' and the police folded together a range of demonstrably recognisable features of regular interaction between CCTV staff and police in response. In this way the CCTV system featured and recorded interactions that demonstrably established the production and corroboration (or dismantling) of folded spatial accounts.

Thus while CCTV staff accounted for a variety of movement through physical space (the town centre) and network space (the changing forms of connectivity in which people and things were engaged, see Mol and Law, 1994; de Laet and Mol, 2000), accountability interactions temporarily achieved stability. Such accounts of the space of the town centre were stored with images of the town centre in CCTV's closed-circuit. However, these accounts were only ever temporarily stable as any account was potentially open to further scrutiny (including further mobilisation, unfolding and re-articulation of the account) in courts of law (see Chapters 3 and 5).

This differed from the 'everyday' accounting accomplishments featured in the videotaping of Burbville. In the everyday account, which used visual anthropology as a form of engaged spatial exploration, certainty was deferred and managed (Lee, 1999). The questions of adequacy in our spatial accounting raised by the series of access problems formed into a series of questions that initially managed deferral ('why can't we film here?', 'what's happened to the car?', 'how do we get it back?') and then subsequently accomplished a further turn in interaction ('we should leave the car-park', 'we should walk away from the "manager" ', 'we should phone the police'). The further turn only became apparent as a form of accomplished spatial manoeuvre after previous turns in interaction. In this way interactions in the town centre were not closely tied into a system for the quick production of (even temporary) certainty. In retrospective analysis of the video-making it is easy to suggest that forms of certainty in spatial accounting were accomplished (e.g. we got the car out of the car park). However, it was not clear in the interactions that certainty would be accomplished (we considered the possibility of further deferrals such as leaving the car in the car-park overnight and then who knew what might happen to it). While the CCTV staff could be certain that their accounts would form part of an interaction that decided on corroboration or dismantling of their account, our moments of accountability were ad-hoc and uncertain and only revealed themselves at particular moments (such as the revelation of the cinema 'manager').

Like the CCTV staff's accounting activities, the video account of the town centre involved movement through physical space (the town centre) and network space (successive connections with a variety of people and technologies). On occasions (particularly with regard to the access problems), these connections formed moments where folded accounts were assessed for their integrity, reliability and utility (e.g. the question might be asked 'to what extent do these accounts help in this interaction?'). However, the video account was not formed within a mechanism (such as the closed-circuit) for the production of (albeit temporary) certainty. Wandering through the town centre was not tied into a mechanism for the production of storable certainty in accounting for 'what was going on'. Thus the relevance of certainty was less clear when wandering through the town centre and the extent to which certainty was achieved was more ambiguous, with a greater emphasis placed on the managed deferral of 'what was going on'. Furthermore the video account was not stored for future reference in the same way as accounts in the closed-circuit. The video account was designed (see 'Local residents' response' section) as a resource for discussion, not as a source for the clear and precise artic- ulation of 'what goes on in Burbville'. However, this emphasises the analyst's own account of the video and video-making process. Consideration needs to be given to local residents' views of the video. 'Local residents' responses' section will describe how their views instigated discussion of space in relation to issues of accountability, forms of technology, privacy and trust.

Local residents' responses

Although Pinney (1992) and Martinez (1992) suggest film is a potentially overpowering medium that should be left open to the inter- pretation of the viewer, the video was replete with numerous images of doors closing or closed, street signs signalling directions, shop notices, cash-points, telephone boxes, television aerials, drain covers, electricity wires, neon adverts, poster adverts, bus-stops, benches and rubbish bins. Like Hirsch's (1992) multi-site ethnographer (see Chapter 1), the video connected multiple spaces into a single narrative, which was then shown to local discussion groups who were offered the opportunity to take those connections apart. For the purposes of a succinct discussion, the local residents' responses have been organised into three areas: accountability, technospace and trust. These three sections were con- structed from the discussion groups' talk, arranged in a similar manner to the broad categories of Chapter 3. These three areas will be utilised in 'An appropriate spatial theory' section detailing an appropriate spatial theory for considering CCTV, privacy, surveillance and trust.

Accountability

Local residents were organised into four groups to watch and discuss the short video. They were video-taped watching and talking about the video to record these discussions. The discussions produced talk of how to understand the town centre in relation to the video. In a sense this talk resembled the CCTV staff's attempts to account for the space of the town centre. Local residents effectively folded together (Hetherington, 1997; Latour, 2002) a range of claims regarding time of day, forms of activity (such as shopping) and specific features of the town centre (such as particular shops, cash-points or benches), alongside orienting accounts through MCDs (Lee, 1984). However, unlike CCTV staff, local residents were not tied into ordered mechanisms for the production of certainty and mechanisms which would hold their accounts to further account. In the discussion groups accounts were produced through local residents' sense-making activities oriented through the video of the town centre and in conversations with other residents. In these conversations adequate spatial accounts were accomplished, but the ways in which these were further accounted for (see later) was characterised by greater fluidity (Mol and Law, 1994) than, for example, CCTV staff's accounts and accountability in courts of law (see Chapters 3 and 5). This first excerpt features one resident discussing signs in shop doorways and is resonant of much of the discussion:

> Discussion Group Number 1:
> (For transcription notes see Appendix).
> *F15*: like **we don't keep cash in our tills** . they're images that
> you're <u>used</u> to seeing so as >soon as you see the first few words
> you know you know what they why< they were there and why
> you were <u>showing</u> them

This resident folded together a variety of claims in a very specific account of features of the town centre. She was 'used to seeing' these signs in shop doorways, she was aware of some implied functionality the signs had and she also claimed to know why they formed a feature of the video. Although this analysis makes the constituent parts of account articulation seem complex, the resident emphasises that she could produce her account of the video's features almost instantly. Her claim to recognise these signs allowed her to see the signs as something familiar to her as 'soon' as she recognised 'the first few words'. A feature of this excerpt was the links which could be drawn between the resident's spatial accounting activity and her occupation. She worked in a shop and suggested the lay-out of shop doorways were very familiar. No other member of this discussion group was as familiar with these signs, and they were included in the video initially as something unfamiliar. Just as Heath, Hindmarsh and Luff's (1999, see Chapter 2) tube drivers make claims for occupationally relevant knowledge, so this respondent's employment interactivity and daily routine were oriented towards the development of a familiarity-based account of features of the video not shared by other residents. Such orientations towards very specific claims to know something about the space of the town centre were a frequent feature of residents' spatial accounting. In the following excerpt this resident orients their account of the town centre through claims to 20 years of interaction in Burbville:

Discussion Group Number 2:
M3:   >i mean i happen to know burbville quite well< and i mean the change in burbville is <enormous> because it was up until recently a fairly sleepy old town and now you suddenly see it with >cash-points and automatic doors and nuclear bunkers this way and that< and you know all the stuff there and it really has changed enormously *in the last 20 years*

Time spent present in Burbville was claimed as a relevant means to account for the space of Burbville. The juxtaposition of two town centres, one 'sleepy' and one full of 'stuff', achieves a disruptive folding (Hetherington, 1997) of past and present Burbville. In the following excerpt Burbville past and Burbville present are oriented as both familiar:

Discussion Group Number 2:
Int: so you would say because you know about burbville it's not that *unusual at all*
F2:   well it looked very much like any other town which is when i used to go to burbville it was individual lots of individual shops and things it's much *more modern and up to date and*
Int: right do you think burbville's become much more like other towns
F2:   yeah i would think so yeah

Claims regarding Burbville's past were oriented in this discussion through familiarity derived from numerous visits, while Burbville's present was accounted for through familiarity with a standardised town centre which (for this resident) Burbville had come to represent. In this spatial account Burbville was thus unlike its past through being like everywhere else. This resident's talk of infrequent visits to Burbville's town centre is a refrain frequently articulated by residents. Since the opening of a major out-of-town retail centre close to Burbville, residents, CCTV managers and local retailers accounted for the town centre in relation to its most notable out-of-town other (see also Chapter 4).

In these discussions, the video was utilised as a focus for articulations of knowledge or familiarity, linking the video of the town centre with a variety of activities, times and locations in which residents had participated. The video was also articulated as unfamiliar or shedding new light on something the residents had not regularly associated with Burbville.

Discussion Group Number 3:

F4: um it's just the odd fact about cctv um (.) [WATCHING THE VIDEO] sort of made the whole cctv more prominent >because when i would normally walk down the high street even if i saw signs for it< i probably wouldn't associate that with what you know that the majority of people don't <u>like</u> it or perhaps now i might think about what it means a little bit more now

In this excerpt the resident suggests shots of CCTV cameras and signs incorporated into the video could be utilised in making sense of and accounting for the space of the town centre. It was in making sense of and accounting for the town centre that a variety of reference points (such as the video, previous town centre interaction, etc.) were made available, made to make sense and folded together. Drawing on Garfinkel (1967) this does not imply that videos, for example, formed straightforward sources of knowledge for residents which could be drawn on in interactions. Instead the video (alongside newspaper stories, programs seen on TV, conversations, etc.) formed one of many reference points to be articulated in any occasion of interactivity where sense was made of the town centre. These reference points were not necessarily articulated in the same way in each occasion in which they formed a feature of sense-making and accounting activity, instead the sense which was made of the reference point was an accomplishment of the interaction. In this way the participants to these discussions offered an account of the video of the town centre by reorienting features of the video in line with claims they deemed significant and may make further claims in the future about these interactions as deemed situationally appropriate (Suchman, 1987). The next excerpt from the same respondent, handles this somewhat differently when the respondent attempts to explain how a space can be accounted for as familiar:

> Discussion Group Number 3:
> F4:   i think you just become um yeah i think we become <u>desensitized</u> to all those things through <u>familiarity</u> so that it would be all those things it would be through seeing images of those things through going yourself
> Int: yeah so it would be like a kind of combination of those things
> F4:   yeah <u>absolutely</u> it would be the same set of factors that would make you familiar of any other area

In a similar manner to discussions of cash-points in Chapter 4, this excerpt suggests familiarity is accounted for through forms of activity ('going yourself'), claims about information (such as the video) oriented toward interaction and the positioning of an account within other times and spaces (other towns and other visits to Burbville). Accounts of the 'desensitising' of technology in relation to particular spaces offer a comparison with the 'obviousness' of cash-points. Just as questions about cash-points confused residents (they asked why such questions were necessary or relevant), the need for residents to ask explicit questions of the technology of the town centre, according to this resident, reduced over time.

In sum, local residents' accounts of the town centre were mundane, everyday and swiftly and routinely produced, while also being complex (involving the folding together of a variety of times, actions and claims to knowledge) and contingent (the outcome of particular instances of interaction). Claims to familiarity in relation to Burbville and other town centres were utilised in orienting accounts of space towards adequate forms of certainty as to what was 'going on'. In a similar manner to the access problems which confronted the process of video-taping the town centre, particular moments when accounts were called into question led to the managed deferral of forms of certainty. A focus for such disruption in local residents' accounting of the town centre was articulated through concerns with technology and space. The 'Techno-space' section will address these issues.

Techno-space

In Chapter 2, Actor-Network Theory (ANT) was utilised to consider the ways in which social and technical entities could be translated into connected networks (Callon, 1986; Latour, 1990). In this chapter it has been argued (drawing on the work of Mol and Law, 1994; and de Laet and Mol, 2000) that such connective networks could be considered as a form of space alongside conventional geographical renditions of the town centre. For local residents, what was and was not technology and how such entities could be articulated in accounts of the town centre formed a focus for discussion. While residents suggested technologies could form a focus for considering familiarity and desensitivity, category judgements regarding the status of technology formed part of the complex accounting for town centre space.

Discussion Group Number 2:

F2: um i mean <u>technology</u> some of it <u>wasn't</u> technology i didn't think i mean some of the <u>man-hole</u> covers and things (.)

Int: right what are they then if they're not a technology

F2: well they're <u>security</u> but are they . they're . not working in any way <u>shape</u> or <u>form</u> are they they're just

Int: right so was there anything else that you looked at that *wasn't a technology would you say*

F2: well i well i would imagine that anything that's a <u>technology</u> would have to be something with working <u>parts</u> or something (.) street signs <u>didn't</u> cash machines <u>did</u>

Int: yeah so was there anything you saw M3 that you thought <u>wasn't</u> a technology at all

M3: no

Int: no?

M3: no i mean i <u>disagree</u> about **manhole covers cause the whole point of that is that once you lift it up there's a whole range** of technology underneath from cabling to whatever <u>telephone</u> wires and all sorts of <u>electricity</u>

This extended excerpt contributed to one discussion of where to draw category judgements regarding technology. The first respondent questioned whether everything in the video was a technology, her definition of technology revolving around something that worked or had working parts. The second respondent, however, robustly asserted a more ubiquitous sense of technology, arguing that manhole covers covered a great deal including cabling, telephone wires and electricity. This difference of opinion highlighted a contrast in category judgements incorporated into forms of folded account production. The video offered the opportunity for articulating the grounds and parameters for achieving such category distinctions. Accomplishing adequacy in accounts of space for the residents involved rendering category distinctions such that space made sense in occasions of interaction. Thus it could be argued sense was made of space through constant ordering of times, places, activities and claims regarding 'what was going on'. These forms of ordering are brought into focus by the following excerpt:

Discussion Group Number Three:
M5:   yeah like when [I SAW] the public phone i didn't think that that was particularly a technological <u>thing</u> **the burglar alarm as well** um i suppose the pedestrian crossing as well i suppose i don't perceive as being <u>extremely</u> technological perhaps because it's been there for such a long time

The category judgement in this excerpt was centred on articulations of familiarity and unfamiliarity. This respondent unfolded a graded space with some elements regarded as 'extremely technological' and some not. Time was claimed as the arbiter of technological sophistication in this account. Familiarity (linked to time present in the town centre) was utilised as the ordering principle for justifying the category distinction between technology and non-technology. The familiar formed the focus for certainty and the unfamiliar formed the focus for deferral and further accounting. Drawing on the work of Hetherington (1997) the familiar and unfamiliar were folded together in this account, the fold forming the focus for potential disruption. However, this group was not in universal agreement:

Discussion Group Number 3:
F4:   i don' think i'd notice trees and benches anymore so than i'd sort of notice any of the technologies
Int: yeah yeah so it's all just part of the same sort of >bundle of things you don't really distinguish anything<
F4:   no i don't think so
Int: between technology or not
F4:   maybe cctv now
M5:   i see them as being quite separate i think
Int: yeah
F4:   they've got separate functions
M5:   supplied by <u>separate</u> people as well in *different places*

The first respondent in this excerpt (F4) accounted for the town centre space by folding together a series of connections apparently without multiple categorical judgements. This respondent suggested she may incorporate 'cctv now' as one technology which required accounting in the space of the town centre, suggesting the video could be articulated in future moments of interactivity and sense-making in order to distinguish CCTV as requiring attention in a distinct category. For the second respondent (M5), though, the items he identified as technological (he had previously suggested CCTV was a technology, while pedestrian crossings, burglar alarms and public telephones were not) remained as separate categories within his folding of an account of the space around him. The distinction drawn through the first respondent's account in this excerpt was that each entity provided or performed a different function. 'Technology' was not the focus for category judgement. For the second respondent, the account of space he folded together incorporated a range of caveats, conditions and categories regarding familiarity, unfamiliarity, technology and certainty.

While category judgements formed one focus for making sense of technology in relation to space, specific forms of activity were also utilised by residents in accounting for the town centre. Local residents offered accounts of how they incorporated CCTV into their sense-making activities for regarding the town centre. The following excerpt is typical of these responses:

Discussion Group Number 1:
Int: do you think if you did see one [A CCTV CAMERA] it would **make you act in a similar sort of way** to a speed camera
F15:   >no no because when i'm looking for a< speed camera i'm doing something wrong and i know i am
Int: you know you're breaking the <law>
F15:   yeah yeah absolutely i can openly admit that yeah because i know i'm doing something wrong i'm looking for it >it's like when you see a police car you slow down< it's just a reaction even if you're not like going above the speed limit you know you just go slow down you know um >well i do anyway< but if i saw a cctv camera um i wouldn't act differently i don't think because (.) one i wouldn't know what they look like and *two* (.) er i might just be walking around and unless i was doing something wrong no i don't think i would act any *differently at all*

This respondent had previously said she did not look out for CCTV cameras in the town centre and, prior to watching the video, would have had trouble pointing a CCTV camera out. Thus her awareness of cameras and her interest in looking out for cameras was articulated in relation to particular spatially-oriented interactivity. She suggested that driving her car required that she looked out for speed cameras. She did not want to receive a police account of her as 'speeding'. She worked within a set of claims regarding authorities such as the police and the kinds of thing they looked out for. Demonstrating awareness of the speed limit, of the presence of speed cameras watching her, of the consequences of not slowing down in front of a camera and so on denied the police the opportunity to reproduce a 'speeding' account. She did not make any of these claims in relation to cameras while shopping in the town centre. She neither looked out for CCTV nor was she certain of what CCTV cameras looked like. This excerpt demonstrates that residents could, on occasions, be held accountable for the accounts they had produced. For example, if the driver wrongly guessed that she was out of range of a speed camera, this may have led to a police assessment of her driving. However, for the majority of the time, accomplishing an adequate spatial account for local residents involved the folding of a range of activities and claims of relevance to that activity, which achieved coherence in such moments of activity. Unlike Foucauldian inspired analyses of governance (see for example, Rose, 1996; Chapter 4), further moments of possible accountability were not a focus for concern nor did such possible moments form into a rationale for organising action.

The following discussion group further emphasised that while their spatial accounts were closely tied to the activities in which they were engaged, CCTV cameras did not form a focus for local residents' town centre activity:

Discussion Group Number 3:
Int: yeah (.) do you ever see like a cctv sign and think <u>ooh</u> that's bad or <u>ooh</u> that's fine
()
F4: i think it's <u>difficult</u> because when you're normally down high street you're there (.) for quite specific purposes you know so you know even though you may be aware that they're there you wouldn't normally focus on that
Int: yeah . so what purposes do you *normally go to the high street for*
M5: <u>shopping</u>
F4: >to meet people socialise go to the pub or whatever<
M5: get some <u>money</u> out of the bank

In this excerpt specific claims were articulated in relation to the space of the town centre with particular regard towards why the person was present in the town centre. Local residents folded such accounts of space in a situationally appropriate manner (Suchman, 1987). CCTV formed a frequent absence in spatial accounting through its lack of situational relevance for local residents. CCTV only shifted into presence through very specific and tightly defined articulations of times, places, activities and claims made regarding forms of information.

This analysis has provided details on local residents' spatial accounting and the broad variety of features folded together within those accounts. It has suggested that a variety of times, places, activities and claims for relevant information or knowledge were oriented towards in these account production processes. This section has further suggested that, given the opportunity to reflect on these processes, residents offered a range of distinct category judgements, the performance of which they deemed necessary for accomplishing adequate accounts of space. Forms of spatial ordering accomplished via the articulation of category judgements enabled local residents to continue accounting for space with certainty adequate for their immediate interactions. Articulating a purpose for these interactions also formed a means to consider issues of technology and space. However, residents' accounts of town centre technologies and activities only occasionally featured CCTV. These local residents' accounts of space were unlike CCTV staff's accounts of space, and were not tied into a mechanism for the production and further accounting of certainty. However, 'Trust, space and CCTV' section will now look in detail at how moments of uncertainty in these account production processes, town centre interactions and category judgements were utilised in assessments of CCTV and trust.

Trust, space and CCTV

This section will draw on both local residents' discussion groups and interviews (see Chapter 1 for more on methodology). The absence of CCTV in the excerpts considering town centre activity highlights the fragility of CCTV's utility. Although Chapter 4 suggested that local residents drew connections between the CCTV system and the bank when using a cash-point and used this connectivity as the location for contingent assessments of trust relations (Szerszynski, 1999) in potential breaches of the social order (Garfinkel, 1963), this connectivity was the product of particular claims made regarding CCTV cameras and what they might offer. Residents unaware of such claims were not in a position to form relations of trust and left CCTV's utility as an unasked question.[5] When residents noted the utility of CCTV in relation to cash-point use, they folded together night-time, lack of people, withdrawing money and claims of 'the kinds of things criminals do' in a spatial account which emphasised the utility of CCTV. On occasions during which the utility of CCTV was considered by local residents, issues discussed in this chapter such as familiarity and unfamiliarity, category distinctions and claims regarding forms of information were drawn together. In order to understand how trust was considered by local residents in these moments of spatial account production, it is necessary to analyse the range of ways in which CCTV, space and trust were articulated. For some residents, as the next excerpts demonstrate, the themes of familiarity and time spent aware of CCTV provided one means through which to express decreasing concern with claims about 'what CCTV could do' and the extent to which CCTV itself might threaten a breach to the ordinary social order:

> Interview With Resident of Burbville:
>
> F9: well i began to think about them [CCTV CAMERAS] when people who were more aware than me of them being er set up began to talk of civil liberties etc um and i did consider what they were um thinking about um tah i think initially i probably thought they were invasive without actually having come across any of the cctv er systems it's just oh big brother you know i mean perhaps we're going down the wrong road but then suddenly you're confronted with it and you're aware that these set ups are around you and you think well what are you going to do leave the area carry on er does it matter actually (.) i thought it really doesn't matter

This articulation of CCTV as having become accepted over time was also related by residents to very specific benefits which they claimed CCTV could offer:

> Discussion Group Number 2:
>
> F2: i mean i think when <u>cctv</u> <u>cameras</u> were first (.) mooted when they were first <u>thought</u> <u>about</u> i thought . god that's an infringement of my <u>civil</u> <u>liberties</u> . being photographed . and . filmed when i don't want to be (.) but <u>um</u> . if it stops my <u>car</u> being stolen from a car park . or . stops somebody being (.) <u>mugged</u> in the street at night time i mean i would <probably> say on balance they're probably a <u>better</u> <u>idea</u> ( )

The second excerpt is focused on a variety of category judgements, suggesting who would be protected by CCTV and who, by implication, would be the target of CCTV. These membership categorisation devices (MCDs; Lee, 1984) of who should and should not be concerned were rendered relevant to particular forms of activity. Car crime (not a great focus for CCTV managers) was articulated as an area where CCTV could prove useful and mugging (a crime CCTV managers were concerned about) was considered as a target for CCTV. These category judgements of relevant activities in which CCTV should be engaged and claims regarding CCTV's ability to intervene, stand distinct from the CCTV managers' attempts (expressed in Chapter 3) to shift the Burbville CCTV system away from a sole focus on crime towards a broader identity of community beneficence. Drawing on these excerpts, both accounts of the town centre space and of CCTV's identity were folded together by local residents in relation to specific forms of activity, through making claims regarding familiarity and unfamiliarity and through the production of particular category judgements and MCDs. These accounts involved assessments of whether or not the CCTV system could prove to be reliable, demonstrate integrity in crime reduction and offer the potential to repair breaches to the social order.

It could be argued that reliability and integrity formed features of trust assessments of CCTV carried out by local residents. However, frequently local residents counterpoised this positive accounting of CCTV's activity with claims they were aware of regarding CCTV's supposed 'big bother' status rendered as a breach to expectations regarding the social order. Each of these assessments of how to account for CCTV involved a balance. The following excerpt illustrates such a form of accounting:

Interview With Resident of Burbville:

M13:   um i just take it for <u>granted</u> these days i mean >you see the cameras< and you <u>know</u> what they're there for . um . er (.) i just <u>er</u> in all honesty i think it is quite a <u>good</u> idea the cctv i mean it doesn't bother me all this <u>big</u> <u>brother</u> watching you business er i've **got nothing to hide** i don't think and er if it's helping to reduce crime then so be <u>it</u> i'm all up for it

Int: er can you think of any points in <u>time</u> where it might have bothered you at all or where you might have noticed *it particularly*?

M13:   <u>er</u> i think perhaps the only time it does bother me is that when you're young when you're <u>larking</u> about you're doing what you want to do yeah um but yeah i think um nowadays i think i'm much *more er much more calmed down* anyway tend not to

doesn't tend to bother me at all anymore but um no there's
not been a particular situation where i've thought oh no hang
on i better stop what i'm >doing because of the cctv camera
around<

In this excerpt the articulation of category judgements (who should and
should not be concerned about CCTV), forms of activity (larking about)
and changes over time (a move from being young to being older and
calmer) are folded together in producing a positive account of CCTV
and the space of Burbvile town centre. The fold (Hetherington, 1997)
again formed the disruptive focus for drawing together distinct times
into a single account. In these excerpts trust could be utilised as the
organising principle for grouping and analysing issues of integrity,
reliability, 'big brother' and the social order. Such issues can be formulated as one means through which residents produced articulations of
trust. Despite claims regarding possible negative aspects of CCTV (i.e.
'big brother' issues), the positive benefits of such systems were said by
these local residents to outweigh the negatives and concerns regarding
negative issues were said to be misplaced. However, for other local
residents, belief in and trust of CCTV's apparent capabilities was more
closely associated with the possibility of adequate legislation:

Interview With Resident of Burbville:
M8:   oh . well . er in *these days where there's* so much <information>
       available about people particularly usually in computer data
       and so forth it's right that >it should be controlled< um as with
       the data protection act um so with the same sort of yardstick i i
       would expect any sort of video film to be controlled and the leg-
       islation to be put in place to *ensure that it's not abused in any way*
       (.) i'm never uncomfortable about the data protection or the
       people using it like it's sometimes irritating on a mailing list to
       receive loads of things and you think how did they did get hold
       of my name ? but i can't say it's anything i waste *any sleep over*

Interview With Resident of Burbville:
M14:   if it's in good hands i know it's corny but i mean if that kind
       of control is governed by a body that's responsible enough . to
       treat it with respect then that's <ok> i mean there's got to be
       something hasn't there they've got to have something there's
       got to be some means of control it's gonna happen sooner or
       later so as long as it's not used for . purposes >that it's not

designed for< as long as it is used to cut out our <u>crime</u> then it can only be a *good thing surely*

Int: >yeah so like you said you have some authority or whatever looking over it< but what kind of authority should you have sort of a local <u>political</u> one or the *police* or

M14: well that's a <u>hard</u> one i <u>think</u> you'd need it **would have to be impartial** above anything (.) but as soon as you've got a <u>governing</u> <u>body</u> you still you can *never ever be sure can you* it's not that i'm a <u>paranoid</u> character or anything <u>but</u> you can never know for sure

In local residents' discussions, CCTV being able to see town activity was generally regarded as unproblematic (see the above excerpt on 'big brother' issues). However, residents who considered aspects of CCTV beyond a focus on the visual to issues of information storage, retrieval and mobilisation raised possible concerns with the extent to which they felt comfortable with CCTV. In place of an articulation of CCTV's apparently positive technological capabilities, the above excerpts suggest that trust in what CCTV could do (rather than what CCTV looked at) was closely bound up with forms of regulation. In these excerpts trust was placed in legislation for holding CCTV to adequate account for its information storage, retrieval and mobilisation activities and preventing breaches of the social order. Emphasising the contingent aspects of trust relations (Szerszynski, 1999), such trust was not uniformly placed in legislation by local residents. Many of the residents could provide stories articulating concerns with what CCTV could do and the difficulties of regulating CCTV:

Interview With Resident of Burbville:

F4: um (.) completely sort of <u>contradictory</u> actually um >on the one hand if i was on my own in the high street< um i would . i mean specially of a <u>night</u> time or something >would feel threatened< . knowing that there were cameras there i'd feel um secure >but at the same time< um . i do feel like my privacy is being invaded as well

Int: right . so . do you see these kinds of systems as predominantly <u>negative</u> or <u>positive</u> or *is it just completely mixed*

F4: er (.) i'd say if <anything> **negative actually**

This excerpt summarises a form of assessment characteristic of much local residents' talk of CCTV, its reliability, integrity and trustworthiness.

In this excerpt the local resident suggests that for her the balance was tipped too far toward privacy invasion and that the supposed benefits of CCTV did not outweigh such a conviction. The next excerpt produces a similarly negative account of CCTV activity, particularly focusing on what might happen to tapes:

Interview With Resident of Burbville:

M6:   it's alright . don't mind it . um (.) well no i don't <u>love</u> it . i find it all really <u>uncomfortable</u> to be honest (.) i don't like the whole <u>idea</u> of people like . <looking> at you and stuff i'm not an <u>attention</u> seeking type person (.) <u>um</u> so i don't like the whole idea that people could tape it and >do what they want with it< you like might walk up the high street and your trousers might fall down and you'll be seen on You've Been Framed and that whole idea is <u>awful</u>

These excerpts switch between concerns, but common threads can be drawn together. Thus the talk of local residents suggests that trust in CCTV and producing a positive account of the CCTV surveyed space of Burbville town centre featured complex and on-going assessments of what CCTV could see, what CCTV could do, claims regarding what local residents were doing and claims regarding the likely actions of others (such as those with criminal intent). Reliability, integrity, utility, 'big brother' issues and forms of legislation were all articulated in assessments of whether or not CCTV could be considered trustworthy (as potentially breaching, preventing or repairing breaches to the social order). This unstable and contingent assessment of trust produced by local residents was closely tied to issues of privacy and surveillance. While the narrow concept of surveillance (particularly focusing on those moments where CCTV images were selected for closer scrutiny) could be utilised to group together the forms of CCTV activity that were noted as unproblematic by local residents, issues of privacy (particularly in terms of what might be occurring in relation to the storage and later use of tapes in the inaccessible closed-circuit of CCTV and what might form appropriate legislation for holding the circuit to account) formed a focus for assessment. This suggests that the adequacy of legislation and an adequate means to make legislation publicly available could form a means through which a positive identity for CCTV and Burbville town centre could be articulated (see Chapter 7).

However, while this articulation of CCTV and town centre space (based on claims regarding particular forms of activity by residents, by possible criminals, a range of category judgements about who should and should not worry about CCTV and the possibility of legislation) formed the dominant contingent and inconsistent basis for assessing ideas of trust and CCTV, these were not the only views expressed. The next excerpt orients accounts of space and issues of trust through suggestions that residents should look out for themselves and not depend on CCTV:

> Interview With Residents of Burbville:
> *Int*: so . you don't ever really feel that the cameras are there for your <protection> at all ? do you feel that they <u>increase</u> your safety *or anything* ?
> *M5*: <yeah> . to a <u>certain</u> extent (.) but i think (.) in this day and age . i think people know that you have to be a <u>bit</u> careful and so you look after yourself (.) i don't think it's completely <necessary> for there (.) for there to be cameras to keep an <u>eye</u> out for you
> *Int*: yeah are there any particular <u>instances</u> that you can think of when you've really <u>noticed</u> cctv cameras in a high street ? (.) any particular events that *stuck in your mind* or ( )
> *M5*: no (.) not really ( )

An alternative articulation of (lack of) trust featured a very brief statement of the (un)reliability of technology. Here little assessment was considered necessary:

> Interview With Resident of Burbville:
> *F1*: i think (.) i don't . trust >you know< <u>technologies</u> not necessarily reliable <u>way</u> of monitoring things (.)

These accounts of technology, CCTV, trust and the space of Burbville town centre which do not match the more prevalent views of the forms of assessment necessary for town centre interaction are a reminder of the diversity of views held by local residents. This diversity retains significance in relation to CCTV managers' attempts to promote a particular account of Burbville and its CCTV system. Although local residents often drew on similar features of assessment (category judgements regarding who should and should not be concerned, issues of familiarity, discussions of reliability, integrity, etc.) these were not oriented towards consistent outcomes and a minority of accounts were focused on very different features of assessment. For the CCTV managers' attempts to promote a particular CCTV identity, this diversity suggests that local residents lacked an easily elaborated or common set of reference points for articulating an identity for Burbville and CCTV. Such an absence of common concern leaves the CCTV managers' articulations of the 'kinds of things local residents worry about' (see Chapter 3) appear misdirected. The following excerpt illustrates the difficulties some residents had in recognising and accounting for the possible utility of CCTV:

> Discussion Group Number 1:
>
> *M12*: things like the <u>cctv</u> cameras
> *F15*: i've never <u>seen</u> one
> *M13*: **have you not**
> *F15*: i don't think i've ever <u>looked</u> for one
> *Int*: ah but you can look for one <u>now</u> [YOU'VE SEEN THE VIDEO] can't you
> *M12*: *something to do innit*
> *Int*: if you felt like there might be someone <u>following</u> you >or something like that< at night-time would you ever look out for a <u>camera</u> then
> *F15*: no
> *M12&M13*: no no
> *F15*: <u>why</u> would you need to see a <u>camera</u> if someone was following you
> *Int*: well because then you'd know there was >someone looking out for you<
> *F15*: no no i'd never think <u>that</u>

This final excerpt suggests that local residents' views of CCTV, its potential benefits, its availability as a focus for trust relations and claims regarding the adequacy of legislation, each need to be considered in relation to frequent assertions regarding a lack of awareness of CCTV. This section has offered detailed insights into the activities of local residents' town centre spatial account production processes. However, how can these insights be drawn together with the spatial account production processes of CCTV staff? What makes these processes distinct? How can such spatial account production processes be utilised in developing an adequate understanding of trust?

An appropriate spatial theory

This chapter has argued CCTV staff articulated observables (Sacks, 1972), folding together (Hetherington, 1997; Latour, 2002) a diverse range of times, places, materials, verbal interactions, forms of professional vision (Goodwin, 1994) and claims regarding 'what is going on' in order to accomplish an adequate spatial account which was situationally appropriate (Suchman, 1987). These accounts were produced in interaction with, for example, police officers while demonstrably recognising the possibility of future accountability relations which might question the folds the CCTV staff had drawn together. Thus the folds were sites of aggregation and possible disruption, drawing together a variety of spaces, crossing conventional geographical boundaries and producing new formations of network relations (Mol and Law, 1994). The closed-circuit of CCTV formed a bounded set of network relations, access to which were closely controlled and through which articulations of the town centre space were held stable until (possibly) later called to account. CCTV staff were thus tied into a mechanism for the rapid production of certainty as to 'what was going on' and how particular spaces should be understood, which also frequently involved paying recognition to the possibility of future accountability which could question such certainty.

Producing a video of the town centre highlighted the ways in which those not in the closed-circuit were involved in distinct forms of spatial accounting. The accomplishment of an adequate spatial account of the town centre via the making of a video involved the on-going production of an account which, while not subject to the same constraints of rapid certainty and possible future accounting, achieved a certainty for 'all practical purposes' (Garfinkel, 1967) or managed uncertainty through processes of deferral (Lee, 1999) as to 'what was going on'. The video folded together a range of times, places, actions and technologies in order to engage with the space of Burbville town centre. The video also provided local residents with an opportunity to engage with these folds, articulating their own accounts of the town centre and their own views as to whether or not CCTV should form the focus for considerations of trust.

Local residents' accounts of space were oriented through particular forms of activity in the town centre which involved claims regarding time of day (e.g. shopping in the day or going to the pub in the evening), forms of knowledge (covering such areas as familiarity and unfamiliarity, or utilising aspects of the video), category judgements (such as what is and is not technology, who should and should not be concerned about CCTV), membership categorisation devices (Lee, 1984) and particular moments of interactivity (between themselves, technological systems and other people in the town centre). Articulating these accounts occasionally focused on CCTV and issues of trust. While Chapter 4 noted that trust relations were considered by local residents in moments of connection between, for example, CCTV and a local bank, this connectivity should not be over emphasised. CCTV was ignored, forgotten, not recognised and occasionally considered in town centre activity. These occasional considerations of CCTV involved articulations of whether or not CCTV was trustworthy in potentially breaching the normal social order on grounds related to privacy (what happened in CCTV's closed-circuit, could the closed-circuit be adequately held to account) rather than in relation to the narrow conception of surveillance (those moments where CCTV staff selected out certain images for closer scrutiny). Such occasional consideration would prove a difficulty for CCTV managers who were concerned with promoting public support for CCTV and the system's community enhancing benefits. Residents only occasionally related to CCTV as holding potential to prevent or repair breaches to the normal social order. Local residents' interests varied in moments of assessment from reliability, integrity, utility and 'big brother' issues to the possibility of adequate legislation. The absence of a set of common concerns for local residents suggested that CCTV managers' attempts to address local residents concerns could be misplaced.

These distinctions of the production of rapid certainty and possibility of future accountability for CCTV staff accounts and the production of adequate certainty for all practical purposes and possibility of managed deferral of certainty in local residents' accounts engaged with distinctions of privacy and surveillance. In terms of surveillance, the narrow conception of surveillance (see Bennett, 2005) – as a focus on those particular moments of accountability scrutiny entered into by CCTV staff amongst a broad range of information collection activities – captures the CCTV staff's selective interrogation of, and accounting for, the space of Burbville town centre. That CCTV staff 'do' surveillance (select moments of space for closer scrutiny) offers a means to distinguish their accounting activity from local residents. The latter engage more pervasively with accounting for the town centre space, broadly accomplishing a reasonably adequate sense of 'what is going on' and very rarely displaying any attention to the idea that their accounts might be held to further formal account. In relation to this lack of a formal mechanism for the production of accounts and procedures for possible future accounting, no local resident suggested that they were engaged in surveillance. At the same time, few local residents raised a problem with activities of surveillance in terms of being seen by CCTV and being the subject of accounting for their activities in Burbville town centre.

Concerns for local residents were more closely tied to the private spaces of CCTV's closed-circuit. However, the maintenance of the closed-circuit and careful direction of forms of access to the spatial account production processes of CCTV staff through the circuit (alongside problems confronted through shifting the access boundaries of the closed-circuit, see Chapter 5), emphasised the utility of privacy for CCTV. The closed-circuit formed the boundary between the inaccessible spatial accounting activities of CCTV staff (where managers identified ambiguity as an important feature of emphasising uncertainty for those with criminal intent keen to decide 'what CCTV could do') and those stories of CCTV as beneficial and community enhancing (where CCTV managers offered at least a form of access to 'what CCTV could do' which was intended to promote a particular systemic identity). This is not to say that access straightforwardly mapped onto public and lack of access straightforwardly mapped onto private and that each could be understood in relation to the other. There was no binary distinction between private and public. Instead, there were a broad range of actions that went into articulating and maintaining a variety of forms of access and non-access (notable in relation to forms of CCTV media activity, CCTV actions in courts of law, attempts to draw connections between residents and CCTV). Furthermore decisions on access shifted such that a clear distinction between those 'with' and those 'without' access was unstable (e.g. after the Mr. B court case, managers were reluctant to work with the media) and what constituted 'public' was a matter of some debate and was articulated spatially and as a membership category (as noted in Chapter 5; see also Chapter 7 and the work of Sheller and Urry, 2003).

While privacy and carefully controlled access to the closed-circuit had utility for CCTV managers, these issues also formed a focus for local residents' concerns with CCTV, particularly in assessments of trust. Assessments of trust were accomplished by local residents in a situationally appropriate manner according to the activities in which they were engaged or were discussing. Accounts of space were offered by local residents which positioned trust in relation to the folding together of times, activity engaged in, claims regarding others peoples' actions, forms of information and (a variety of forms) of social order. In these folded accounts of the space of the town centre, trust was assessed in a variety of different ways. There was little consistency in the concerns which residents' claimed should form the appropriate basis for assessing trust and the social order and there was little consistency in the outcomes of trust assessments. Whether or not CCTV should be considered trustworthy (particularly in relation to what might happen to tapes in the privacy of CCTV's closed-circuit), whether or not CCTV could be adequately regulated (particularly in relation to whether or not the privacy of CCTV's closed-circuit could be held to adequate account) and whether or not a trust relationship could be formed with CCTV for particular moments of activity (such as withdrawing money from a cash-point, where a potential breach to the social order was articulated) were all considered as appropriate or inappropriate bases for assessing trust. The outcomes of such trust assessments positioned CCTV as unreliable, difficult to legislate, a good thing, a beneficial presence when withdrawing money, a worry for particular groups and so on. While the details and concerns of trust assessment may have varied a great deal between local residents, the most frequently articulated features of such accounts can be drawn out. Thus claims to knowledge were frequently reoriented in assessing trust and in activities of accomplishing social ordering (in relation to what residents claimed to have read or seen on TV or what residents 'knew from experience'), category judgements were performed to order the spaces of the town centre in making sense of trust (particularly in assessing what was technology, what was not technology, what was familiar and what was unfamiliar, who should and should not worry about CCTV) and particular forms of activity were considered as necessitating assessments of trustworthiness (involving assessments of both what residents were doing themselves and claims regarding what other people in the town centre might do). These regularly recurring features of trust assessment and social ordering then found a focus in a wide variety of assessments of CCTV's reliability, integrity, utility and in relation to 'big brother' issues and the possibility of adequately legislating for CCTV. Thus trust could be understood as an ongoing principle for social ordering in the sense that CCTV could be considered as constituting both a potential breach and repair to social order.

Privacy, surveillance and trust can be understood as concerns oriented towards by local residents in folding together accounts of the space of Burbville. Such folds formed the focus for aggregations of conventional geographical space and aggregations of network space (Mol and Law, 1994; de Laet and Mol, 2000) in the relations plaited between a range of social and technical entities. Folds formed the focus of tension or disruption with many of the local residents disputing the particular ways in which some spatial accounts of Burbville were articulated. CCTV staff also folded together a range of geographic and network spaces, forming relations between times, places, materials and verbal interactions in making an account which made sense of Burbville. However, through recognition of, and the on-going constitution of, the closed-circuit of CCTV, these spatial account production processes were tied into demonstrably recognisable, regularly repeated forms of interaction through which awareness of possible future formal means of accountability assessment could be performed. While privacy, surveillance and trust could be understood as organising principles of local residents' spatial accounting activity, for CCTV staff their frequent reiterations of the accountability principles of the closed-circuit formed a distinct set of organising principles.

Conclusion

In drawing this spatial discussion together, it can be argued that space formed a focus point for articulating accounts of Burbville, of 'what was going on' in Burbville and what might happen next in Burbville. Both CCTV staff and local residents folded together a range of times, places, actions and claims about information in making Burbville make sense. These accounts of space were practically accomplished by CCTV staff tied into the closed-circuit of CCTV which formed the privately bounded site for surveillance activities. The closed-circuit of CCTV was characterised by the frequent reiteration of the necessity of producing rapid certainty in accounts of 'what was going on', fulfilling criteria for adequacy articulated in interactions between CCTV staff and managers and police officers. These adequate accomplishments frequently alluded to, and used as an organising principle, the possibility of future accountability relations which might unfold carefully elaborated spatial accounts. Such spatial accounts were also practically and contingently accomplished by local residents who produced accounts for all practical purposes and with less reference to the possibility of formally being held to future account. For local residents the production of such spatial accounts provided a forum through which decisions could be made regarding CCTV, privacy, surveillance and trust. These discussions of space and trust have shifted dependency on what can be quite abstract theoretical issues towards the empirical analysis of practical, contingent, accomplishments available for interrogation by social scientists (for more on shifting conceptions of space and spatial empirics, see Osborne and Rose, 2004).

The next and final chapter will now utilise these insights on spatial accounting and assessment, along with insights from previous chapters on forms of public, media engagement, issues raised by courts of law and questions of identity and accountability in detailing the analytic and methodological insights of this study. Chapter 7 will ask: how can the empirical and theoretical strategy employed in this book engage with the increasing number of technologies of information collection, storage, analysis and mobilisation? The chapter will then engage with the policy and legislative implications of this study. Finally questions will be posed for future research on privacy, surveillance and trust.

7
Conclusion

Introduction

Socio-technical systems for the collection, storage, analysis and mobilisation of information on specific populations are increasing rapidly in number and scope. Systems for the regulation of identification (such as biometrics), movement (such as traffic management) and non-movement (such as airport security), disposal (such as waste management), saving (such as banking regulations), spending (such as point of sale machines) and retrieval (such as illegal download tracking) form just some of the many developments in this area. In line with this systemic expansion has come a rapidly developing legislative environment characterised by rapidly expanding funding for forms of data protection and monitoring. Alongside these legislative endeavours the industry of protest has grown significantly with ever greater number of organisations, websites, publications and public protests dedicated towards antagonising socio-technical systems of information collection.

This book has suggested that privacy, surveillance and trust can be used as three organising principles for interrogating the activities, content and questions raised by these socio-technical systems. However, privacy, surveillance and trust are not universal or stable concepts, sticking rigidly to single definitions across a variety of times and places. Instead they have been fluidly interpreted across locations and used as a focus for elaborating concerns, complete lack of concern and the identification of who should be concerned in relation to new systems. This fluidity has utility for drawing together and providing a structure for the data gathered in this research. Ethnographic observations, interviews, video-taping, documentary analysis, media coverage, discussion groups and existing social science research have been used to illuminate the study. This chapter will now engage with the insights provided by preceding chapters in order to establish the basis on which articulations of privacy, surveillance and trust are constituted. In this sense this chapter will not form a repeat or a summary of previous ideas, but will instead instigate an engagement with the ideas presented.

First this chapter will consider the concept of privacy and offer an analysis of the concerns raised by social scientists and participants to this research. Rather than aligning with recent arguments that privacy is dead, it will be argued that privacy has never been more alive. Second the chapter will engage with surveillance as one of several accountability activities in which socio-technical systems are engaged. This section will suggest that surveillance is what renders society available for consideration. Third the chapter will consider issues of trust. In place of the common social science assumption that trust underpins social action, this section will argue that trust is used by participants to this research in orienting social ordering. Fourth the chapter will use these engagements to illuminate the policy and legislative relevance of insights presented. It will argue that current privacy protection legislation may be deficient. Fifth the chapter will look to the future of privacy, surveillance and trust. Utilising other conclusions on the future of socio-technical systems, this section will warn against the development of deterministic declarations of what the future will bring. In place of such a declaration, a series of questions will be offered as one means to address future concerns of privacy, surveillance and trust.

Privacy

The recent life and times of privacy

It has recently been claimed that privacy has either come to an end (see for example, Sykes, 1999; Whitaker, 2000), been destroyed (see for example, Rosen, 2001) or died (see for example, Garfinkel, 2000). Although this 'death' may sound terminal, it is little more than fervent sloganeering. Claims of a death, end or destruction of privacy are frequently founded on one of the following arguments. First, it is claimed that an interconnected global flow of data, people and technology has been established in recent years which has shifted 'us' into an era of so many privacy concerns that the term itself has become defunct. There are just too many variations on what a privacy concern could be for the term privacy to be able to cope. Second, it is suggested that an interconnected global flow of data, people and technology has been established in recent years which has shifted 'us' into an era where there are no longer any spaces, actions or forms of information which can be considered immune from collection, storage, analysis and further mobilisation. In this sense privacy as a concept is dead as boundaries prove an insufficient impediment to activities of data scrutiny and management.

Detailed consideration of these claims suggests a variety of problems. First, the proposal that society is now characterised by an interconnected mass of people, technology and flows of information, what Castells (1996) terms the network society, offers a socio-technical gloss to a range of complex and on-going relations. These relations (as demonstrated in Chapter 4) involve the complex plaiting and bounding of social and technical entities for the production, mobilisation and direction of forms of information. Hence in the CCTV system we can see staff, monitors, radios, police officers, pens, paper, regulations, codes of practice and fibre optic connections drawn together. However, it is not the case that such connectivity results in global information flows or an automated functioning of power. In attempts to connect the CCTV system to the bank (Chapter 4), discussions were entered into by managers over finance and customer protection. The two systems did not enter into discussion regarding opening the bounded information flows characteristic of each organisation. This lack of informational interaction between the bank and CCTV system acts as one example of the global valuing, bounding and restraining of information flows which renders the network society unlikely. Of course there are always examples of information that has leaked, perhaps inappropriately, from an organisational container. However, such leaks are partial, mostly unpredictable, mostly involving a small amount of information and hardly illustrative of a global and automated, privacy-ending, network society. Indeed residents who participated in this research often identified the bounded closed-circuit of CCTV as a problematic, inaccessible and private space. Attempts to constitute and maintain bounded information systems thus constitute new concepts and spaces of privacy.

A second problematic feature of the death of privacy arguments relates to the 'we' or 'us' which, it is claimed, is now experiencing a global flow of information, ending boundaries to data collection, storage and analysis. Who is the 'we' that might be experiencing such a phenomena? As Bennett and Raab (2003) argue experiences of privacy are not evenly socially distributed. Those in need of state welfare are involved in the submission, collection and use of information that otherwise would not be required. Those with credit cards, access to the internet and telephone, those who pay bills, who shop in areas covered by CCTV, who are required to carry ID cards, may each engage in a range of activities, traces of which are collected, stored, analysed and further mobilised. However, these are by no means global experiences and are by no means universally experienced even by those who do participate. The claim that everyone participates in such activities and that partici- pants share the same experiences of such activities appears simplistic. A history of research on technology (see Mackenzie and Wajcman, 1985; Bijker, Hughes and Pinch, 1989; Woolgar, 1991; Bijker and Law, 1992; Mansell, 1994; Grint and Woolgar, 1997; amongst others) provides multiple examples of the variety of experiences which engagement with the 'same' technology can bring. In light of this, careful consideration is required of what is meant by privacy, when and for whom.

A third feature of death of privacy arguments involves the claim that the rise in number and scope of systems designed to collect, store, categorise and analyse information on the population has led to an explosion of privacy concerns so diverse that the term privacy is no longer appropri- ate or meaningful. This implies that at a previous time there has been a universal, agreed-upon definition of privacy that has now become obsolete. This does not appear to be the case. Privacy has consistently formed a focus for questions. What might be an appropriate form of privacy? What types of information should be held on the population? Which freedoms should the population be expected to concede through the performance of what kind of tasks to meet the demands of the state? These questions constituted the basis for the (successful) 1952 challenge to repeal UK wartime identity cards and have been reiterated on each occasion since when identity cards have been proposed by successive governments over five decades. In this sense privacy has always been a focus for multiple concerns and, although there may be a larger number of technologies of information compilation, it is not clear that the types of privacy concern have significantly altered. The frequency with which participants to research (see for example, Hine and Eve, 1998; this research, Chapter 6) are able to elucidate questions of privacy suggests that it still fulfils a meaningful role as an organising principle for articu- lating concerns. Furthermore the continuing appeal of films on privacy themes and the number of books published on privacy, suggest it con- stitutes a compelling, albeit varied focus for discussion. In place of the dissolution of privacy through multiple claims regarding what it might mean, increasing discussion of privacy and the development of modes of privacy legislation may now mean that privacy has greater coherence than ever before. For example, although the European Human Rights Act (1998) is subject to multiple interpretations (see Chapter 5), it does articulate for the first time in the United Kingdom a right to privacy.

Privacy as a focal point in this research

A feature of the on-going importance of privacy as a focus for discussion in this research was the variety of issues drawn together for discussion. Residents talked of privacy concerns in relation to the body, for example suggesting they would not be happy to be seen being clumsy or drunk in the town centre. Further privacy concern was raised regarding particular activities, with one resident focusing her concern on the possibility of being taped using a toilet in a fast food restaurant. Information was a privacy concern for local residents with wariness exhibited, for example, over the possibility of connecting the bank and CCTV system. Finally privacy concerns also found a focus in discussions of particular spaces, involving both articulation of spaces which should not be videotaped (e.g. schools) and a wish to see the spaces of videotaping (see 'CCTV legislation' section).

These privacy concerns were not restricted to a discussion of the appropriate content of such concerns. A feature of these discussions were attempts made to attribute who should hold the concerns, when, where and for what reason. These attributions shifted around so that one resident expressed concern that although he had nothing to hide from CCTV now, he may have done in his youth. Another resident suggested she had no concerns over CCTV, but was worried about its impact, particularly on young people, who might spend more time in the town centre. Further attributions were made by a resident who considered that he might be the focus of CCTV camera attention, something which he found problematic. With these attributions of who should hold particular privacy concerns, when and in relation to what action, came assessments of the justification of CCTV more broadly. For some residents privacy concerns outweighed any of the benefits CCTV might offer; for others a balance between CCTV and privacy invasion was currently tipped negatively towards unwarranted invasion of privacy; for other residents CCTV was worth what they perceived to be minimal privacy sacrifices. Residents talk of concerns regarding CCTV was not matched by the CCTV managers' and local police officers' attempts to constitute a set of public concerns which could be reassured through publicity. In this publicity attempts were made to constitute a link between increased CCTV cameras and police on the beat, CCTV cameras and a general fall in crime, and CCTV cameras and an absence of increase in violent crime. These concerns and connections were not raised by residents who participated in this research.

This talk of the times, places, actions and justifications for concerns over privacy and CCTV appears so varied as to be difficult to summarise in a succinct conclusion. However, one area where residents shared and mutually elaborated concern with regard to the CCTV system and privacy was in the inaccessibility of CCTV's closed-circuit.

CCTV's closed-circuit of interaction

The CCTV system operated as a closely bounded system through which access was tightly controlled. The CCTV staff, cameras, managers, monitors, control room and police officers were connected as a socio-technical forum for interaction. This interaction was focused on a series of accountability activities (see 'Surveillance' section). Access to this interaction was offered through further carefully bounded entries into the closed-circuit through courts (see 'Surveillance' section) and through the media such as in the Mr. B story (Chapter 5). The CCTV managers were caught in what they acknowledged was a difficult position. Opening up the closed-circuit may have enabled those with criminal intent to devise ways of outwitting the CCTV system. Keeping the closed-circuit closed may have maintained residents' concerns with what might be occurring in the closed-circuit. However even partially opening the closed-circuit to mobilise footage from CCTV to national TV came to be regarded as a risky endeavour in the aftermath of the Mr. B story where footage intended to portray the community beneficial aspects of CCTV was reinterpreted as privacy invading. For the residents not used to Burbville gaining a great deal of media coverage, the Mr. B story formed a prime focus for the articulation of privacy concerns. The closed-circuit of CCTV, what might occur beyond residents' vision, the ways in which tapes might be stored, re-articulated and mobilised to further organisations contributed to claims amongst residents that invasion of privacy (in the sense of being seen by CCTV) was not their main concern. Instead the preparation, movement and possible broadcast on national TV of CCTV tapes of their activity became the focal point for their concerns. In place of invasion of privacy came concerns regarding possible invasion of publicity.

Surveillance

Residents' concerns

Although the closed-circuit of CCTV formed a focus for local residents' concerns of privacy, the interactivity which occurred in the closed-circuit can be considered as a form of surveillance. The current literature on surveillance (see Chapters 1 and 2) provides a varied backdrop for considering the interactivity made witnessable as a result of this research. Surveillance can be considered politically in relation to the state's activities in collecting information to effectively manage the population (see for example, Norris and Armstrong, 1999; Fussey, 2004). Alternatively, surveillance can be considered as a feature of more pervasive governance techniques (see for example, Andrejevic, 2005). On occasions surveillance is approached as partial and fragmentary (Dubbeld, 2004, 2005). In the work of Lyon (2001) surveillance is construed broadly to encompass a wide variety of information gathering. For Bennett (2005) such a view of surveillance is too broadly construed. A more appropriate approach to surveillance, Bennett argues, is to consider specific and detailed moments of data scrutiny as moments of surveillance within broader practices of information gathering.

The narrow approach to surveillance appears to fit more closely with the views of residents participating in this research who suggested moments of data scrutiny, rather than more general activities of data gathering, were activities of surveillance. However residents expressed a broad distribution of views on the appropriateness of such activities (see particularly Chapter 6). Only a few residents expressed concern with being seen by CCTV cameras and being held up to possible scrutiny, made notable when they happened to notice a camera. More residents expressed concern with the tape storage facilities of CCTV. Here concerns were expressed in regard to where the tapes were stored, what CCTV staff did with tapes, the possibility of tapes being moved on from the CCTV system to a variety of other locations (e.g. in the criminal justice system or broadcast on TV). Yet these latter concerns were not considered as moments of surveillance but were elaborated in relation to privacy concerns (as highlighted in the 'Privacy' section). The storage and movement of tapes did not form a focus for discussions of data scrutiny, but were a matter of concern in relation to their inaccessibility and a broadly construed mystery with what might happen inside the CCTV system. It should be noted that these concerns did not constitute a regular aspect of life in Burbville: many of the residents expressed the view that this research project was one of the few occasions when they had paused to reflect on the content of CCTV activity and made few efforts to discover more information about CCTV (see Chapter 3).

CCTV modes of accountability

Moments of surveillance scrutiny formed one of three cross-cutting modes of accountability through which Burbville's CCTV system operated. In Chapter 3 it was noted that these three modes were characterised by activities to render available various publics. The CCTV system was involved in forms of accountability of the public, accountability in public and accountability for the public. Chapter 3 argued that each of these modes could be engaged in tandem with a particular approach to social science. In this sense, accountability *of* public in Burbville's CCTV system involved the CCTV staff and local police officers interacting to produce and corroborate accounts of particular images. It was argued that this accountability of the public could be approached using insights from neo-Foucauldian work on governance (such as the work of Rose, 1996) and accountability (such as the work of Miller and O'Leary, 1994) and critical studies of surveillance (such as Norris and Armstrong, 1999; drawing on Poster, 1990). What these studies suggest is that mechanisms of accountability are involved in the production of rationales for action, communicated to specific populations, enwrapped in webs of knowledge (Rose, 1999) which form the basis for the collection, storage and categorisation of information on that population (Norris and Armstrong, 1999). However, as Chapters 2 and 3 noted, the uncertainty of CCTV staff police interaction and local residents' lack of awareness of CCTV rendered these social science approaches somewhat limited. It was in the interactions (drawing on Sacks, 1972; Garfinkel, 1967) between CCTV staff and police officers that sense was made of 'what was going on' and in place of rules which drove CCTV staff activity (Norris and Armstrong, 1999), there was regular and somewhat routinised activity which was consistently oriented towards the production of a sense of 'what was going on'. Thus the local population were not enwrapped in webs of knowledge, and the CCTV staff's accounts featured as one turn in interaction made available to, most frequently, the police who would produce a further turn. The outcomes of such activities often produced and maintained a sense that there was nothing going on. Even in events which eventually required a significant police response, turns in interaction could be characterised by uncertainty ('there are some kids standing still and we don't know what they are doing', or 'there is a man with what appears to be a knife and we don't know what he is going to do').

These uncertain accounts were often used by CCTV staff in order to shift responsibility to the police to complete the account of the event. The CCTV staff and police were mutually tied into a series of interactions through which they were expected (by CCTV managers, codes of practice, operational guidelines and county police regulations) to produce a viable account of what was going on (if anything) for all practical purposes (Garfinkel, 1967) which would be adequate to satisfy potential future accountability audiences such as courts of law. Courts of law formed one focus for CCTV's second mode of accountability *in* public. Here ethnomethodological studies of courtroom activities (Lynch, 1998; Cole, 1998; Daemmreich, 1998) were used to consider the ways in which the possibility of courtroom accountability was oriented towards in the production of accounts of the public in order to ensure that CCTV staff and police officers would be able to reproduce an account of CCTV activity in public which would be adequately routine and standardised (a form of professional vision, Goodwin, 1994). In the courtroom, it was suggested by CCTV managers that the content of the tapes was not a matter of dispute (although see Chapter 5 for a slight alternative). Instead the focus of interrogation was on the tape itself, the methods of recording which went into it, who had accessed the tape and its movement from control room to courtroom. In court the adequate re-performance of CCTV was as important as the adequate re-performance of the content of the tape.

This courtroom activity was only one part of CCTV's accountability in public. The CCTV managers also entered into a variety of activities to try and make available a version of CCTV in public. Posters, signs and newspaper stories were differentially drawn on by the CCTV managers. They worked with the police to constitute what they thought might be concerns local residents had with CCTV and attempted to assuage those concerns through running stories which apparently demonstrated that CCTV could cut crime, did not lead to displacement of crime and did not reduce the number of police on the street. The CCTV managers put together an informal ranking for such forms of publicity suggesting signs were of little use (as they could not contain much information on CCTV activity) and local newspaper stories were of greatest value (as stories of CCTV's success could be elaborated). The managers hoped to use these newspaper stories to promote CCTV's community enhancing benefits as they suggested the costs of CCTV were sufficiently significant that CCTV needed to be seen to be doing more than cut crime. The problem for CCTV managers was not that local residents sought to explicitly challenge the positive stories mobilised to promote CCTV's community beneficence. Instead it was residents' ignorance of these stories (very few participants could recall CCTV coverage except for that devoted to the Mr. B story) that posed the biggest challenge to communicating positive stories of CCTV.

Local residents were equally unaware of the third mode of accountability *for* public. Although much is made in the literature (see for example, Gray, 1992) of the importance of getting organisations to make available information for audiences to make a judgement on the organisation and its activities, residents of Burbville remained unaware of the legislative mechanisms in place on their behalf. While CCTV might be subject to aspects of the European Convention on Human Rights and the Information Commissioners' Code of Practice for CCTV (2000), only the Data Protection Act (1998) was familiar to residents (and then only in a passing manner, see Chapter 6). These aspects of CCTV will be dealt with in more detail later, suffice to say that although legislation might be putatively enacted on behalf of the resident population, the population showed little awareness of it and placed their concerns with CCTV in areas that the legislation only barely covers (see 'CCTV legislation' section).

Rendering society available to behold in real-time and through history

CCTV surveillance activity (primarily focused on accountability of the public) has become a significant UK reference point for making sense of society. Although Latour (2004) claims (drawing on Thatcher) that there is no society, CCTV control rooms are one location where society is rendered amenable to analyses. In producing accounts of 'what is going on' CCTV staff and police officers together make available claims regarding people's current actions and likely future actions, based on apparent age, dress, style of walking, time of day, location, direction, the weather and anything else deemed apparent. These claims perform a variety of ordered socio-material collectives (people, times, place, things) in real-time. Furthermore CCTV's taped archives have become a reference point for attempting to understand the recent history of such collectives and for drawing distinctions of notable (social and technical) others who should be regarded as separate from the collective. Examples of such othering include the Jamie Bulger case (see Chapter 3) where footage from multiple CCTV systems was used to replay the panoply of social and material things surrounding the disappearance of a child in a city centre. The children responsible for the kidnapping and the child kidnapped were rendered (eventually) as the notable others, appearing demarcated from a mass of collective normality in CCTV images on the TV news, and circled and highlighted to denote their effective separation from the collective. In the aftermath of the terrorist attacks in London in 2005 a similar process occurred with TV news calling upon CCTV to replay society for the morning of the 7th of July within hours of the devices exploding. In this replaying of collectives, the process of othering sought out the relevant people and things which might be circled, highlighted and drawn out. In line with analyses of media othering (see for example, Lee, 1984), in these cases CCTV renders society available and the notable socio-material other (from child kidnappers to bombs, suspect packages and terrorists) forms the focus for constituting and holding together the collective, unified in its recognition of the distinctiveness of the other.

Trust

Trust underpinning social order

Residents lack of concern over surveillance and range of concerns over privacy found a focus in discussions of trust (see Chapters 4 and 6). Social scientists often consider trust as a foundational aspect of collective social action. Shapin (1994) for example suggests 'Knowledge is a collective good. In securing our knowledge we rely upon others, and we cannot dispense with that reliance. This means that the relations in which we have and hold our knowledge have a moral character, and the word I use to indicate that moral relation is trust' (1994: xxv). Using Shapin's approach to trust the local residents would secure knowledge of CCTV through reliance on particular sources and would then depend or rely upon that knowledge in producing a sense of CCTV and the world in which it operates. For Shapin 'To accept the relation of another is ... to give that other the right to furnish our minds' (1994: 34). This would suggest that buying into, for example, CCTV managers' attempts to promote an identity for CCTV (a form of accountability in public) would be influential in local residents' accounts of CCTV. In line with this argument, whichever source was deemed reliable by local residents would establish expectations for the ways in which interactions with CCTV would turn out. This would concur with Barber's (1983) approach which suggests that trust lies in 'expectation of the persistence and fulfilment of the ... social orders' (1983: 9). Here trust underpins or makes possible social action and makes possible expectations of consistent future social action rendering a social order possible and meaningful. For local residents, this would suggest that trust is formed through reliance on knowledge of CCTV and through on-going expectations that CCTV would continue to act in line with expectations.

Trust through breaches to social order

Analysing trust through expectations, reliance on forms of knowledge and assumptions regarding the stable social order is not the only approach offered by social science. Garfinkel (1963) takes a distinct view of trust. He suggests: 'In accounting for the persistence and continuity of the features of concerted actions, sociologists commonly select some set of stable features of an organisation of activities and ask for the variables that contribute to their stability' (1963: 187). This would be exemplified by the Shapin (1994) approach which looks at reliance on sources of knowledge and moral relations as the basis for stable social order. Garfinkel (1963), however, recommends a distinct course of action: 'An alternative procedure would appear to be more economical: to start with a system with stable features and ask what can be done to make for trouble. The operations that one would have to perform in order to produce and sustain anomic features of perceived environments and disorganised interaction should tell us something about how social structures are ordinarily and routinely being maintained' (1963: 187). Garfinkel deployed a variety of breach experiments in which the conventions for social action, including any sense of trust, would be made available as participants attempted to make sense of 'what had happened' in the course of the experiment. In constituting a variety of repair mechanisms for coming to terms with apparent breaches in social convention, participants to experiments would make available the means by which their ordinary everyday social actions were constituted and maintained. In this approach trust was not conceived as underpinning social order, but instead 'trust is a condition for "grasping" the events of daily life' (1963: 190). Thus trust as an organising principle was used by participants in the breach experiments to express views regarding their conventional expectations, but these were made available in moments of breach (rather than in many successive moments of ordinary social actions).

This approach has led Misztal (1996) and Szerszynski (1999) amongst others to consider trust as an 'active political accomplishment' (Misztal, 1996: 7). The argument here is that trust is not a stable feature of social interaction which can be taken for granted, but needs to be considered as an on-going and worked for accomplishment. Rather than consider trust in terms of expectations, in this approach residents would work at building an understanding of CCTV and would work at maintaining a sense that CCTV could be trusted to fulfil routine expectations. However such an approach to trust as an accomplishment is not the only possible interpretation of Grafinkel's (1963) work. Another way of thinking through the breach experiments would be to analyse them as moments where considerations are explicitly articulated regarding trust. Taking such an approach suggests that trust is not a routine form of social expectation which underpins social order. Neither would trust form an on-going political accomplishment resulting from successive and on-going work to maintain trust on a day to day basis. Instead, trust would form the focus for consideration on occasions through which apparent breaches to the social order were made manifest. Trust would then act as the organising focus for articulating what relevant expectations were, what the breach appeared to be and what repair mechanisms may be required to get the interaction back on track or to make sense of what has gone on. Trust is thus not the foundation for social order but a principle for focusing concerns on occasions of a noted breakdown in social order. Such an approach requires further elaboration of what is meant by the breach, by social order and by repair mechanisms.

Breaches, repairs and the social order

Garfinkel (1963, 1967) utilised a range of breach experiments in order to grasp the ways in which members made sense of the social world. In one such experiment Garfinkel asked students to return home and act as if they were lodgers in their own homes rather than members of the family. Students were asked to maintain the task for as long as possible and report on the outcomes. Students reported referring to their parents by their surnames rather than by more familiar terms, being polite at the dinner table and talking to family members as if they were part of an economic relationship rather than a family. The students produced a variety of responses to these activities. Several students found the terms of the experiment particularly difficult to maintain in the face of questioning, upset family members. Other students reported that the experiment revealed things about family members and partners that they had always expected. Other students reported the extremely short-lived nature of their experiments. The students' reports revealed detail on the way members of the experiments (both students and family members) were attentive in attempts to first, figure out the apparent breach in social order (what was going on? why were individuals acting in this way?) and second, constitute repairs to the social order. Attempts at repair included figuring out rationales for why individuals were acting in the way they were (by suggesting, for example, individuals were obviously sick) and attempts to get individuals to act in ways to which other members of the social interaction now suggested they had become accustomed (by articulating the ways in which family members were expected to act). These expectations were made available through consideration of the apparent breaches.

The breaches and repairs (or attempted repairs) offered opportunities to consider the social order of these forms of interaction. Thus the expectations that students were to act in particular ways as members of a family which involved sitting in certain ways at the dinner table, addressing family members using certain terms, talking about particular subjects and so on, were made available through the breach experiment. In these articulations of the social order clear reference was made to expectations as to how members of the social interaction should act, thus suggesting a form of trust. However, this does not necessarily lead to the straightforward conclusion that were it not for the breach experiments these relationships would be characterised by trust. That is, although it could be said that these familial relationships were relatively stable and routine and were disrupted by the breach, it was in the moments of breach that clear articulations of expectations, considerations of social order and trust were made available. Thus trust was an organising principle for orienting concerns regarding what was going on, what expectations were characteristic of these forms of social interaction, what constituted the ordinary social order and what was required to repair the social order and get interactions back on track.

CCTV, trust and socio-material ordering

In this research participants articulated vague concerns over privacy and mostly viewed surveillance as an unproblematic extension of being seen in particular spaces. Such visibility was construed as a convention for social action. However, specific and detailed concerns regarding privacy were offered at moments constituted as breaches or potential breaches to the social order. These constitutions took two forms. First, CCTV formed the focus for considerations of its potential in repairing apparent breaches or preventing apparent breaches to the social order. In Chapters 4 and 6 local residents talked of occasions in the town centre through which the social order, potential breaches to the social order and the necessity of repairs or means to prevent breaches to the social order could be articulated. One such type of occasion was withdrawing money from a cash-point at night. Through this occasion the social order was constituted in terms of the necessity of withdrawing cash and the link between cash and social activity (particularly if the individual was on a night out and wanted to continue in their activity). The socio-material order thus drew together themselves, friends, the town centre, money, the pub and mechanisms such as the cash-point. These were each considered mundane, ordinary and unexceptional features of the social order (to the extent that residents asked me why these questions were necessary). Threats to this socio-material order were constituted in relation to the apparent emptiness of the town centre at night, possibilities that cash-points could form the focus for criminal attention and the potential for losing money, being physically assaulted and being the victim of a crime. Although not strongly emphasised, several residents noted the potential for CCTV to form the focus for preventing this breach to the social order. Through being visible, through being recognisable to those with criminal intent and through forming a connection to the cash-point user in an empty town centre, CCTV could form a notable constituent of the socio-material order, effectively maintaining that order through deterrent to potential breaches.

Second, CCTV was considered (particularly in the aftermath of the Mr. B story, see Chapter 5) as having the potential to breach the social order. Specifically the closed-circuit of CCTV, its tape storage facilities and the possibility of tapes being mobilised from this apparently private space into a public arena (most notably on TV) as a form of invasion of publicity were articulated as a potential breach to the social order. It was in relation to this breach that sense was made of what CCTV could do, what an appropriate concern with CCTV might be and the appropriateness of forms of legislation which could hold CCTV to account. Trust was considered in line with what it might take for CCTV to slip back into the background activities of the town centre. Trust was thus a characteristic of occasions when consideration was given for what CCTV might be able to do and the results of CCTV action, oriented towards articulations of when CCTV might form less of a notable other and no longer form the focus for such trust assessments. 'CCTV legislation' section on appropriate legislation will investigate this point further.

In sum, trust was not articulated as underpinning social order and trust was not a frequent consideration for participants in this research. Instead trust was considered at apparent moments of breach or potential breach to the socio-material order. During such moments residents most clearly articulated the components of the socio-material order, the consequences of a breach or potential breach to the order and the role of CCTV in the constitution of both the breach and the order. On occasions where CCTV was considered as having the potential to repair or prevent breaches to the social order, residents were glad of their accountability and constituted a use for CCTV. On occasions where (many of the same) residents considered CCTV as potentially breaching the socio-material order, consideration was given to CCTV's accountability. In place of desiring greater mechanisms through which they could hold CCTV to account, local residents most frequently sought an appropriate body to hold CCTV to account (see Chapters 3 and 4 for more detail), if not on their behalf, then at least in a way that would not form a focus for further articulations of breaches to the socio-material order.

CCTV legislation

Residents' concerns with CCTV can be briefly summarised in three areas. First, residents were concerned with the closed-circuit of the CCTV system and the interaction which they deemed to occur in that closed-circuit to which they had no access. Second, residents were not concerned with being seen and recorded, but worried that in this closed-circuit, images may be accounted for at future times and mobilised into locations beyond the closed-circuit. Third, however, residents also expressed little concern in finding out more about CCTV, the way it works and what happens in the closed-circuit (see Chapters 3 and 4). This lack of concern was justified on the grounds that CCTV must be held to account by a legislative body acting on their (the residents') behalf. In this sense accounting for CCTV was assumed to be the concern of another body and personal interest in such accountability was delegated to an unspecified other on the assumption that there was someone (or something) else taking responsibility.

CCTV Code of Practice

In the United Kingdom the variety of legislative acts connected to CCTV (including the European Human Rights Act, 1998; Regulation of Investigatory Powers Act, 1998; Data Protection Act, 1998; Freedom of Information Act, 2000) find a focus in the Information Commissioner's CCTV Code of Practice (2000). To what extent does the Code match the residents' concerns over privacy and the public, lack of access and expectations of delegated accountability responsibility? The Code was developed as a result of the House of Lords Select Committee view that public confidence in CCTV needed to be maintained through control over cameras' deployment and use (Ibid., 2000: 2) and in line with the updated Data Protection Act (from 1984 in 1998). According to the information commissioner: 'The changes in data protection legislation mean that for the first time legally enforceable standards will apply to the collection and processing of images relating to individuals' (Ibid., 2000: 2). The Code sets out to inform CCTV systems of their legal obligations while also informing and reassuring members of the public about legal protections. However, the following analysis needs to be considered in line with the commissioner's suggestion that Codes are ' "living" documents which are updated as practices, and understanding of the law develops' (2000: 2).

The Code is clear that accountability responsibility in CCTV systems falls on the data controller (and in the case of systems such as Burbville, run jointly by the police and local political authority, the data controller is a jointly held position). The data controller has the defined role of ensuring that the Code is put into practice and can be held legally responsible for failure of the CCTV system to comply. The commissioner can also: serve an information notice on a data controller in order to check compliance with the code; issue a decision notice on a system regarding compliance with the Code and Data Protection Act and, in cases of non-compliance, the steps to be taken to remedy the situation; and serve an enforcement notice on a public authority regarding compliance with the Freedom of Information Act (2000) and a timescale for compliance. Legal enforcement of these notices is dealt with in the same manner as if the offence committed were contempt of court. The authority served notice can appeal to an information tribunal which can uphold, substitute or dismiss the notice. Individuals can also seek a court order if they feel that the CCTV system has contravened the Data Protection Act (1998). The order can insist that the data controller comply with the act. Individuals can also seek compensation in response to a contravention.

The content of the CCTV Code of Practice (2000) deals with the location of cameras, quality of images, processing of images, access and disclosure of images, access by data subjects and monitoring of compliance with the Code. The directives for each of these areas are based on the Data Protection Act (1998) principles that information is: fairly and lawfully processed; for limited processes which are adequate, relevant and not excessive; are accurate; not kept for longer than necessary; processed in accordance with individual rights; secure; and not transferred to countries without adequate protection.

Can the Code meet residents' concerns?

This appears initially to be a stringent, coherent and flexible set of principles to adequately render CCTV accountable and meet the concerns of the local residents who participated in this research. However, on close inspection the detail of these principles may be considered problematic in relation to residents' expectations. Residents' first concern was lack of access to CCTV's closed-circuit. The Code (2000) sets out in detail the ways in which information should be made available on a CCTV system's compliance with the code. Data controllers should produce annual, publicly available, reports of the number of complaints received, how these were dealt with and include information on the operational practices of the CCTV system and the ways in which these comply with the code. This adheres to broad calls in recent years for (particularly publicly funded) organisations to be transparent through reporting of their internal activities and thereby recognising their responsibility to particular public audiences (see for example the work of Gray, 1998). A problematic feature of these moves to transparency is the extent to which the 'transparent' reporting mechanisms adopted by an organisation offer a view of internal organisational activities. Do reports of activity, make available and accountable 'what's going on' in the organisation? Alternatively do the reports reflect attempts to adopt new information production processes which produce reports packed with information designed to succeed on the terms of the transparency mechanism with little connection to the day to day activities of the organisation? Strathern (2002) suggests that academic accountability exercises designed to make available a rendition of internal university activity involve a complex series of abstraction and decontextualisation practices which translate day to day activities into easily digestible reports which end up bearing only a passing connection to the organisational activity they are intended to reflect. This might suggest that the CCTV Code of Practice (2000) would make available only a partial and fragmentary, abstracted and decontextualised version of the activity of CCTV's closed-circuit. Rather than open up the closed-circuit for public scrutiny, the reports might just reflect the extent to which the system is successfully dealing with the reporting terms established by the Code (which include number of complaints, how these were dealt with, and whether or not the system complies with the Code). For the purposes of holding the closed-circuit to account such reports appear limited.

These reporting problems lead into a second problematic feature of the Code and connect with residents' assumptions that they have delegated responsibility for holding CCTV to account. Built into the Code is a model of the 'data subject' – the individual likely to be held to account and forming the focus of CCTV images. Constituting an individual data subject is the first problem. Often collectives are constituted and held to account as notable representatives of those who need no further attention (such as shoppers on a Saturday afternoon) or as notable others who require clear demarcation from the mundane masses and further accounting scrutiny (such as groups of kids standing still, crowds outside pubs, queues forming outside nightclubs, by taxi ranks and bus stops). Under the terms of the Code it is not clear who should take responsibility for reducing, for example, excessive accounting scrutiny of such 'data collectives' rather than 'subjects'. Who is to hold CCTV to account to assess whether or not kids, for example, as a collective gain excessive attention?

A second problem with the notion of a 'data subject' is the suggestion that the subject should be given sufficient information about the CCTV system; should know when they are being taped, who is responsible and how they can contact the system; should have a right to apply to the CCTV system for access to data on the subject; should have access to the annual report of the CCTV system, its complaint procedures and efforts to reduce or respond to complaints; should be offered a leaflet on the operations of the system and a copy of the Code of Practice (2000) if necessary; should be offered the opportunity to make a complaint to the information commissioner; should have a right to prevent automated data processing in certain circumstances (particularly employment situations); should be able to apply for a court order stopping contravention of the Data Protection Act; and should be able to apply for compensation as a result of contravention.

These apparent opportunities for access, complaint and problem resolution require an active 'data subject' who is not merely a subject of data capture, but is instead an active, knowledgeable citizen interested in rights (and wrongs), privacy protection and maintenance of the law. This does not match the residents of Burbville who participated in this research. Although it is not the intention here to buy into a deficit model (Wynne, 1996; see Chapter 1) of local residents' knowledge, it appears that residents do not match up to this model of the active 'data citizen'. In place of knowledge about complaints procedures, knowledge of who runs the CCTV system, concern for the maintenance of the law and a desire for compensation, Burbville residents who participated in this research delegated responsibility for holding CCTV to account to an unspecified other who they assumed would act on their behalf. Residents were not active 'data citizens' of the type built into the Code of Practice (2000), neither were they suffering from a general deficit in knowledge. Instead residents were deficient (in comparison with the Code's 'data citizen') in concern with what CCTV might be doing.

Residents neither sought to, nor did they want to, have to find out about CCTV or hold CCTV to account. As residents displayed such a deficit in concern over CCTV, it could be said that privacy is not a significant concern and the Code should be made available to those active 'data citizens' who do care. However, if the Code of Practice (2000) along with the various legislative acts upon which it draws are recognition of the importance of privacy protection, then the Code does not appear to meet the view of the residents of Burbville who assume that an authority is holding CCTV to account on their behalf. Furthermore, if the Code is designed to protect privacy, then the form of privacy written into the Code depends on knowledge (see Chapters 3 and 4) actively oriented towards by residents who might participate in their own protection. Most of the residents who participated in this research based their deficit of concern regarding CCTV and privacy invasion on the assumption that a government funded system, such as CCTV, would operate in such a way that they did not have to actively participate in protecting themselves against the system. Thus it can be argued that the model of the active 'data citizen' built into the Code does not match the activities of residents who live near a CCTV system and thus the Code fails to meet their needs.

A third problematic feature of the code connects with residents' concern over the accounting of tapes at future dates and mobilisation of images and accounts into further (public) locations without consent. The Code (2000) offers some detail on the processing (recording, storing, labelling/documenting) and accessing (by employees, in courtrooms and third parties such as the media) of images. The Code suggests tapes can be mobilised to the media if 'the public's assistance is needed in order to assist the identification of victim, witness or perpetrator in relation to a criminal incident', but tapes should 'not be routinely made available to the media or placed on the internet' (2000: 13). This appears to offer a stringent defence against a repeat of the Mr. B story (Chapter 5). However, the Code (2000) proceeds to suggest 'If it is decided that images will be disclosed to the media (other than in the circumstances outlined above), the images of individuals will need to be disguised or blurred so that they are not readily identifiable' (2000: 14). This is a dilution of the first statement and suggests that the treatment of the image itself (through blurring) is sufficient to provide privacy protection in the mobilisation of images onto TV. In the Mr. B story such protection proved insufficient. Masking of images often only serves to give viewers clues to use to construct an appropriate identity for individuals in their account of a series of images. The absence of 'consent' to mobilisation of images in the Code renders such masking the only attempt to protect the privacy of (and prevent invasions of publicity for) those in the footage.

Furthermore the Code (2000) continues to suggest the grounds on which it might be appropriate to mobilise footage to the media.

For example, it might be appropriate to disclose to the media images of drunken individuals stumbling around a town centre on a Saturday night to show proper use of policing resources to combat anti-social behaviour. However, it would not be appropriate for the same images to be provided to a media company merely for inclusion in a 'humorous' video (2000: 25).

This extended excerpt from the Code suggests that different uses can be made of the 'same' set of images. However, what controls would be placed on the ways in which TV viewers would account for, make sense of and use these images once mobilised to TV? The Mr. B story and history of social science research on TV viewing (see for example, Ang, 1985) suggests that, for example, people stumbling around the streets of Burbville would be accounted for in any number of ways by TV viewers who may try to pick out friends, relatives and near neighbours and may make sense of their activities in a variety of ways (as Mr. and Mrs. Smith from down the road having a bit of fun, being drunk and aggressive as usual, not being the sort of people I will invite round to dinner again, etc.). There can be no guarantee that TV viewers would account for images as demonstrable of the intent of TV programme producers, with images acting as examples of the policing of anti-social behaviour or humorous clips for entertainment. The clauses in the Code (2000) regarding the grounds on which tapes can be mobilised do not appear to match the concerns of residents who did not want footage of themselves to be stored in CCTV's closed-circuit, accounted for at a later date and mobilised back into a public space such as TV. The Code thereby appears to offer an insufficient defence to invasions of publicity.

In sum, residents articulated concerns with: the activities of the closed-circuit of CCTV and their lack of access to such activity; the possibility that images might be accounted for at a later date and mobilised into public spaces such as TV without their consent; and assumed they need not care too much about CCTV and delegated responsibility for their concern and privacy/publicity protection to an unspecified other who they assumed would hold CCTV to account on their behalf. The CCTV Code of Practice does not appear to cover these concerns in detail, leaving CCTV systems to report on their activities, assuming that residents are active 'data citizens' and act individually, and suggesting that CCTV systems simply mask footage in mobilising data to further public spaces in which images will be understood in a uniform and stable manner. 'Futures of privacy, surveillance and trust' section will take up these legislative issues.

Futures of privacy, surveillance and trust

It is a trend amongst social science research, particularly books on socio-technical systems involved in the collection, storage, analysis and mobilisation of information on the population, to conclude with suggestions on the future of the technology in focus. This appears to recommend a conclusion on the future of privacy, surveillance and trust. However, despite books on socio-technical systems taking a stance against technological determinism (suggesting technologies can turn out otherwise and technologies can be used in many ways), the conclusion of such books often make statements constituting visions of the future of the technology in question. For example, the introduction to Norris and Armstrong's (1999) study of CCTV suggests that we should avoid 'technological determinism' and the assumption that 'CCTV actually produces the effects claimed for it' (1999: 9). The conclusion (entitled 'Seeing the Future') argues that the United Kingdom is moving from a mass surveillance to a maximum surveillance society, with cameras and other technologies increasingly combined, leading to a 'profound transformation in the surveillance capacity' (1999: 221). Thus anti-determinist sentiments seem to fall away in considering the future. While the present (multiple) usages, understandings and identities related to any technology can be called on to hold to account any apparent determinist or essentialist rendition of a technology, renditions of the future appear to be held less accountable. This relative freedom from academic accountability through shifting attention towards future orientation is often achieved through timescale. Declarations of the future of the technology in question are targeted towards five or ten years time (Suchman, 2005), rendering close accountability scrutiny for the declaration unlikely.

In place of such determinist declarations of what the future holds, this chapter will introduce two areas which require further exploration in developing an understanding of on-going developments in privacy, surveillance and trust. First, the area of privacy legislation and protection (as noted in 'CCTV legislation' section) raises questions. The data subject written into legislation such as the Data Protection Act requires further scrutiny. When, and under what conditions, does the collective for whom the act is designed, match this model? It appears that in Burbville residents were neither so individuated as the data subject nor were they as active and concerned as suggested by the version of citizenry implicated in the model subject. Residents assumed that there was a notable authority holding CCTV to account on their behalf. Furthermore, residents expressed concern with the possibility that images of them could invade the public (through TV) and be accounted for in many ways and worried about the private spaces of CCTV's closed-circuit. Taken together, these concerns suggest future research should focus on: the possibilities of the data subject and alternatives which might form a closer match for those who live, work and shop near CCTV systems; possible means for holding CCTV to account on behalf of local populations; and alternative ways to render the private spaces of CCTV's closed-circuit amenable to accounting by a notable authority. This research suggests that appropriate developments would be a less active version of the data subject (or citizen) and a new model of the data collective on whose behalf a more stringent watchdog than the current information commissioner could hold CCTV (and other systems of information collection and processing) to account.

Away from privacy legislation and protection, a second area for the development of future research on privacy, surveillance and trust is provided by questions raised by new pervasive forms of technology development. To name a few examples, the global development of the recording, carrying, retrieving and matching of biometrics appears to raise questions regarding the ways in which identities can be accounted. Also the development of pervasive and apparently subtle information storage, mobilisation and transmission technologies such as Radio Frequency IDentity (RFID) chips and tags in shopping, in ID cards and places of work appear to introduce further questions of surveillance awareness. Increasing concerns regarding people's responsibility for environmental impact and the number of new systems for compiling information on what people do (in terms of, for example, waste, car driving and home heating), what people use and dispose of, where and when, each lead to questions of how much information on the population should be compiled, for what use should such information be put and who (or what) is holding such processes to account.

This is not to suggest that these examples of new technologies in information collection, storage and management can be approached deterministically as definitively ushering in new social orders and forms of social ordering. Instead questions need to be asked about whether or not these technologies work on the terms proposed by, for example, technology developers and governments, how these technologies might be involved in the re-orientation of mundane, day to day social activities and the specific versions of privacy, surveillance and trust that they imply. It may not be that these technologies introduce profoundly new questions. Instead forms of privacy, surveillance and trust provided in this book could be utilised to form the basis of interrogating these new developments.

Conclusion

This chapter has suggested that privacy is by no means dead. Privacy provides the focus for articulating a range of concerns about likely rights and wrongs, forms of access and problems with the bounded spaces of technologies involved in the collection, storage, analysis and mobilisation of information on specific populations. Surveillance has formed an organising rationale for understanding the ways in which the public (as the mundane, not particularly notable mass of, for example, shoppers in the town centre) are watched and constituted as unworthy of greater attention. Surveillance has also been used to organise an understanding of the specifics of data scrutiny through which various notable (social and material) others are demarcated from the mass and subjected to closer account. It is through surveillance that a socio-material sense of society is constituted in real-time in the CCTV control room and in retrospective replaying through tapes made available from CCTV's archive to courtrooms and on national TV. Such accountability of the public is one of three modes of CCTV system accountability also involving accountability in public (in court rooms, through publicity campaigns) and accountability for public (through legislation). Trust has been used as the third principle to organise understanding of the specific occasions on which clear concerns are articulated regarding the social order and possible threats and repairs to that order. In place of considering trust as underpinning social order, trust has been approached as a focus for getting to grips with potential and manifest breaches and breakdowns in the social order. This chapter has suggested that current legislation does not adequately cover the concerns of participants to this research. The inaccessible private spaces of CCTV's closed-circuit, the possibility of invasion of publicity, the absence of a body to hold CCTV to account on residents' behalf and the lack of consideration given to data collectives, each constituted a particular deficiency in current legislation. Finally it has been argued that the forms of privacy, surveillance and trust introduced here have utility for considering new legislative forms and new technology developments.

Appendix

Guide to Transcription Devices

[......] Author's comments IN CAPITALS in brackets are for clarification

<u>Underlining</u> signals vocal emphasis

. (.) ( ) pauses, increasing in length

? signals stronger questioning emphasis despite grammar

< ...... > slowing of speech, > ...... < speeding up of speech
Italics denotes quieter speech

Bold denotes louder speech

Int:	Interviewer
F1, 2, M3 (etc):	Interviewees (F: Female, M: Male)
JM and SM:	CCTV managers
CPO:	Crime Prevention Officer
BM:	Bank Manager

Notes

1 Introduction

1. The number of CCTV cameras operating in Britain (and elsewhere) continues to be a matter of lively debate. The frequently re-iterated figure for the number of CCTV cameras in the United Kingdom has recently shifted from two-and-a-half million (BBC, 2002) to four million (*The Independent Newspaper*, 2004). This shift is one part of the on-going debate as to how CCTV cameras should be counted and categorised (see Norris, McCahill and Wood, 2004). There is no national register of *all* cameras (i.e. including those used in 'public,' those used covertly, those used in private residences, those used in workplaces, mobile CCTV units, etc.). Hence all figures for 'number of CCTV cameras' in Britain vary according to where boundaries are drawn, on what counts as a CCTV camera and what, thereby, gets counted as a CCTV camera. A great deal of work goes into the production of these boundaries.
2. These two views of surveillance are a close match for what Agre (1994) terms two models of privacy (one which he terms the surveillance model and one he terms the data capture model). This highlights the fluidity of the use of terms privacy and surveillance in social science research and beyond. This chapter can only serve to begin to steer a way through this diversity of usage of the same terms.
3. Rousseau *et al.* (1998) consider this view of trust as a sociological approach to the issue. They suggest this view is contrasted by an economic approach to calculative or instrumental trust and a psychological view of internal cognitions relating to trust.

2 Who are These Kids and Why are They Standing Still? Questions on the Telling of CCTV Stories

1. The story of kids standing still also appears in Neyland (in press).
2. Police officers do sometimes use the radio that connects them to CCTV staff to provide a commentary on events. The radio can also be used by the CCTV staff to guide officers to a particular target.
3. For more detail on Foucault's approach to governmentality, see Lemke (2001). For an alternative approach, see Cruikshank (1999).
4. For an alternative take on circuits and surveillance, see Williams and Johnson (2004).

3 CCTV Modes of Action: Accountability, Surveillance and Privacy

1. These accountability pressures also operated in the real-time accounting of activity in the town centre. Since the introduction of CCTV to Burbville, the

police were expected to implement a quicker response to the activity of a scene as they had quicker access to a scene. The recording system of CCTV could effectively time the police response and keep on record with any event, how long it took for the police to get to the scene. For more on police and images, see Mawby (2002). For more on police use of CCTV, see Goold (2004) and for an alternative view, see Newburn and Hayman (2002).

2. The eight principles of the Data Protection Act are that data should be:

   Fairly and lawfully processed
   Processed for legitimate purposes
   Adequate, relevant and not excessive
   Accurate and up-to-date
   Not kept longer than necessary
   Processed in line with the data subject's rights
   Secure
   Not transferred to countries without adequate protection.

3. There are further areas of public not touched on in this chapter such as concepts of 'public opinion' (see Cutler, 1999, for a discussion) and the 'public sphere' (see Habermas, 1989; and Ku, 2001). These areas have been left out as they were not referred to by participants in any detail and may add unnecessary further complexity to the analysis. Other researchers also distinguish between publicly and privately owned CCTV (see for example, Klauser, 2004). This is not a major discussion point in Burbville where the system is owned and run by the local authority.

4 Trust and Informational Mobility: CCTV, Local Retailers and Local Residents

1. Studies of mobility also find a focus in research on, amongst other things, social movements (Sheller, 2001), mobile workers (Laurier, 2004), cars (Dant, 2004; Thrift, 2004; Featherstone, 2004) and road safety (Beckmann, 2004).

2. The data for this section of the chapter is drawn from interviews with a bank manager in Burbville and a guided tour of his bank branch. This will not be the first piece of CCTV research which draws in a retail voice. See Martinais and Betin (2004) for more on CCTV and retailers' views, particularly with regard to retailers' wish to exclude certain groups from parts of cities (this is not something expressed in Burbville).

3. Although it has been argued that moves to produce a UK national ID card suggest the availability of such a database is a matter of time, it is not clear that having many photographs will enable a computer to definitively pick out who is who in a busy town centre, and it will not provide CCTV staff with information on who is doing what. Much of their accounting activity will thereby remain the same (see Neyland, 2005).

4. While analysts such as Graham and Marvin (2001) talk of the splintering of such networks, this does not provide the same focus as considering technological networks (such as banks and CCTV) active resistance to connection.

5   'We Sold Pictures of a Man Cutting His Hands Off For Entertainment Purposes': The Story of Mr. B and CCTV

Mr. B, the Daily Monograph and Freedom are all names adopted for the purposes of anonymity in this chapter. The limitations of anonymity are discussed in the Analysis section. A version of the Mr. B story appears in Neyland (2004).

1. CCTV images speaking for themselves can be considered in relation to claims that with CCTV if you are not doing anything wrong, you have nothing to hide. Webster (1999) calls this 'nothing to hide, nothing to fear' argument, the dominant view of CCTV (1999: 122). It can also be considered in relation to claims regarding the evidential strength of CCTV images. This is analysed in more detail by Graham, Brooks and Heery (1996). CCTV managers and police officers in this research suggested that CCTV images were of such good quality that they spoke for themselves. Police officers suggested that confronted with a CCTV image of their activity, defendants could not help but admit their guilt. CCTV managers said that they do nothing wrong, they simply lift images from a public space. For more on evidence speaking for itself, see Daemmreich (1998).

2. Although it might be possible to use Latour's notion of immutable mobility (1990) here to say that the CCTV staff worked hard to produce a sufficiently durable association of account and image that it travelled in a stable manner from CCTV staff, to police, to High Street, back to CCTV staff, this chapter will argue it is more appropriate to draw on Garfinkel's (1967) work to suggest the CCTV staff make identifications for all practical purposes, articulating various expert discourses and things which are available to hand, to produce an association of account and image which they hope will be corroborated. The 'for all practical purposes' clause allows them to incorporate sufficient ambiguity into their accounts ('there is a man with a knife and we don't know what he's doing') that their authority in account production is not challenged by later, seemingly contrary evidence (Mr. B's own version of events). Furthermore this suggests that rather than rules driving activity (Norris and Armstrong 1999), CCTV staff actively orient their activity toward maintaining notional forms of continuity within myriad expectations from managers and police officers (see Chapter 2 for more on rules).

3. The CCTV managers had previously used an obscured image of Mr. B in three of their local newspaper stories in order to promote the beneficial aspects of CCTV (see Chapter 3 for more on local newspaper stories).

4. European rulings are directed at the level of member states rather than local authorities such as Burbville.

5. Versions of the Mr. B article, which include his medical history and family background, continue to appear in a variety of publications, from academic publications to supermarket magazines to on-line discussions. To give a list of these references would only serve to undermine further the precarious anonymity attempted in this chapter.

6. The masking efforts of the author of this chapter could be seen as a reflexive exercise in attempting to achieve 'correct' status. However, the masking exercise is intended to highlight the limitations of the concepts of masking and consent. Any form of masking provides clues to be pursued in uncovering the

'true' identity of the subjects made anonymous and the concept of consent provides a set of questions to be answered (when to gain consent, what form should consent take, etc.).

6   Constituting the Town Centre: Space, Trust and Accountability

1. Livingston (1987) is critical of MCDs, suggesting they can be seen as objective rules of behaviour. This chapter will approach MCDs as local interactional achievements.

2. These spatial folds also feature in the work of Thrift (1996) who asks how areas become folded together, how technologies, for example, become folded into realms previously reserved for human action. Folds can also be traced through Mol and Law's (1994) version of Actor Network Theory in which the points of the network dispersed by conventional geography are folded together in the network (see also Law, 1991, 1986; and for a commentary, see Latour, 1997; 1999; Hetherington and Law, 2000).

3. This is not a call for a further reflexive turn (Woolgar, 1988; Ashmore, 1989). If this chapter is considered reflexively, it should be in line with Lynch's (2000) conception by which reflexivity 'is an unavoidable feature of the way actions (including actions performed, and expressions written, by academic researchers) are performed, made sense of and incorporated into social settings' (2000: 26).

4. Of course the question could be asked, to what extent does an everyday account of space involve carrying a video camera? The camera is a heuristic device to aid engagement with questions regarding adequate accomplishments of space and for producing material for local residents to discuss.

5. While CCTV managers shifted responsibility for many privacy concerns onto the local residents, effectively requiring residents to have a reasonable knowledge of CCTV, a lack of awareness of CCTV has privacy and policy implications (see Chapter 7).

References

Adey, P. (2004) 'Surveillance at the airport', *Environment and Planning* A 36: 1365–80.

Agre, P. (1997) 'Introduction', in Agre, P. and Rotenberg, M. (eds) *Technology and privacy: The new landscape* (MIT Press, London), pp. 1–28.

—— (1994) 'Surveillance and capture: Two models of privacy', *The Information Society* 1: 101–27.

American Civil Liberties Union (2005): available at http://www.aclu.org/Privacy/Privacy.cfm?ID=17298&c=27

Andrejevic, M. (2005) 'The work of watching one another: Lateral surveillance, risk and governance', *Surveillance and Society* 2(4): 479–97.

Ang, I. (1985) *Watching Dallas* (Methuen, London).

Ashmore, M. (1989) *The Reflexive Thesis: Wrighting sociology of scientific knowledge* (University of Chicago Press, London).

Atkinson, P. (1992) *Understanding Ethnographic Texts* (Sage, London).

—— (1990) *The Ethnographic Imagination – Textual Constructions of Reality* (Routledge, London).

Ball, K. (2002) 'Elements of Surveillance: A new framework and future directions', *Information, Communication and Society* 5(4): 573–90.

Barber, B. (1983) *The Logic and Limits of Trust* (Rutgers University Press, New Jersey NJ, USA).

Baxter, J. and Chua, W. (2003) 'Alternative management accounting research – whence and whither', *Accounting, Organisation and Society* 28(2): 97–126.

BBC (2004): available at http://news.bbc.co.uk/2/hi/uk_news/4020023.stm

—— (2002): available at http://news.bbc.co.uk/1/hi/sci/tech/1789157.stm

Beck, U. (1992) *Risk Society: Towards a new modernity* (Sage, London).

Beckmann, J. (2004) 'Mobility and safety', *Theory, Culture and Society* 21(4/5): 81–100.

Benn, S. and Gauss, G. (1983) *Public and Private in Social Life* (Croom Helm, London).

Bennett, C. (2005) 'What happens when you book an airline ticket (revisited): The collection and processing of passenger data post 9/11', in Salter, M. and Zureik, E. (eds) *Global Surveillance and Policing* (Willan, Devon), pp. 182–208.

Bennett, C. and Grant, R. (eds) (1999) *Visions of Privacy: Policy choices for the digital age* (University of Toronto Press, Toronto, Canada).

Bennett, C. and Raab, C. (2003) The governance of privacy – policy instruments in global perspective (Ashgate, Hampshire).

Bijker, W. and Law, J. (eds) (1992) *Shaping Technology/Building Society: Studies in sociotechnical change* (MIT Press, London).

Bijker, W., Hughes, T. and Pinch, T. (1989) *The Social Construction of Technological Systems: New directions in the sociology and history of technology* (MIT Press, London).

Bowker, G. and Star, S. L. (2000) *Sorting Things Out: Classification and its consequences* (MIT Press, Cambridge MA, USA).

Boyd, J. (2002) 'In community we trust: Online security communication at E-Bay' *Journal of Computer Mediated Communication* 7(3): available at http://jcmc.indiana.edu/vol7.html

Braithwaite, J. (2000) 'The new regulatory state and the transformation of criminology', *British Journal of Criminology* 40: 222–38.

Brekhus, W. (1998) 'A sociology of the unmarked: Redirecting our focus', *Sociological Theory* 16(1): 34–51.

Brown, B. (1999) 'Unpacking a timesheet: Formalisation and representation', *Computer Supported Cooperative Work* 10: 293–315.

Brown, N. and Michael, M. (2002) 'From authority to authenticity: The changing governance of biotechnology', *Health, Risk and Society* 4(3): 259–72.

Callon, M. (1986) 'The sociology of an actor-network: The case of the electric vehicle', in Callon, M., Law, J. and Rip, A. (eds) *Mapping the Dynamics of Science and Technology* (Macmillan, London), pp. 19–34.

Cameron, H. (2004) 'CCTV and (in)dividuation', *Surveillance and Society* 2(2/3): 136–44.

Castells, M. (1996) *The Rise of the Network Society* (Blackwell, Oxford).

CeMoRe: Centre for Mobility Research, Lancaster University: available at www.lancs.ac.uk/fss/sociology/cemore

Chaudhuri, A. and Holbrook, M. B. (2001) 'The chain of effects from brand trust and brand effect to brand performance: The role of brand loyalty', *Journal of Marketing* 65: 81–93.

Cole, S. (1998) 'Witnessing identification: Latent fingerprinting evidence and expert knowledge', *Social Studies of Science* 28(5/6): 687–712.

Coleman, R. (2004) 'Reclaiming the streets: Closed Circuit Television, Neo-liberalism and the mystification of social divisions in Liverpool, UK', *Surveillance and Society* 2(2/3): 293–309.

Collier, S., Lackoff, A. and Rabinow, P. (2004) 'Biosecurity: Towards an anthropology of the contemporary', *Anthropology Today* 20: 5.

Coulon, A. (1995) *Ethnomethodology* (Sage, London).

Crabtree, A. (2000) 'Remarks on the social organisation of space and place', *Journal of Mundane Behavior* 1(1): available at http://mundanebehavior.org

Crang, M. (1996) 'Watching the city: Video surveillance and resistance', *Environment and Planning* A. 28(12): 2099–104.

Cruikshank, B. (1999) *The Will to Empower* (Cornell University Press, New York, USA).

Cutler, F. (1999) 'Jeremy Bentham and the public opinion tribunal', *Public Opinion Quarterly* 63(3): 321–46.

Daemmreich, A. (1998) 'The evidence does not speak for itself: Expert witnesses and the organisation of DNA-typing companies', *Social Studies of Science* 28(5/6): 741–72.

Dant, T. (2004) 'The Driver-car', *Theory, Culture and Society* 21(4/5): 61–79.

Data Protection Act (1998): available at http://www.informationcommissioner.gov.uk/

Davies, S. (1996) *Big Brother – Britain's Web of Surveillance and the New Technological Order* (Pan Books, London).

de Laet, M. and Mol, A. (2000) 'The Zimbabwe bush pump: Mechanics of a fluid technology', *Social Studies of Science* 30(2): 225–63.

Deleuze, G. and Guattari, F. (1986) *Nomadology* (Semiotext(e), New York, USA).

Derrida, J. (1976) *Of Grammatology* (John Hopkins University Press, Baltimore MD, USA).

Ditton, J. (2000) 'Crime and the city: Public attitudes towards open-street CCTV in Glasgow', *British Journal of Criminology* 40(4): 692–709.

Dubbeld, L. (2005) 'Protecting personal data in camera surveillance practices', *Surveillance and Society* 2(4): 546–63.

—— (2004) 'Limits on surveillance: Frictions, fragilities and failures in the operation of camera surveillance', *Information, Communication and Ethics in Society* 2: 9–19.

Ericson, R., Doyle, A. and Barry, D. (2003) *Insurance as Governance* (University of Toronto Press, Toronto, Canada).

European Human Rights Act (1998): available at http://www.crimereduction. gov.uk/infosharing22-3.htm#echr

Fahey, T. (1995) 'Privacy and the family: Conceptual and empirical reflections', *Sociology* 29: 687–702.

Featherstone, M. (2004) 'Automobilities: An Introduction', *Theory, Culture and Society* 21(4/5): 1–24.

Foucault, M. (1977) *Discipline and Punish* (Allen Lane, London).

—— (1970) *The Order of Things* (Tavistock, London).

Fraser, N. (1994) 'Rethinking the public sphere', in Giroux, H. and McLaren, P. (eds) *Between Borders: Pedagogy and the politics of cultural studies* (Routledge, London), pp. 109–42.

Freedom of Information Act (2000): available at http://www.information commissioner.gov.uk/

Frewer, L. (2004) 'Consumers, food, trust and safety: The need for collaboration between the social and natural sciences': available at http://www.wageningen-ur.nl/ oraties/Frewer270504.doc

Frewer, L., Howard, C., Hedderley, D. and Shepherd, R. (1996) 'What determines trust in information about food-related risks? Underlying psychological constructs', *Risk Analysis* 16: 473–86.

Fussey, P. (2004) 'New labour and new surveillance: Theoretical and political ramifications of CCTV implementation in the UK', *Surveillance and Society* 2(2/3): 251–69.

Fyfe, N. and Bannister, J. (1996) 'City watching: Closed Circuit Television surveillance in public spaces', *Area* 28(1): 37–46.

Gallagher, C. (2004) 'CCTV and human rights: The fish and the bicycle?', *Surveillance and Society* 2(2/3): 270–92.

Gambetta, D. (2000) 'Can we trust trust?', in Gambetta, D. (ed) *Trust: Making and Breaking Cooperative Relations* (Department of Sociology, University of Oxford, Oxford): available at http://www.sociology.ox.ac.uk/papers/ gambetta213-237.pdf

Gandy, O. (1993) *The Panoptic Sort: A Political Economy of Personal Information* (Boulder, Westview).

Garfinkel, H. (1967) *Studies in Ethnomethodology* (Polity Press, Cambridge).

—— (1963) 'A conception of and experiments with 'trust' as a condition of stable concerted actions', in Harvey, O. (ed) *Motivation and Social Interaction* (Ronald Press, New York, USA), pp. 197–238.

Garfinkel, S. (2000) *Database nation: The death of privacy* (O'Reilly, California CA, USA).

Giddens, A. (1990) *The Consequences of Modernity* (Polity Press, Cambridge).

Goodwin, C. (1995) 'Seeing in depth', *Social Studies of Science* 25(2): 237–74.

—— (1994) 'Professional vision', *American Anthropologist* 96(3): 606–33.

Goodwin, C. and Goodwin, M. (1996) 'Seeing as situated activity: formulating places', in Engestrom, Y. and Middleton, D. (eds) *Cognition and Communication at Work* (Cambridge University Press, Cambridge), pp. 61–95.

Goold, B. (2004) *CCTV and Policing: Public area surveillance and police practices in Britain* (Oxford University Press, Oxford).

—— (2003) 'Public area surveillance and police work: The impact of CCTV on police behaviour and autonomy', *Surveillance and Society* 1(2): 191–203.

Goombridge, N. (2002) 'Crime control or crime culture TV?', *Surveillance and Society* 1(1): 30–46.

Goombridge, N. and Murji, K. (1994) 'As easy as A, B and CCTV?', *Policing* 10(4): 283–90.

Graham, S. (1998) 'Spaces of surveillant simulation: New technologies, digital representations, and material geographies', *Environment and Planning* D 16: 483–504.

Graham, S. and Marvin, S. (2001) *Splintering Urbanism: Networked infrastructures, technological mobilities and the urban condition* (Routledge, London).

Graham, S., Brooks, J. and Heery, D. (1996) 'Towns on television: Closed Circuit Television surveillance in British towns and cities', *Local Government Studies* 22(3): 1–27.

Gray, R. (1992) 'Accounting and environmentalism: An exploration of the challenge of gently accounting for accountability, transparency and sustainability', *Accounting, Organizations and Society* 17(5): 399–425.

Grimshaw, A. (2001) *The Ethnographer's Eye: Ways of seeing in modern anthropology* (Cambridge University Press, Cambridge).

—— (1997) 'The eye in the door: Anthropology, film and the exploration of interior space', in Banks, M. and Murphy, H. (eds) *Rethinking Visual Anthropology* (Yale University Press, London), pp. 36–53.

Grint, K. and Woolgar, S. (1997) *The Machine at Work: Technology, work and organisation* (Polity Press, Cambridge).

Guardian (23 August 2000): available at http://www.guardian.co.uk/internetnews/story/0,7369,357580,00.html

Habermas, J. (1989) *The Structural Transformation of the Public Sphere: Inquiry into a category of Bourgeois society* (Polity Press, Cambridge).

Haggerty, K. and Ericson, R. (2000) 'The surveillant assemblage', *British Journal of Sociology* 51(4): 605–22.

Heath, C. and Luff, P. (1999) 'Surveying the scene: The monitoring practices of staff in control rooms', in Noyes, J. and Barnsby, M. (eds) *Proceedings of People in Control: An international conference on human interfaces in control rooms, cockpits and command centres* (University of Bath, UK; IEE Press), pp. 1–6.

Heath, C. Hindmarsh, J. and Luff, P. (1999) 'Interaction in Isolation: The dislocated world of the London underground train driver', *Sociology* 33(3): 555–75.

Heritage, J. (1984) *Garfinkel and Ethnomethodology* (Polity Press, Cambridge).

Hetherington, K. (2002) 'The unsightly: Touching the parthenon frieze', *Theory, Culture and Society* 19(5): 187–205.

—— (1997) 'Museum topology and the will to connect', *Journal of Material Culture* 2(2): 199–218.

Hetherington, K. and Law, J. (eds) (2000) 'Special issue – after networks', *Environment and Planning* D 18(2): 127–32.

Higgs, R. (2001) 'Guarding the home front: Will civil liberties be a casualty in the war on terrorism?': available at http://www.reason.com/0112/fe.symposium. shtml

Hilgartner, S. (1990) 'The dominant view of popularisation: Conceptual problems, political uses', *Social Studies of Science* 20: 519–39.

Hine, C. (2000) *Virtual Ethnography* (Sage, London).

Hine, C. and Eve, J. (1998) 'Privacy in the Marketplace', *The Information Society* 14(4): 253–62.

Hirsch, E. (1992) 'The long-term and the short-term of domestic consumption: An ethnographic case study', in Silverstone, R. and Hirsch, E. (eds) *Consuming Technologies* (Routledge, London), pp. 208–26.

Home Office (1993) 'Understanding car park crime & CCTV: Evaluation lessons from safer cities' by Tilley, N., Policing Research Group Pamphlet No. 42, CPU, Home Office, London.

—— (1992) 'Closed Circuit Television In Public Places' by Honess, T. and Chapman, E., Home Office Pamphlet No. 35, CPU, Home Office, London.

The Independent Newspaper (2004) 'Big Brother Britain' (front page story, Monday 12 January).

Information Commissioner's Office (2004) 'Public attitudes to the deployment of surveillance techniques in public places': available at http://www. informationcommissioner.gov.uk/cms/DocumentUploads/cctv%20report.pdf

Information Commissioner's CCTV Code of Practice (Code, 2000): available at http://www.informationcommissioner.gov.uk/

Irwin, A. (1995) *Citizen Science* (Routledge, London).

Jasanoff, S. (1998) 'The eye of everyman: Witnessing DNA in the Simpson trial', *Social Studies of Science* 28(5/6): 713–40.

—— (1990). *The Fifth Branch. Science Advisors as Policy Makers* (Harvard University Press, Cambridge, Massachusetts MA, USA).

Jordan, K. and Lynch, M. (1998) 'The dissemination, standardisation and routinisation of a molecular biological technique' *Social Studies of Science* 28(5/6): 773–800.

Kitcher, P. (2001) *Science, Democracy and Truth* (Oxford University Press, Oxford).

Klauser, F. (2004) 'A comparison of the impact of protective and preservative video surveillance on urban territoriality', *Surveillance and Society* 2(2/3): 145–60.

Kleinman, D. (2000) (ed) *Science, Technology and Democracy* (State of New York University Press, Albany NY, USA).

Koskela, H. (2003) ' "Cam Era" – the contemporary urban Panopticon', *Surveillance and Society* 1(3): 292–313.

—— (2000) ' "The gaze without eyes": video-surveillance and the changing nature of urban space', *Progress in Human Geography* 24(2): 243–65.

Ku, A. (2001) ' "The Public" up against the State: Narrative cracks and credibility crisis in postcolonial Hong-Kong', *Theory, Culture and Society* 18(1): 121–44.

Latour, B. (2004) *Politics of Nature* (Harvard University Press, Cambridge MA, USA).

—— (2002) 'Morality and technology: The end of means', *Theory, Culture and Society* 19(5/6): 247–60.

—— (1999) 'On recalling ANT', in Law, J. and Hassard, J. (eds) *Actor-Network Theory and After* (Blackwells, Oxford), pp. 15–25.

—— (1997) 'On actor network, a few clarifications', CSTT, Keele University: available at www.lancaster.ac.uk

—— (1990) 'Drawing things together', in Lynch, M. and Woolgar, S. (eds) *Representation in Scientific Practice* (MIT Press, Cambridge MA, USA), pp. 19–68.

—— (1987) *Science in Action* (Open University Press, Milton Keynes).

—— (1986) 'Will the last person to leave the social studies of science please turn on the tape-recorder?', *Social Studies of Science* 16(3): 541–48.

Latour, B. and Woolgar, S. (1979) *Laboratory Life: The construction of scientific facts* (Sage, London).

Laurier, E. (2004) 'Doing office work on the motorway', *Theory, Culture and Society* 21(4/5): 261–77.

Law, J. (2002) 'Objects and Spaces', *Theory, Culture and Society* 19(5/6): 91–105.

—— (1996) 'Organising Account Ethics: Ontology and the Mode of Accounting', in Munro, R. and Mouritsen, J. (eds) *Accountability: Power, ethos and the technologies of managing* (International Thomson Business Press, London), pp. 283–306.

—— (ed) (1991) *A Sociology of Monsters* (Routledge, London).

—— (ed) (1986) *Power, Action and Belief – A New Sociology Of Knowledge* (Routledge and Kegan Paul, London).

Law, J. and Mol, A. (1998) 'On Metrics and Fluids – Notes on Otherness', in Chia, R. (ed) *Organised Worlds: Explorations in technology and organisations with Robert Cooper* (Routledge, London), pp. 20–38.

Lee, J. (1984) 'Innocent victims and evil-doers', *Women's Studies* 7(1): 69–73.

Lee, N. (1999) 'The challenge of childhood – distributions of childhood's ambiguity in adult institutions', *Childhood* 6(4): 455–74.

Lee, N. and Hetherington, K. (2000) 'Social order and the blank figure', *Environment and Planning* D 18(2): 69–184.

Lee, N. and Stenner, P. (1999) 'Who pays? Can we pay them back?', in Law, J. and Hassard, J. (eds) *Actor-Network Theory and After* (Blackwell, Oxford), pp. 90–112.

Lemke, T. (2001) 'The birth of bio-politics: Michel Foucault's lecture at the College de France on neo-liberal governmentality', *Economy and Society* 30(2): 190–207.

Levin, T., Frohne, U. and Weibel, P. (eds) (2002) *CTRL [Space] : Rhetorics of surveillance from Bentham to Big Brother* (MIT, London).

Livingston, E. (1987) *Making Sense of Ethnomethodology* (Routledge and Kegan Paul, London).

Lomell, H. (2004) 'Targeting the unwanted: Video surveillance and categorical exclusion in Oslo, Norway', *Surveillance and Society* 2(2/3): 346–60.

Luff, P. and Heath, C. (1993) 'System use and social organization: observations on human-computer interaction in an architectural practice', in Button, G. (ed) *Technology in Working Order: Studies of work, interaction and technology* (Routledge, London), pp. 184–210.

Luhman, N. (2000) 'Familiarity, Confidence, Trust: Problems and alternatives', in Gambetta, D. (ed) *Trust: Making and breaking cooperative relations* (Department of Sociology, University of Oxford, Oxford): available at www.sociology.ox.ac.uk/papers/luhmann94-107.pdf

Lynch, M. (2000) 'Against reflexivity as an academic virtue and source of privileged knowledge', *Theory, Culture and Society* 17(3): 26–54.

—— (1998) 'The discursive production of uncertainty: The OJ Simpson 'dream team' and the sociology of knowledge machine', *Social Studies Of Science* 28(5/6): 829–68.

Lyon, D. (2001) *Surveillance Society: Monitoring everyday life* (Open University Press, Buckingham).

Lyon, D. (1994) *The Electronic Eye* (Polity Press, Cambridge).

—— (1993) 'An Electronic Panopticon? A Sociological Critique Of Surveillance Theory', *Sociological Review* 41(4): 653–78.

Mackenzie, D. and Wajcman, J. (eds) (1985) *The Social Shaping of Technology* (Open University Press, Milton Keynes).

Mansell, R. (ed) (1994) *Management of Information and Communication Technologies – Emerging Patterns of Control* (Aslib, London).

Martinais, E. and Betin, C. (2004) 'Social aspects of CCTV in France: the case of the city centre of Lyons', *Surveillance and Society* 2(2/3): 361–75.

Martinez, W. (1992) 'Who constructs anthropological knowledge? Towards a theory of ethnographic film spectatorship', in Crawford, P. and Turton, D. (eds) *Film as Ethnography* (Manchester University Press, Manchester), pp. 131–61.

Marx, G. (2002) 'What's new about the new surveillance? Classifying for change and continuity', *Surveillance and Society* 1(1): 9–29.

Mason, D., Button, G., Lankshear, G. and Coates, S. (2002) 'Getting real about surveillance and privacy in the workplace', in Woolgar, S. (ed.) *Virtual Society? Technology, Cyberbole, Reality* (Oxford University Press, Oxford), pp. 137–52.

Mawby, R. (2002) *Policing Images: Policing communication and legitimacy* (Willan, Devon).

McCahill, M. (2002) *The Surveillance Web: The rise of visual surveillance in an English city* (Willan, Devon).

McCulloch, A. (1997) 'On the public and the private – a comment on Fahey', *Sociology* 31(4): 793–99.

McGrail, B. (2003) 'Confronting electronic surveillance: Desiring and resisting new technologies', in Woolgar, S. (ed) *Virtual Society? Technology, Cyberbole, Reality* (Oxford University Press, Oxford), pp. 115–36.

Milberg, S. *et al* (2000) 'Information Privacy: Corporate management and national regulation', *Organization Science* 11(1): 33–57.

Miller, P. (1992) 'Accounting and objectivity: The invention of calculable selves and calculable spaces', *Annals of Scholarship* 9(1/2): 61–86.

Miller, P. and O'Leary, T. (1994) 'Governing the calculable person', in Hopwood, A. G. and Miller, P. (eds) *Accounting as Social and Institutional Practice* (Cambridge University Press, Cambridge), pp. 98–115.

Misztal, B. (1996) *Trust in Modern Societies* (Polity Press, Cambridge).

Mol, A. and Law, J. (1994) 'Regions, networks and fluids: Anaemia and social topology', *Social Studies of Science* 24: 641–71.

Mondada, L. (2003) 'Working with video: How surgeons produce video records of their actions', *Visual Studies* 18(1): 58–73.

Muller, C. and Boos, D. (2004) 'Zurich main railway station: A typology of public CCTV systems', *Surveillance and Society* 2(2/3): 161–76.

Newburn, T. and Hayman, S. (2002) *Policing, Surveillance and Social Control* (Willan, Devon).

Neyland, D. (in press) 'Moving images: The mobility and immobility of "Kids Standing Still" ', *Sociological Review*.

—— (2005) 'Who's who? The politics of identity and the biometric future', paper presented at HCTP workshop, Toronto, Canada, May.

—— (2004) 'Closed-circuits of interaction? The mobilisation of images and accountability through High Street CCTV', *Information, Communication and Society* 7(2): 252–71.

Neyland, D. and Woolgar, S. (2002) 'Accountability in action?', *British Journal of Sociology* 53(2): 259–74.

Norris, C. (2003) 'From Personal to Digital: CCTV, the panopticon and the technological mediation of suspicion and social control', in D. Lyon (ed) *Surveillance as Social Sorting: Privacy, risk and digital discrimination* (Routledge, London), pp. 249–81.

Norris, C. and Armstrong, G. (1999) *The Maximum Surveillance Society – The Rise Of CCTV* (Berg, Oxford).

Norris, C., McCahill, M. and Wood, D. (2004) 'Editorial: The growth of CCTV: A global perspective on the international diffusion of surveillance in publicly accessible space', *Surveillance and Society* 2(2/3): 110–35.

Norris, C., Moran, J. and Armstrong, G. (eds) (1998) *Surveillance, Closed Circuit Television and Social Control* (Ashgate, Aldershot).

Osborne, T. and Rose, N. (2004) 'Spatial phenomenotechnics: Making space with Charles Booth and Patrick Geddes', *Environment and Planning* D 22: 209–28.

Oxford (2003) 'Community and mobility: Living with the technologies of mobile communication', Said Business School, Oxford University, 2 October.

Pink, S. (2001) *Doing Visual Ethnography* (Sage, London).

Pinney, C. (1992) 'The quick and the dead: Images, time and truth', in Crawford, P. Turton, D. (eds) *Film as Ethnography* (Manchester University Press, Manchester), pp. 26–49.

Pollner, M. (1987) *Mundane Reason: Reality in everyday and sociological discourse* (Cambridge University Press, Cambridge).

Poster, M. (1990) *The Mode of Information* (Polity Press, Cambridge).

Power, M. (1997) *The Audit Society* (Oxford University Press, Oxford).

Privacy Rights (2004): available at www.privacyrights.org

Raab, C. and Bennett, C. (1998) 'The distribution of privacy risks: Who needs protection?', *The Information Society* 14(4): 263–74.

Rappert, B. (2001) 'The distribution and resolution of the ambiguities of technology or why Bobby can't spray', *Social Studies of Science* 31(4): 557–92.

Regulation of Investigatory Powers Act (1998): available at http://www.homeoffice.gov.uk/crimpol/crimreduc/regulation/index.html

Ris:Ome: Centre for mobility research, University of Surrey: available at www.risome.soc.surrey.ac.uk

Rogers, M. (1983) *Sociology, Ethnomethodology and Experience – A Phenomenological Critique* (Cambridge University Press, Cambridge).

Rory, F. (1996) *The Third Eye – Race, Cinema and Ethnographic Spectacle* (Duke University Press, London).

Rose, N. (2000) 'Government and control', *British Journal of Ciminology* 40: 321–39.

—— (1999) *Powers of Freedom* (Cambridge University Press, Cambridge).

—— (1996) 'Governing "advanced" liberal democracies', in Barry, A., Osborne, T. and Rose, N. (eds) *Foucault and Political Reason* (UCL Press, London), pp. 37–64.

Rosen, J. (2001) *The Unwanted Gaze: The destruction of privacy in America* (Vintage Press, New York, USA).

Rousseau, D. *et al.* (1998) 'Not so different after all: A cross-discipline view of trust', *Academy of Management Review* 23(3): 383–404.

Rowe, G., Marsh, R. and Frewer, L. J. (2004) 'Evaluation of a Deliberative Conference using Validated Criteria', *Science, Technology and Human Values* 29(1): 88–121.

Ruby, J. (2000) *Picturing Culture* (University of Chicago Press, London).

Rule, J. (1973) *Private lives, Public Surveillance* (Allen Lane, London).

Ryave, A. and Schenkein, J. (1974) 'Notes on the art of walking', in Turner, R. (ed) *Ethnomethodology* (Penguin, Middlesex), pp. 265–74.

Sacks, H. (1972) 'Notes on police assessment of moral character', in Sudnow, D. (ed) *Studies In Social Interaction* (Free Press, New York, USA), pp. 280–93.

Schlesinger, P. and Tumber, H. (1994) *Reporting Crime* (Clarendon Press, Oxford).

Serres, M. (1991) *Rome: The book of foundations* (Stanford University Press, California CA, USA).

Shapin, S. (1994) *A Social History of Truth: Civility and science in 17th century England* (University of Chicago Press, London).

Shapiro, S. (1987) 'The social control of impersonal trust', *The American Journal of Sociology* 93(3): 623–58.

Sheller, M. (2001) 'The mechanisms of mobility and liquidity: Re-thinking the movement in social movements': available at http://www.lancs.ac.uk/fss/sociology/staff/sheller/sheller.htm

Sheller, M. and Urry, J. (2003) 'Mobile Transformations of "Public" and "Private" Life', *Theory, Culture and Society* 20(3): 107–25.

Shove, E. (2003) 'Things in the making and things in action: A discussion of design, use and consumption', Science and Technology Studies seminar, Said Business School, University of Oxford, 24 January.

—— (2002) 'Rushing around: coordination, mobility and inequality': available at http://www.its.leeds.ac.uk/projects/MobileNetwork/downloads/rushing_around.doc

Shove, E. and Southerton, D. (2000) 'Defrosting the freezer: From novelty to convenience', *Material Culture* 5(3): 301–19.

Smith, G. (2004) 'Behind the screens: Examining constructions of deviance and informal practices among CCTV control room operators in the UK', *Surveillance and Society* 2(2/3): 363–95.

Soetnan, A. *et al.* (2004) 'Controlling CCTV in public spaces: Is privacy the (only) issue?', *Surveillance and Society* 2(2/3): 396–414.

Stalder, F. (2002) 'Privacy is not the antidote to surveillance', *Surveillance and Society* 1(1): 120–24.

Star, S. and Griesemer, J. (1989) 'Institutional ecology, "translations" and boundary objects: amateurs and professionals in Berkley's museum of vertebrate zoology', *Social Studies of Science* 19(3): 387–420.

Strathern, M. (2004) 'Laudable aims and problematic consequences, or: the "flow" of knowledge is not neutral', *Economy and Society* 33(4): 550–61.

—— (2002) 'Abstraction and decontextualisation – An anthropological comment', in Woolgar, S. (ed) *Virtual Society? Technology, Cyberbole, Reality* (Oxford University Press, Oxford), pp. 302–13.

—— (2000) 'Introduction', in Strathern, M. (ed) *Audit Cultures: Anthropological studies in accountability, ethics and the academy* (Routledge, London), pp. 1–18.

—— (1999) 'The aesthetics of substance', in Strathern, M. (ed) *Property, Substance and Effect* (Athlone, London), pp. 45–64.

—— (1991) *Partial Connections* (Savage, Maryland MD, USA).

Street, J. (1992) *Politics and Technology* (Macmillan, London).

Strum, S. and Latour, B. (1999) 'Redefining the social link: From baboons to humans', in Mackenzie, D. and Wajcman, J. (eds) *The Social Shaping of Technology* (2nd Edition) (Open University Press, Milton Keynes), pp. 116–25.

Suchman, L. (2005) 'Ordinary rhetorics of extraordinary futures', Globalization in Practice seminar, Said Business School, University of Oxford, 10 February.

—— (1993) 'Technologies of accountability: Of lizards and aeroplanes', in Button, G. (ed) *Technology in Working Order: Studies of work, interaction and technology* (Routledge, London), pp. 113–26.

—— (1987) *Plans & Situated Actions* (Cambridge University Press, Cambridge).

Sudnow, D. (ed) (1972) *Studies in Social Interaction* (Free Press, New York, USA).

Surrey. (2004) 'The life of mobile data: Technology, mobility and data subjectivity', University of Surrey, 15–16 April.

Surveillance and Society (2004) 'Special issue: Surveillance and mobilities' 1(4): 449–587: available at www.surveillance-and-society.org

Sykes, C. (1999) *The End of Privacy* (St. Martin's Press, New York, USA).

Szerszynski, B. (1999) 'Risk and trust: The performative dimension', *Environmental Values* 8: 239–52.

Taylor, N. (2002) 'State Surveillance and the right to privacy', *Surveillance and Society* 1(1): 66–85.

Thrift, N. (2004) 'Driving in the city', *Theory, Culture and Society* 21(4/5): 41–59.

—— (1996) 'New urban eras and Old technological fears: Reconfiguring the goodwill of electronic things', *Urban Studies* 33(8): 1463–93.

Urry, J. (2001) 'Mobile cultures': available at www.comp.lancs.ac.uk/sociology/soc030ju.html

—— (2000) *Sociology Beyond Societies: Mobilities for the twenty-first century* (Routledge, London).

Viseu, A., Clement, A. and Aspinall, J. (2004) 'Situating privacy online', *Information, Communication and Society* 7(1): 92–114.

Webster, C. W. R. (1999) 'Closed Circuit Television and Information Age Policy Processes', in Hague, B. and Loader, B. (eds) *Digital Democracy: Discourse and decision making in the information age* (Routledge, London), pp. 116–31.

Webster, W. and Hood, J. (2000) 'Surveillance in the community: Community development through the use of Closed Circuit Television', International Conference at CIRA, University of Teesside, 26–28 April.

Whitaker, R. (2000) *The End of Privacy: How total surveillance is becoming a reality* (New Press, New York, USA).

Williams, R. and Johnson, P. (2004) 'Circuits of surveillance', *Surveillance and Society* 2(1): 1–14.

Woolgar, S. (1991) 'Configuring the user: The case of usability trails', in Law, J. (ed) *A Sociology of Monsters* (Routledge, London).

—— (1988) *Science: The very idea* (Tavistock, London).

Woolgar, S. and Cooper, K. (1999) 'Do artefacts have ambivalence? Moses' bridges, Winner's bridges and other legends in STS', *Social Studies of Science* 29(3): 433–49.

Wynne, B. (1996) 'May the sheep safely graze? A reflexive View of the Expert-Lay Knowledge Divide', in Lash, S., Szerszynski, B. and Wynne, B. (eds) *Risk, Environment and Modernity: Towards a new ecology* (Sage, London), pp. 44–83.

Young, A. (1996) *Imagining Crime* (Sage, London).

Index

Access
  CCTV and residents 64–66, 71–73,
    87, 102–3, 111, 167
  Methodology 14, 124–25
Accountability
  In ANT 36
  Of public 47, 49, 74, 158
  In public 48, 54, 74, 159
  For public 48, 59, 74, 159
  Responsibility shifts 43, 70–71
Actor-Network Theory (ANT) 33–38,
  40, 121
Archiving 52–53, 174
Armstrong, Gary 1, 21–25, 29, 38–39

Bank
  Call centre 77–78
  Closeness 82
  Customer identification 78–82
  Databases 77, 79–80
  Manager 77–78, 82
  Staff 77, 79–80
BBC 4
Biometrics 12, 75, 116, 173
Blank figure 36–38
Border crossing 1, 19
Boundaries 3, 15, 92, 101, 120,
  153
Boundary object 35–37, 105
Breaching social order 9, 90, 103,
  162–65
Bulger, Jamie 53, 160
Burbville
  Familiar 129–31
  Hi-tech 132, 135–37
  Sleepy 130
  Under threat 84–85, 141–44

Calculability 87, 92
Cash-points 88–90, 129–30, 164
Category judgements 133–35,
  139–40, 148
Civil liberties 1, 17–18, 113–14

Closed-circuits of CCTV 2, 42,
  71–73, 94–96, 101–3, 145–47,
  149, 156
Connectivity 15, 86–89, 92–5, 137
Consent 111–13, 170–71
Courts of law
  Accountability in public 54–57
  CCTV integrity 56
  Losing the plot 54–55
Crime Prevention Officer 54–56,
  67–68
Critical approach 21–25

Data-flow 77–78
Data Protection Act 60, 166–67
Data subjects
  Data citizens 169, 172
  Data collectives 168–69, 173
Denim 49, 126
Deterrence 57, 165
Digital cameras 66–67
DNA 54–55
Documentary analysis 14, 151

Engineering CCTV 61
Environmental accountability 173
Ethnography
  Mobile 14
  Multi-site 15
Ethnomethodology 25–33,
  118–20
European Human Rights Act 16, 60,
  160, 166
Evidence
  Courts 34, 54–57, 103–5, 111,
    114–15
  Images speaking for themselves
    97, 99, 111

Fair Information Principles 4–5, 69
Field notes 20
Fibre-optics 20, 34–35, 99
Fluidity 35

Folds 121–22, 145, 148
  Connecting network entities 35, 61, 120–21
  Of images 35, 40
Foucault, Michel 7, 23, 41, 47, 121
Futures
  Predicting 170
  Of privacy, surveillance and trust 171–73
  Technologies 172

Garfinkel, Harold 8–9, 28, 39–40, 158, 161–3
Governance 23, 41–42, 82, 92, 157
Governmentality 41–44, 83

Health services 98, 100
High Court 105, 107, 111–12, 115
History
  Categorising, archiving and storing 174
  Retrospective relevance 53–54

ID cards 153, 173
Immutable mobile 34, 121
Industry of protest 1, 101, 151
Information Commissioner's CCTV
  Code of Practice 51–52, 60, 67, 166–69
Interviews 15
Invasions
  Of privacy 13, 67, 104, 156
  Of publicity 156, 165, 171

Kids 21, 30, 63, 116
Knives 110, 126

Latour, Bruno 26, 34, 77, 120–21, 126, 160
Legislation 4, 22, 46, 60, 166–71
Local council 14, 15, 105, 124
Logbooks 98, 99
London terrorist attacks 160
Lyon, David 6, 22, 25, 157

Managers
  Bank 76–78
  CCTV 13, 17, 40, 60, 161
Mardi Gras bomber 49–51

Masking 112–15, 170
McDonald's 25
Media
  CCTV coverage 105
  CCTV use 58, 100–1
  And courts of law 109
Membership Categorisation Device
  (MCD) 119, 124, 139, 145
Methodology
  Access 14
  Reflexivity 26
  Representation 14–15
  Researcher influence 15–16
  Selection of CCTV 11–12
Mobilisation
  Bodies 76
  Exclusion 75
  Information 76, 77–78
  Research centres 75
Monitors 13, 25, 31, 100
Mundane 9, 30
  Everyday 26, 31, 53, 75, 119

Network Society 87, 94, 153
Newspapers
  Local 101, 102
  National 103–5
Norris, Clive 1, 21–25, 29, 38–39
Nothing to hide, nothing to fear 97

Others
  And blank figures 36–38
  Othering 160, 161
  And social ordering 160–61, 163
Out of town retail developments 84, 131

Panopticon 7, 23–25, 114
Pervasive technologies 157, 173
Police officers
  Focus for negotiations 99
  Guidelines 60
  Information provision 32, 52, 110
  Interaction with CCTV staff 49–51
Policy relevance 166–71
Poster 7, 22, 24, 158
Privacy
  Death/End of 152–55
  In legislation 4–6

Privacy – *continued*
  Knowledge 66–69
  Multiple forms 87
  And the public 3–4
  And publicity 67
  As radically contingent 5–6
Professional vision 50–56, 118, 159
Profiling 1, 55
Protocols 50, 55
Public
  The absence of collectives 160, 173
  Adequate, mundane
    accomplishment 30
  Funding 57, 59, 61
  Performative criteria 72–73, 110
  Spatial relation 72–73, 109–10
Publicity 57–59, 100–3

Radio 13, 32, 98, 176
Real-time 13, 21, 62, 98
Reflexivity 26
Regulation of Investigatory Powers Act
  60, 166
Representation 16, 26, 56
Residents
  As a collective 59, 160, 172
  Individualised 4–5, 87, 167
  As notable other 165
  As public 72–73
Retailers 76–80
Radio Frequency Identity (RFID) 173
Rose, Nikolas 41–42, 82, 114
Routinisation 49, 51
Rules
  Driving behaviour 29
  Oriented towards 50–51

Sacks 22, 27, 29, 158
Science and Technology Studies
  33–38, 121
September 11th 3, 16
Shapin, Steve 9, 90, 161–62
Social Construction of Technology
  33, 120, 154
Social order
  Breach 9, 10, 90, 161–63
  Potential breach 90, 148, 165
  Repair 9, 139, 146, 148

Society and CCTV 160–61
Staff
  Bank 77, 79–80
  CCTV 13, 21, 51, 119–20
State regulation 5
Statistical analysis of CCTV 13
Strathern, Marilyn 48, 59, 80, 168
Suchman, Lucy 48, 132
Super-panopticon 7, 23–24, 114
Surveillance
  Broad definition 7
  As interactive accomplishment
    32
  Narrow definition 7, 51, 102
  And state politics 7

Technological determinism
  And the future of technology
    172
  Problematic 22, 33
Television 102, 111, 174
Town Centre
  Burbville 30
  Car park 124
  Cinema 124
  Ethnomethodological studies
    118–20
  Technospaces 132–37
  Trust 137–44
Trust
  Fear and night time 90, 138
  Fear and the use of cash-points 91,
    92, 107
  As a political accomplishment 11,
    162
  And risk 9–10
  Socio-material orders 161
  Temporal, spatial and knowledge
    claims 137–44
  As underpinning the social order
    9, 161
  Understood at moments of breach
    10, 161–63

Uncertainty
  CCTV's activity 109
  CCTV's identity 20, 158
  In identification 81, 98

Uncertainty – *continued*
   Inconcludability   102, 112
   Managed deferral   70, 107, 127
   Resolution of ambiguity   70, 98,
      102, 107
   Utility of uncertainty   71
Utility   58, 92, 128, 137, 146

Video ethnography   122–23

Villains   52
Violent crime   58, 72, 155
Visual   26, 31, 50, 110–11, 117–18
Visual anthropology   122–23

War on terror   1
Woolgar, Steve   1, 10, 14, 33, 70
Workplace studies   4, 48
Wynne, Brian   10, 16